ESSAYS ON THE HISTORY OF ETHICS

ESSAYS ON THE
HISTORY OF ETHICS

Michael Slote

OXFORD
UNIVERSITY PRESS
2010

OXFORD
UNIVERSITY PRESS

Oxford University Press, Inc., publishes works that further
Oxford University's objective of excellence
in research, scholarship, and education.

Oxford New York
Auckland Cape Town Dar es Salaam Hong Kong Karachi
Kuala Lumpur Madrid Melbourne Mexico City Nairobi
New Delhi Shanghai Taipei Toronto

With offices in
Argentina Austria Brazil Chile Czech Republic France Greece
Guatemala Hungary Italy Japan Poland Portugal Singapore
South Korea Switzerland Thailand Turkey Ukraine Vietnam

Copyright © 2010 by Oxford University Press, Inc.

Published by Oxford University Press, Inc.
198 Madison Avenue, New York, New York 10016

www.oup.com

Oxford is a registered trademark of Oxford University Press.

Library of Congress Cataloging-in-Publication Data
Slote, Michael A.
Essays on the history of ethics / Michael Slote.
   p. cm.
ISBN 978-0-19-539155-8 (hardback: alk. paper)
1. Ethics—History. I. Title.
BJ71.S59 2009
170.9—dc22   2009002755

9 8 7 6 5 4 3 2 1

Printed in the United States of America
on acid-free paper

To Carol Gilligan and Nel Noddings

ACKNOWLEDGMENTS

Two of the essays in this book have been published elsewhere. I want to thank Lawrence and Charlotte Becker for permission to reprint an article on "Teleological Ethics" from the second edition of their *Encyclopedia of Ethics* in this book (under a new title). I would also like to thank the journal *Dao*—and Springer Science and Business Media—for permission to reprint my "Comments" on Bryan Van Norden's *Virtue Ethics and Consequentialism in Early Chinese Philosophy*. Those comments are appearing as part of a symposium on that book that *Dao* is publishing.

I am indebted to many individuals for comments on one or more of the essays collected here. My thanks to Julia Annas, Marcia Baron, Rachel Cohon, Roger Crisp, Virginia Held, Barbara Herman, Richard Kraut, Elizabeth Radcliffe, Georges Rey, Henry West, Nicholas White, and Richard Wollheim for their helpful suggestions. I also want to thank Peter Ohlin of Oxford University Press for all his support for this project.

My most general debt is to Carol Gilligan and Nel Noddings, to whom this book is dedicated. I say something about that debt in "Under the Influence" and "Carol Gilligan and History of Ethics," the two final essays in this book. But I want to add that their work has influenced my own *much more generally* than the present book, which focuses mainly on history, can really indicate.

CONTENTS

ESSAYS ON THE HISTORY OF ETHICS

INTRODUCTION

I am not a scholar of the history of philosophy or of the history of ethics; and anyone who reads the essays that follow will soon become aware of that fact if they aren't already aware of it from reading things I have previously written. Nonetheless, I think there is a significant place for a book like this one that seeks to use ideas from or interpretations of the history of ethics to illuminate present-day issues. Present-day ethics needs its history more than philosophy of mind, epistemology, and philosophy of language seem to need their histories, though I am not sure I have anything very enlightening to say about why that seems to be so.

But if I may approach matters from the other end, I think it is also true that historians of ethics and of philosophy more generally look to present-day developments to give them clues for interpreting the past. (At least this is true of the kind of historians who are trained in and come out of analytic philosophy departments.) The minds and the creativity of great historical figures are often so great that subsequent and even much, much later generations may see what those figures were moving toward or developing only after their inchoate or tentative ideas are rediscovered in possibly clearer and more articulate form. Aristotle or Hume, for example, may simply be greater than we at any given time can understand them to be. (Artur Schnabel once said that Schubert's piano music is better than it can be played.) And this gives historians a chance and a right, among other things, to investigate the history of philosophy through the magnifying lens of contemporary philosophizing. Historians who know enough about the present can see better than others how certain important historical figures adumbrate current ideas. So even a philosopher who doesn't know the past as well as others may be able to use current ideas to cast light on that past, and to do so in a way that real historians of ethics could find interesting. And, once again reversing direction, what that philosopher finds, the way he or she interprets the past, may have useful bearing on how we (should) think about current issues—even on how we should formulate them or whether we should reformulate them.

However, in speaking, as I just have, of what the philosopher—and so perhaps this philosopher—*finds*, I don't mean to be claiming that the interpretations I shall be offering are always going to be what the best present historical scholarship would agree upon (and, of course, scholars will invariably

3

disagree among themselves on many historical questions). I am not going to be emphasizing scholarly issues here nor, therefore, will I dig as deeply into the scholarly literature on the history of philosophy as scholars might prefer to do themselves or prefer that others should do. The ideas and arguments I attribute to historical figures in the course of and for purposes of making philosophical points will sometimes just be ideas and arguments that *have* been attributed to them and that in my estimation it makes *interesting sense* to attribute to them. And it is my belief that history offered with a view more to philosophical interests than to historical ones has a definite place in our field.

These, then, are some of my reasons for offering the present essays to public scrutiny (rather than merely inflicting their contents on classes and seminars). I have been teaching the history of ethics either in courses under that title or in seminars/courses that draw on the past in attempting to treat current issues, for many years; and I have found it enjoyable to bring together some of what I have said in those courses/seminars and to develop that material, those ideas, further. Whether the philosophically enlightened and/or historically savvy reader will enjoy it all is, of course, another matter. But it might help that reader if, instead of just leaving the essays to themselves in the order in which they appear in this book, I said something by way of introducing them and perhaps in some instances also connecting them.

The order of the essays in this book follows a rough trajectory of earlier to later in the history of ethics. But since I think it can be helpful to understand theories or approaches by reference to other theories and approaches, even the first essay here on "The Opposite of Reductionism" brings in later philosophical developments in its effort to clarify and defend a roughly Platonic view of human well-being. The essay derives its antecedently obscure title from the fact that Plato, Aristotle, and Stoicism understand the relation between virtue and well-being or happiness in a way that is the very opposite of the reductive way in which Epicureanism and, later, utilitarianism understand that relationship. We have no historiographic or philosophical term for that opposite way, and in "The Opposite of Reductionism," I suggest that we designate this opposite relationship using the term "elevation(ism)." This is a somewhat awkward and certainly not a very elegant term for the opposite relationship, but I have found no better way of referring to it (and it would have been even more perplexing if I had used this new term in the title of the essay). "The Opposite of Reductionism" goes on to show that the opposition between reductionism and elevationism has application outside of ethics to issues like the mind–body problem, the debate between rationalism and empiricism, and differing theories about the nature of social entities.

It also turns out that in all these areas, one can deny both reductionism and elevationism and hold what I call a dualist view about the particular issue in question. One can hold, for example, that neither virtue nor well-being can be understood entirely in terms of the other, and such a dualistic ethical view was held, as I show, by Kant. Similarly, instead of reducing concepts to percepts in the manner of empiricism or elevating percepts to the (mentally higher) status of concepts in the manner of rationalism, one can say, as Kant did, that both categories (in the ordinary, not the Kantian sense) are cognitively fundamental, and this too represents a (different) form of dualism. These historiographic distinctions have some interest in their own right and the essay attempts to show or illustrate that. But it also argues that the elevationist idea of understanding human well-being in terms of (the higher notion of) virtue needn't be as implausible or far-fetched as the Stoic version of that idea, which simply identified the two, can make it seem. Utilitarianism has some significant unifying power as a theory through the way (among other things) that it reduces all virtue to what produces human or sentient well-being; but a Platonic elevationism that understands *each objective human good* as requiring or involving its own kind of virtue avoids the excesses of Stoicism (and, I argue, of Aristotle) and can be defended quite promisingly in contemporary terms. Or so "The Opposite of Reductionism" seeks to argue.

The second essay, "The End of Teleological Ethics," is very short and comes from an article in the *Encyclopedia of Ethics*. It argues that the notion of teleological ethics is difficult to make coherent sense of, given the advances that have occurred in our understanding of ethical and ethics-historical issues in recent decades; and it says that we probably don't need to make use of the teleological/non-teleological distinction any more. Perhaps the plausibility of the conclusion will help justify the shortness, and not just the title, of the essay.

"Ancient Ethics and Modern Moral Philosophy," the third essay in the book, seeks to say something useful about the distinction between ancient and modern (including contemporary) thought. The title is, of course, taken at least partly from Elizabeth Anscombe's "Modern Moral Philosophy," a paper that launched the recent revival or renaissance of virtue ethics and that harped on the importance of the difference between ancient and modern ways of seeing things. I have not found the distinctions Anscombe was making to be of much help, however, in defining or marking the difference(s) between ancient and modern, and the reason for this, I think, is that Anscombe drew her distinction(s) in highly polemical terms. She hated what had happened in modern times, and I don't. And in any event, the essay I have written seeks to be generally neutral on questions about the merit or validity of the theories or approaches it compares and connects. Like others in the past (most notably Sidgwick), I hold that one of the most interesting differences between ancient and modern lies in the (variously) dualistic character of modern theories and the absence of dualism in the ancient. (I point to other important differences, but spend the most time discussing the difference just mentioned.)

Now the first essay, "The Opposite of Reductionism," introduces a notion of dualism that relates to (quasi-)ontological issues of reduction or elevation; but in "Ancient Ethics and Modern Moral Philosophy," the notion of ethical dualism is somewhat different and refers, roughly, to differences in and conflicts between the way we are (supposed to be) *motivated to relate to different sorts of ethical values*. The essay argues that there are some important motivational differences or conflicts within (individual) modern approaches that were absent in ancient views. But this generalization turns out to be true only for the most part, and the most interesting thing, perhaps, is to see how dualistic views differ among themselves in the *way* they lead to or encompass duality or dualism.

The fourth essay in the book comes from some comments I made at the Pacific APA on a then new book on early Chinese philosophy by Bryan Van Norden. Chinese philosophy (unlike the Indian) is primarily preoccupied with ethical issues, and in recent years it has been argued and widely concluded that Confucian ethics in a sense broad enough to include Mencius and later figures is largely virtue-ethical, and virtue-ethical in a way that specifically resembles Aristotelian virtue ethics. Van Norden develops this understanding further in his book, but my comments suggest that the discussion of Chinese virtue ethics needs to be broadened. Yes, Chinese ethics can, for the most part, be seen as virtue-ethical, but with some figures, and especially Mencius, the comparison with Aristotle is less illuminating than a comparison with Humean virtue ethics and with British moral sentimentalism (and its contemporary descendants) more generally. Some scholars of Chinese philosophy have recently been moving in this direction, but my contribution pushes the comparison harder and I hope more deeply than has otherwise been done. My comments on Van Norden's book also focus on the consequentialist ethics of the early Chinese philosopher Mo Tzu. Van Norden's discussion doesn't nail down the consequentialist character of Mo Tzu's ideas as thoroughly as I think it needs to be, and I show there are passages in Mo Tzu that Van Norden doesn't mention and that serve to prove the consequentialist credentials of Mo Tzu better than the passages Van Norden *does* cite. I also point out that the arguments Mo Tzu gives for consequentialism don't show why we should accept consequentialism in preference to a totally impartialist version of *virtue ethics* (what I called "morality as universal benevolence" in a book entitled *Morals from Motives*, published by Oxford University Press in 2001).

More than any of the other essays in this book, the fifth essay, "Hume on Approval," carries forward the work I have recently been doing outside the history of ethics. It is more philosophically important to me than any of the other essays because it seeks to make good an ambition or aspiration I have had for many years now: to combine normative moral sentimentalism with a sentimentalist view of metaethics. This is something Hume sought to do and that I found myself unsuccessfully pursuing some years back. But having written up my ideas about normative sentimentalism in the form of a book, *The Ethics of Care and Empathy* (*ECE*), that was published by Routledge in 2007, I believe I have found a way to say something that isn't obviously mistaken about the metaethical side of sentimentalism, and "Hume on Approval" attempts to do this.

ECE argued that the normative distinctions we intuitively wish to make can be made in terms of sentimental distinctions of empathy or, more precisely, of empathic caring/concern about others. Even deontological distinctions turn out to be understandable in these terms, and *ECE* cites some recent work in neuroscience that supports my sentimentalist way of approaching deontology. "Hume on Approval" argues that the phenomenon or concept of empathy can also help us understand what it is to morally approve or disapprove of someone('s actions). But the empathy involved in moral approval is not the empathy felt by agents for the suffering, say, of others, but, rather, is empathy *felt by observers* for the empathy or lack of it that *agents* exhibit toward third parties, the people they either help or don't help. In other words, the empathy involved in approval and disapproval is directed toward agents and *their* empathy or lack of it, and the essay then goes on to argue that approval understood in this fashion can help us understand the nature of explicit moral judgments in a noncircular way.

The literature of developmental psychology indicates that empathy has motivational force (and may be essential to moral motivation in general), but if approval involves empathy and approval enters into the making of moral judgments, that will serve to explain why moral claims or judgments are intrinsically motivating. But I also argue that this needn't undercut the possibility of our moral judgments or utterances having cognitive validity. Following Thomas Nagel, I argue that the "objective prescriptivity" J. L. Mackie once characterized as "queer" in fact makes sense in the realm of moral judgment. However, the prescriptivity needn't be conceived in the rationalist terms Nagel developed, but can be understood, rather, in sentimentalist terms that can be used to describe the phenomenon of approval/disapproval and connect it with the making or understanding of moral judgments.

If talking about empathy allows us both to defend a sentimentalist account of normative ethics and to understand the metaethical nature of moral judgment(s) in sentimentalist terms, then a revival of sentimentalism on the large and systematic scale that Hume himself pursued may actually be possible. If such an approach can be made to appear plausible in contemporary terms, then there is more to be said for moral sentimentalism as a general approach to morality than most philosophers have thought possible. But I am not proposing to extend a Hume-like approach into epistemology, metaphysics, and the philosophy of mind generally; it is difficult enough to work out sentimentalism within or about morality or ethics more generally.

The sixth essay in this book, "Hume on the Artificial Virtues," discusses Hume's attempt to understand virtues like justice/honesty with respect to other people's property and fidelity to one's promises in sentimentalist terms. Hume curiously combines a Kant-anticipating insistence on the strictness of our moral obligations of honesty and fidelity with a commitment to virtue ethics, and this combination forces him to conceive our common thinking about strict obligations as in certain ways circular (what is sometimes called "Hume's circle"). Whether the *philosopher* can avoid such circular thought is a major issue for Hume, but the arguments he gives in defense of this possibility turn out, as I try to show, to be incompatible with (the rest of) his own empiricist thinking and to depend on something like rule-utilitarianism. "Hume on Artificial Virtues" ends with a negative verdict on the success of Hume's efforts to understand the artificial virtues—but deliberately leaves open the possibility that virtues like fidelity and honesty might be understood in the sort of "natural" terms that don't rely on human conventions and self-consciously strict explicitly moral thinking. I have pursued such a "natural virtues" (empathy-emphasizing) approach to fidelity and honesty, and to deontology and social justice more generally, in *ECE*.

"Kant for Anti-Kantians," the seventh essay in this book, is my acknowledgment of a great indebtedness to Kantian thought. I may be a thorough-going moral sentimentalist and Kant may be an arch-rationalist, but Kant made contributions to our understanding of morality and rationality that cut across different schools or approaches. I argue, for example, that we should accept what Kant says about the categorical character of moral judgments whether or not we believe what Kant specifically claims about the content or source of such judgments. I also defend the idea that Kant was the first to be explicit and clear about a distinction that nowadays we all need to make, the distinction, namely, between what is good *for* people and what is good impartially considered. The latter notion is involved when we talk about good states of affairs, but philosophers (not even Kant) don't seem to have explicitly spoken of good states of affairs before the time of G. E. Moore. However, the idea of a good state of affairs is implicit in Kant and Bentham and even earlier, and the seventh essay spends some time discussing how this idea, and the idea of a contrast between good states of affairs and personal well-being, slowly developed and emerged during the history of ethics.

"Kant for Anti-Kantians" ends with a discussion of the value and importance of Kant's insistence on the internal or inner character of moral judgment, on the idea that external results are irrelevant to our moral judgment of someone's actions. Kant thinks a moral agent will and should focus on producing results—for example, happiness for others, self-development for oneself—but also holds that if through bad luck and despite our best efforts we fail to achieve what morality tells us we should try to achieve, our actions are in no way morally criticizable. However, many contemporary approaches to ethics find this Kantian internalism to be extreme and implausible; and in the present essay, I attempt to show that they should think again. If we approach moral matters in commonsense terms, we find, I argue, a large measure of vindication for the Kantian emphasis on the inner.

In the eighth essay in this volume, "Reconfiguring Utilitarianism," I take a look at the varying ways utilitarianism has been seen over the past hundred years or so. How we conceive utilitarianism partly depends, perhaps largely depends, on how we conceive its relation to intuitive or commonsense moral thinking, and that relationship has in fact been intellectually reconfigured (at least) twice since the time of Sidgwick. Sidgwick saw utilitarianism as accounting for and partly justifying commonsense thinking, rather than clashing with it. But by the time we get to Ross the incompatibility between common sense and utilitarianism is a given. Ross thinks, in addition, that common sense is intuitively justified and that utilitarianism fails the test of intuitiveness; moreover, he regards utilitarianism as an unjustifiably truncated version of what common sense tells us. This means that utilitarianism is understood by Ross *in relation to* our commonsense thinking about prima facie duties.

However, by the time we get to the late twentieth century, things are different. We nowadays tend to understand common sense *by contrast with* and thus in relation to utilitarianism, the very opposite of what is suggested by Ross's account of morality. Nowadays, anti-utilitarian deontology and anti-utilitarian prerogatives to favor one's own projects and well-being are presented as *qualifications* of or *exceptions* to some basic, simple utilitarian account/statement of what is right and wrong. "Reconfiguring Utilitarianism" seeks to offer an explanation of why these changes, and especially this last reversal of the Rossian order of explication, have historically occurred.

I found "Under the Influence: A Very Personal Brief History of Late-Twentieth-Century Ethics," the ninth essay in this book, to be the most fun to think about and write of all the essays included here. It charts the history of the period through the lens of my own philosophical education and career, and explicitly focuses on the people who influenced me the most. It is, indeed, a very personal history, but in addition to telling the reader something about the philosophical/ethical thought of some important late-twentieth-century figures, the essay has a larger historical/historiographic purpose. It talks a great deal about the differing philosophical mentalities or differing intellectual talents that lay behind the accomplishments of philosophical ethicists like John Rawls, Philippa Foot, Thomas Nagel, Derek Parfit, Bernard Williams, and Michael Stocker; and I am not sure that other approaches to the history of philosophy have focused in this way on similarities and dissimilarities between the "casts of mind" of different philosophical figures. The essay hopes to demonstrate that it is worth doing this sort of thing when writing about the history of philosophy, but the reader will have to judge for herself or himself whether it was worth my effort. The essay ends with a discussion of two other important thinkers who have affected my work in recent years, Carol Gilligan and Nel Noddings, and the way this essay ends leads us right into the tenth and final essay of the book.

"Carol Gilligan and History of Ethics" begins by saying something about the enormous contribution Gilligan has made to the field of ethics. Care ethics is increasingly and prominently pursued by philosophers and nonphilosophers, and Gilligan's influence (together with that of Nel Noddings and also of Sara Ruddick) has been in large measure responsible for this development. (People like Virginia Held who came to care ethics a bit later also deserve some of the credit.) But this tenth and final essay does two other things as well. It argues that Gilligan's revolutionary ideas within ethics can and should make a difference to how we write about the history of ethics. And it also, very briefly, discusses Gilligan's mentality, the character of her thinking and of her creative contribution, in the sort of terms that were used in the previous essay to talk about Rawls, Foot, et al.

After reading what I have just been saying about the essays in this book, the reader might have (at least) one rather large question about the overall structure or character of my ethical views. The first essay here, "The Opposite of Reductionism," tentatively defends a rather Platonic conception of human well-being, or the good life, and yet in "Hume on Approval" and later essays in this book, I argue for or presuppose a moral sentimentalism that is more in line with Hume than with anything that can be derived from Platonic (moral) rationalism. Are these views mutually inconsistent or at least in some tension with each other?

I think not. The sentimentalism I defend applies only to morality and *moral* virtue, and I have no doubt that there are plenty of virtues that are not specifically (or exclusively) moral and that need a more extensive treatment than I have offered here or anywhere else. So when I say, in the first essay, that every class of human good may entail a corresponding and distinctive form of virtue, the virtues I specify for particular human goods are virtues like courage and perseverance that may well forever remain at least partly outside the ambit of (my) moral sentimentalism. Clearly, what I say in "The Opposite of Reductionism" doesn't flow out of or create the basis for any form of moral sentimentalism, but I see diversity or complexity here, not any sort of tension.

However, my commitment to sentimentalism is stronger than my commitment to what I have called Platonic elevationism, and it is not clear to me that sentimentalism wouldn't be more comfortable with a less elevationist and more reductionist (e.g., a hedonistic or desire-based) account of human well-being. But even this isn't obvious because (as I argue in *ECE* and at greater length in a paper called "Empathy and Objectivity" that can be found in my *Selected Essays*, Oxford University Press, 2009) empathy, which I treat as the psychological/ethical basis for a sentimentalist ethics of care, doesn't have to be directed at hedonic, emotional, or orectic states/events. Psychologist Martin Hoffman, who is briefly discussed in "Hume on Approval" and who has written more and better about empathy than anyone else I know, holds that we can be empathic with a person's situation or condition somewhat independently of what the person is feeling or desires. His example is that of a person who knows that someone has terminal cancer and feels empathy for them (and their condition) even though the person with the cancer doesn't yet know about it. This possibility leaves it open that morality should, through empathy, have a sentimentalist foundation and yet, again through empathy, allow of a wider range of fundamental human goods than empiricists/associationists like Hume were willing to acknowledge. Some day I may be able to integrate what I think about human well-being with my sentimentalist views about both morality and rationality. (*ECE* contains a long discussion of sentimentalist practical rationality; and I say something about this in "Ancient Ethics and Modern Moral Philosophy," the third essay of the present book.) But for now it seems worthwhile to have worked up and to be publishing all the essays offered in this book, even if they can't be placed together in a simple or unified package.

It has, honestly, been fun writing this book. That is partly because I had never before written so much about the history of ethics, and the fact that I was doing so represented, to me, a kind of novelty. Still, the essays collected here defend serious philosophical and historical ideas; it's not supposed to be, and neither was it, all fun and games. I think a moral philosopher like myself can learn a great, great deal by becoming more deeply and more broadly (think of the fourth essay here on Chinese ethics) engaged with the history of ethics and with thinking of philosophical ideas and arguments in relation to that history. But the reader will have to judge for herself whether, at least regarding my own case, I have been right about this.

I

THE OPPOSITE OF REDUCTIONISM

The present essay has been a long time in the writing. The question of how virtue and well-being, or self-interest, connect has interested me since at least the early 1980s; but in the course of developing my thoughts on that issue, I began to see that the differing positions various schools or philosophers take in this area illustrate a wider sort of difference of opinion and approach. When the utilitarian or Epicurean understands or explains morality/virtue in terms of considerations of human (or sentient) well-being, this constitutes a form of reduction(ism), because morality/virtue is typically or naturally regarded as something higher than the sheer enjoyment of well-being. But in that case, we need a name for the opposite sort of move that the Stoics make when they explain human well-being or happiness in terms of the higher, or more exalted, notion of (having) virtue, and as far as I was able to tell, historians of ethics or philosophy more generally hadn't come up with such a name. The name I came up with, "elevation(ism)" is certainly not very elegant; but it is accurately descriptive of the way Stoicism opposes, moves in the opposite direction from, Epicureanism and utilitarianism. If the latter understand the putatively higher in terms of what is putatively lower, then Stoicism understands the putatively lower in terms of the higher.

But once one makes this distinction and has this vocabulary, it becomes possible to see that the opposition between elevationism and reductionism is illustrated in a number of areas outside of ethics. The two terms or notions therefore offer us a very general method or prism for viewing large swaths of the history of philosophy, and in what follows I shall be taking up all these themes and relating them to particular issues and controversies both inside and outside the field of ethics.

1.1 Elevation versus Reduction

One of the main strengths or attractions of act-utilitarianism is that it allows for a reduction of all our ethical ideals and standards to the ethical notion of well-being or welfare. Actions count as right, roughly speaking, to the extent they bring about (the greatest possible) well-being; and utilitarianism also reduces other moral notions to the notion of well-being suitably supplemented by appropriate causal and other concepts. An act counts as blameworthy, for example, if the act of blaming or negatively reinforcing it will have the best or good enough consequences for human or sentient well-being, and a trait counts as a (moral) virtue if it generally leads to well-being rather than to its opposite. Similarly, states of affairs count as intrinsically (and morally) good if they *contain* more of well-being than of its opposite.

Utilitarianism also tends to treat (practical) rationality (or reasonableness) as reductively understandable in terms of well-being. But different utilitarians effect this reduction in different ways. For example, when he isn't worrying about what he takes to be an unresolvable conflict between ethical egoism and utilitarianism, Sidgwick regards rationality (and reasonableness and, of course, rightness too) as understandable in terms of what makes the greatest contribution to overall human/sentient well-being.[1] But in recent years, Peter Railton, while defending an act-utilitarian view of right action, has accepted a conception of rational choice and action that differs from Sidgwick's.[2] According to Railton, individual rationality is understood as a form of instrumental rationality, as the agent's efficient pursuit (roughly) of his own ends or, perhaps, of his own interests or his own good. But whether one ties rationality to the general welfare or to the agent's, the effect is reductive in the same way that utilitarian accounts of rightness, blameworthiness, and virtue are reductive. So I think it is safe to say that utilitarianism reduces all prominent ethical notions to concepts of well-being or personal good.

But then the fundamental ethical category of well-being is treated by the utilitarian as *further reducible* to empirical or nonethical notions like preference satisfaction or pleasure/pain. So utilitarianism not only reduces the major concepts of ethics to a single ethical notion, but then reduces the whole realm of ethical value and evaluation to naturalistic and value-free facts. This unifying reduction occurs at a considerable price, since utilitarianism notoriously clashes with commonsense judgments about what is morally right or blameworthy (or rational). However, at this point, I think we need to become a bit clearer about the double reduction that I have just attributed to utilitarianism and about the notion of reduction in general.

In philosophical parlance, one kind of reduction occurs or is attempted when one seeks to understand the macro in terms of the micro (the whole in terms of its elements or parts), as, for example, when we identify salt with sodium chloride. But, as I indicated above, another form of reduction takes place when an attempt is made to understand what is "higher" in terms of what

---

1. In *The Methods of Ethics* (7th edition, London: Macmillan, 1907), Sidgwick claims that "rational," "right," and "reasonable" all express a single property or concept, and for someone who is otherwise so attentive to usage and examples, this seems a surprising ground-floor mistake. After all, there are many things we consider irrational or foolish without regarding them as immoral, or involving wrongdoing: for example, trying to jump over a barrier that is simply too high for one (and hurting oneself in the process).

2. See Peter Railton, "Moral Realism," *Philosophical Review* 95: 163–207, 1986.

is "lower."[3] Thus when the utilitarian identifies well-being or doing well in life with pleasure or desire satisfaction, this is plausibly regarded as a *reduction* because the realm of value seems in some way *higher* than the merely empirical or natural (is that because it involves *standards for judging* what actually occurs or might occur in human life or *ideals to aspire to* in our lives?). For the same reason, it makes sense to say, for example, that Freud and Adler *reduced* all putatively higher activities and aspirations, respectively, to mere sexual strivings and desire for power.

However, as I have already mentioned, when utilitarianism seeks to understand all rationality, virtue, and morality in terms of facts about well-being, that also counts as a reduction, because it is natural or commonsensical to think of the ethical category of well-being as in some sense *lower* than the categories utilitarianism seeks to understand in terms of it. To that extent, the unification utilitarianism seeks and achieves *within* the realm of the ethical is reductive quite apart from the further attempt to reduce well-being (and thus all other ethical concepts as well) to naturalistic terms, but I think we need to say a bit more about why well-being (or personal good) is regarded as *lower* than virtue, morality, and rationality.

The first point, I think, to be made in this connection is that what counts as an element in our well-being or as good for us may in no way be admirable. For example, in the *Eudemian Ethics* (1248b 17–27), Aristotle makes the commonsense point that unlike the virtues, (sheer) health is good but not praiseworthy. Now health can perhaps be thought of as praiseworthy or admirable when it is regarded as the result *of prudent* exercise and self-controlled dieting, as an *achievement*. But a sheer state of good health, or a healthy constitution that owes nothing to one's efforts (or any one else's), is presumably not praiseworthy, and this would appear to be what Aristotle had in mind. A similar point can be made about pleasure and common enjoyment. These involve something good happening to us, but because they don't seem to require any virtue, rationality, or morality on our part, there seems to be nothing admirable or praiseworthy about the capacity for and occasions of (appetitive) pleasure and enjoyment.

But the distinction between what is *merely* enjoyable, pleasurable, and good (for us) and what is admirable or praiseworthy seems to involve a distinction between lower and higher ethical values—what else can the word "merely" be doing in this sentence? Claims about rationality, morality, and what is admirable in other spheres express *ideals*, and in becoming generous or prudent or trained in physics or philosophy, we would normally be thought to be realizing certain actual or possible ideals of character or human aspiration, in a way that enjoyment, feeling secure, and a healthy constitution do not require. Of course, it is also possible to be immoral, irrational, and vice-ridden, but even these

---

3. One can also try to reduce the number of entities or concepts one refers to or makes use of in a theory, but this notion of reduction cuts across the distinctions I shall be making in the main text, and I shall ignore it in what follows.

negative attributes, like their positive counterparts, seem to involve and make reference to more *highly evolved* capacities than those required for sheer well-being and its opposite. (Again, think of why the term "sheer" seems appropriate in this context.) So in understanding rationality, virtue, moral goodness, and their opposites as (mere) means to well-being and its opposite, utilitarianism is reducing (what is intuitively and antecedently taken to be) the ethically higher to (what is intuitively and antecedently taken to be) the ethically lower. And to that extent, utilitarianism deflates ethics internally by telling us that there is nothing to the apparent distinction between higher and lower ethical values, telling us that the virtue, rationality, etc., that we tend to think of as higher than mere or sheer well-being or welfare is really at the same level as (what we antecedently regard as) the lower.[4]

Note, however, that such reduction(ism) *isn't* the inevitable effect of any attempt to unify the concepts of ethics, a price we have to and should be willing to pay if we value theoretical systematization and unification highly and are willing to pay the price of rejecting many of our ethical intuitions.[5] There is another mode of intra-ethical unification that involves just the opposite of reductionism. Above, I called this elevationism,[6] but in order to understand how such a different mode of unification is possible and may even be ethically plausible, we would do well to begin by considering the difference between Stoicism and Epicureanism.

4. In speaking just a moment ago of more highly evolved capacities, I wasn't necessarily referring to or making use of the theory of evolution, something that would have been unavailable to the ancients and to many modern thinkers. But the capacity for thought or virtue does, I think intuitively, seem like a higher capacity than the capacity for enjoyment and (sheer) well-being. It didn't take the theory of evolution to make these things seem higher on the scale of values or ideals. The very fact that we naturally speak of ideals of virtue/rationality but not of well-being already indicates the thought of something higher, because although we can speak of low aspirations, there is something oxymoronic about the idea of low ideals. The naturalness of the idea of height here may be further evidenced by the fact that it is/was natural to think of God or the gods as *physically* higher than we humans: as in heaven or on Mount Olympus (Hades would then be an exceptional place for a god or gods to be). And, of course, the gods or God were also (before the theory of evolution) conceived as higher *beings* than we are, and higher in something like the way that we, in turn, are higher than nonrational animals. We can certainly then ask whether it is physical or ontological height that comes/came conceptually or historically first. The idea, furthermore, that the realm of value as a whole is higher than that of sheer or mere (empirical) factuality also seems to have a place in our minds (and not just, e.g., in Plato's mind). We can talk of mere fact in a way that we aren't inclined to talk of "mere value(s)"—unless we are strongly, perhaps brutally, reductionistic. In the wake of what I have just been saying, I think more historical work needs to be done on the question of how we come by our (intuitive) notions of higher and lower. But, in any event, the use I have made of these notions here seems to me to have a ring of intuitiveness, and I hope the reader agrees. (I am indebted on these issues to discussion with Richard Kraut.)

5. I am not going to try to discuss here whether such quasi-scientific attitudes toward the doing of ethics are entirely appropriate given the practical aims of morality and the richness and complexity of our ordinary understanding of moral phenomena.

6. I haven't been able to find any more idiomatic, natural, or attractive term for conveying the opposite of *both* higher/lower *and* macro/micro reduction.

Epicureanism is reductive in the manner of utilitarianism, though on an (arguably) egoistic, rather than universalistic, basis. What is antecedently regarded as higher is understood in terms of what is antecedently thought of as lower via its claim that practical rationality and (the) virtue(s) generally are nothing more than effective means to—and thus exist at the same level as—a person's well-being. (Like utilitarianism, Epicureanism then effects a second reduction by treating well-being or human good as a matter simply of pleasure, or, more accurately, freedom from pain.)

But if Epicureanism, like utilitarianism, assimilates the admirable and putatively higher to the desirable and putatively lower, Stoicism works in just the opposite direction, understanding or explaining the putatively lower values of well-being or personal good in terms of the supposedly higher ones of rationality and virtue. And I have suggested that we introduce the term "elevation" for this second form of assimilation. (As I also mentioned, however, historians of philosophy haven't previously come up with any term for this phenomenon; and this is odd and surprising because, as we shall be seeing in a moment, many kinds of theories both inside and outside ethics assimilate levels of entities/concepts/phenomena in the manner of Stoicism.) So we can say that Stoicism *elevates* human well-being to the level of human virtue/morality/rationality.

For the Stoics, human well-being (or happiness) *consists* in being virtuous. Virtue or the virtues taken together are the sum and substance of human well-being: nothing beyond (the attainment of) rational virtue is required for us to be well-off or have good lives, and nothing that fails to improve us in virtue/rationality can be, therefore, of any real benefit. A virtuous individual bereft of wealth, friends, bodily/appetitive pleasures, and good health—indeed even on the rack and in great permanent pain—can be as well-off as it is possible for a human being to be, and so on a Stoic account human well-being is regarded very differently from the way it ordinarily is. For common sense, whether or not virtue, or various virtues, are part of a good life, certain enjoyments and activities that seem neither admirable nor the means to anything admirable are definitely seen as constituents of living well, of a good life, of personal good, or well-being. But Stoicism denies the intrinsic personal goodness of so-called worldly and appetitive goods, and it doubts even the universal instrumental goodness of such things because it questions whether they usually lead to the virtuousness of those who enjoy them. And so the following contrasts can be drawn between the Stoic and Epicurean treatments of the relation between personal good/well-being and the virtues.

The Epicurean deflates our ideas about virtue and admirability by regarding these things as simply a matter of what is conducive or not conducive to the well-being (or happiness) of individuals. What is normally seen as higher than mere personal well-being (as being, e.g., admirable in a way well-being or enjoyment isn't and/or as depending on evolutionarily higher capacities than well-being depends on) turns out, on the Epicurean account, to be of a piece with, at the same level as, facts solely about human well-being and its causes or effects.

But rather than reduce virtue/admirability to personal well-being (or happiness), the Stoic inflates or elevates our ideas about personal good (or well-being or happiness) by thinking of the latter solely in terms of (what constitutes) human virtue or admirability.[7] What is normally seen as lower than (ideas of) virtue turns out, on the Stoic account, to be of a piece with facts about virtue. And if, for the Epicurean, virtue is nothing more than a factor in personal good or happiness, then, for the Stoic, happiness and well-being are nothing *less* than virtue or virtuous living; and these contrasts should at this point make it understandable that Stoicism should be deemed a form of elevationism if Epicureanism is regarded as a form of reductionism.

Having set elevationism and reductionism at odds, I think it is now important to note what they have in common. It is well known, for example, that reductions needn't preserve meaning—"salt is sodium chloride" is not an analytic or a priori truth. Similarly, neither utilitarian nor Epicurean reductionism need claim an analytic status for itself, and the same holds true for Stoic elevationism. These are *theories*, and they can be true in the way theories are true rather than definitionally or by virtue of some form of ethical mathematics.

In addition, the idea of reducing one kind of entity or property to another is often clarified by invoking the notion of certain *distinctions* being reducible to certain others. For example, we naturally think of the mental as in some sense higher (evolutionarily and perhaps spiritually) than the purely (or *merely*) physical, and if the mental then turns out to be reducible to the physical, then every valid mental distinction can be reduced to or identified with some distinction made in physical terms. According to such reductionism, then, where no physical distinction/difference obtains, no distinction/difference will (be able to) occur at the mental level either. But none of this entails that every physical distinction will be accompanied by some mentalistic one. As long as the mental is a function of the physical, the reducing relation can obtain even if no function from the mental to the physical can be found, and so, more briefly, we can characterize typical reductions of the mental to the physical as claiming that physical distinctions are *necessary but not sufficient* for the existence of mental distinctions.

By the same token, when Epicureanism (or utilitarianism) reduces virtue to well-being, it treats all distinctions of virtue as accompanied by distinctions in (causal, relational, and other) facts about individual well-being or happiness. But it needn't claim that every distinction in facts about the production

---

7. The word "inflation" actually won't do as a general term for the opposite of the deflation or reduction advocated by Epicureanism, because it strongly suggests the falsity of any theory or view to which it applies. We shall be seeing that at least one form of ethical elevationism (though not Stoicism!) is far from implausible in contemporary terms. The term "sublimation" won't do for other reasons. So I think we may be stuck with "elevation" for the broad range of phenomena we shall be talking about here.

of well-being (distinctions, e.g., about *who* certain character traits benefit or about *when* those benefits occur) will be accompanied by or give rise to a distinction having to do with virtue.

Elevation can be understood in essentially similar terms. When the Stoic elevates the personally good (up) to the virtuous or admirable, he or she is committed to saying that every distinction with regard to the former can be thoroughly understood or accounted for in terms of distinctions relating to the latter, just as, when the Epicurean reduces the virtues or virtue (down) to matters of well-being, he or she is committed to saying that every distinction with regard to the former can be thoroughly understood or accounted for in terms of distinctions involving the latter. The only difference between the two processes or results lies in the respective *heights* of "the former" and "the latter" in the two cases. In elevations, distinctions with regard to the presumptively lower are always correlated with distinctions that involve the presumptively higher, but the reverse need not be true. In reductions, distinctions regarding the presumptively higher are always accompanied by distinctions relating to the presumptively lower, though, again, the reverse need not be true. So in some sense, reduction and elevation are the same thing operating in *opposite* (vertical) directions.

Moreover, the distinction between reduction and elevation also applies well beyond the confines of ethics. For example, just as in ethics we can be dualistic about virtue and well-being (I shall have more to say about this possibility shortly) or else identify these concepts either reductively or elevatively, one of our main choices in metaphysics is between mind–body dualism and monism of an either reductive (materialist or physicalist) or elevative (idealist or phenomenalist) character. Indeed, quite a number of disagreements outside of ethics allow of historiographic clarification through these categories. We think of concepts, for example, as higher (as depending on more highly evolved capacities) than percepts or sensations, yet British empiricism basically reduces all concepts to percepts, whereas Continental Rationalism treats sensation/perception as a matter of obscure conception and thus counts as a form of elevationism. Kant's insistence on the distinction between percepts and concepts would then represent the "dualistic" option in this area of philosophical thought.

Similarly, and thinking now in terms of wholes and parts (rather than in terms of the higher and the lower), the choice among reduction, elevation, and dualism can also be seen to apply in the field of social philosophy. Social atomism is the reductionistic option regarding the relation between individuals and the societies of which they are members, whereas an organicism that treats the individual as a mere aspect or reflection of society constitutes a form of elevationism, and the view that the social and individual levels need to be differentiated represents dualism in this area. But however historiographically significant these extra-moral applications of our distinction may be, we have more than enough to occupy us in considering its relevance, and, in particular, the relevance of elevationism, to ethics and its history.

1.2 Is Elevationism Viable?

Stoic elevationism is implausible as a theory of human well-being. It notoriously considers ordinary appetitive pleasures to constitute no part of human
well-being, and it regards (nonmoral) pain as in no way intrinsically contrary
to human well-being or good. Such conclusions about human good and ill are
highly counterintuitive, perhaps more counterintuitive than anything utilitarianism is committed to, and although the Stoics offer a variety of arguments
for their views, those arguments are widely regarded as unpersuasive and will
not concern us here. Let us see, rather, whether any other kind of historically
significant (or historically rooted) virtue-ethical elevationism can avoid the
excesses of the Stoic view of human good and ill.

At first glance, this might seem to be impossible. If a virtue ethics is to be
elevationistic, it must understand all distinctions relating to well-being in terms
of distinctions having to do with virtue. Doesn't this mean that how well-off
one is will depend on how virtuous one is and doesn't this precisely deliver us
up to the forbidding conclusion that pain is no evil for the virtuous person on
the rack? It is certainly natural to think so. It is natural to think that if virtue
and well-being don't, so to speak, coincide, then neither can be understood in
terms of the other (suitably supplemented by nonevaluative notions); and it is
interesting, in this connection, to consider what Kant says about Stoicism and
Epicureanism in the *Critique of Practical Reason*.[8]

Kant recognizes that these ancient views are not merely inconsistent with
one another, but are in an important respect opposites—his discussion to some
extent anticipates, though in a less general and self-conscious fashion, the distinction we are making between elevationism and reductionism. Kant holds
that individual virtue cannot be identified with what effectively serves the
well-being or happiness of the individual, in the manner of Epicureanism, but
also that individual well-being or happiness cannot, in the Stoic manner, be
identified with the individual's (consciousness of his or her own) virtue. (He
refuses to accept the Stoic's claim that pain is for him no evil.) Kant is in fact
a dualist about our higher and lower ethical values, about the admirable and
the personally desirable, and he claims that well-being and virtue are "entirely
heterogeneous" concepts.

But it in fact doesn't follow from the fact, assumed by Kant, that virtue and
well-being don't coincide in either the way Stoics believe or the way Epicureans believe that these notions are entirely heterogeneous. Kant doesn't say
that this follows, and he seems to have independent reasons, to be discussed
briefly in a moment, for holding that we cannot understand virtue in terms of
well-being or vice versa. But what is most important at this point is to see why
"entire heterogeneity" doesn't follow from noncoincidence, since that will precisely leave open the possibility of a historically interesting elevationism that

---

8. See especially part I, book I, ch. 2.

avoids the problems of Stoicism. And we can see this most easily, I think, if we consider utilitarianism (which isn't mentioned in Kant's discussion).

Utilitarianism at one and the same time denies the coincidence of virtue and well-being and insists that the former can be understood or explained in terms of the latter, taken together with nonethical, empirical notions. For under utilitarianism, the virtuous individual is one who contributes to the general well-being at the possible *expense* of her own, and the familiar criticism that utilitarianism is too demanding is based upon the realization that utilitarian morality puts at considerable risk, rather than insuring, the well-being of the virtuous individual. So for utilitarianism, virtue and well-being don't at all have to coincide in individuals. Yet utilitarian reductionism treats virtue and morality as understandable in terms of well-being rather than as entirely heterogeneous with the latter notion, and in that case, there is room in ethical/conceptual space for an elevationist (virtue) ethics that understands well-being in terms of virtue without assuming, in the way that has such damaging consequences for Stoicism, that virtue and well-being coincide in individuals. It must be possible for there to be a view or views that bear to Stoicism something like the relation that utilitarianism bears to Epicureanism, a possibility that I myself have sometimes ignored in writing about elevationism and that Kant doesn't seem to regard as a serious option for ethical theory.

I believe that the overall Critical Philosophy gives Kant a reason to ignore this option and to look askance at all monistic theorizing about virtue and personal well-being, a reason emerging from the approach to metaphysics and epistemology taken in the First Critique. Kant thinks that in ethics, well-being represents or corresponds to sensibility and virtue represents or corresponds to the understanding; and to the extent the Critical Philosophy rests on a dualism of sensibility and understanding (and of percepts and concepts), Kant seems to want a corresponding dualism in ethics; and that may be why he insists that well-being and virtue are entirely heterogeneous. So Kant's larger or more systematic dualism seems to predispose him not only against any form of ethical reductionism, but also against the possibility I want to defend here in both historical and theoretical terms, the possibility of understanding well-being in elevationist terms but not as *coincident* with virtue or morality. (Samuel Kerstein has pointed out to me that Kant's position here may have in part also derived from an intuitive conviction that virtuous people are sometimes very unhappy and the wicked sometimes "flourish as the green bay tree.")

But doesn't the drive for a unifying system, to the extent we consider such a thing appropriate in doing ethics, actually favor the Kantian ethical dualism at this point over any form of elevationist monism, even one that would be more plausible than Stoicism? To be sure, monism allows us a greater unification within ethics than dualism does, but to the extent Kant's ethical dualism allows him to dovetail his ethics with his metaphysics/epistemology in a way that ethical elevationism doesn't claim to do, doesn't Kant's *ethical* dualism come out ahead of any monistic (virtue-ethical) elevationism we might be able to locate in the history of philosophy and/or develop in contemporary terms?

That depends, I think, on what one says about the First Critique. If one has doubts about the way Kant treats concepts and percepts and about his general metaphysical and epistemological methods and conclusions in that context, then that may actually rebound *against* the approach Kant takes in ethics. Basing an ethics on an epistemology-cum-metaphysics is a double-edged sword, but rather than attempt here to investigate all the epistemological and metaphysical issues that we would need to examine in order to determine which way the sword cuts, it seems reasonable to explore the historical and contemporary possibilities of monistic, elevationistic virtue ethics in order to see whether, quite apart from any connection to epistemology or metaphysics, such an ethics can fulfill the (somewhat independent) criteria of a good systematic ethical theory. Those criteria are demanding and interesting enough, so that it seems worth our while to see whether any form of elevationist virtue ethics can meet them, and I shall proceed accordingly.

I think a more plausible example of virtue-ethical elevatonism than Stoicism offers us can in fact be found in a certain way of understanding or interpreting Aristotle's views in the *Nicomachean Ethics*. The so-called function (or *ergon*) argument of book I of the *Ethics* concludes that the good life for human beings consists in a long and active life of virtue. But Aristotle immediately qualifies this claim by pointing out that how pleasant or painful, successful or unsuccessful one's life is also helps to determine how good it is (whether it is "blessed"). This further point seems to take Aristotle away from any attempt to explain human well-being in terms of the higher categories of virtue and rationality and toward some sort of dualistic conception of the ethical. But that interpretation is not actually forced on us, because of some of the things Aristotle says later about pleasure. In book X (chs. 3–5), he says that pleasures deriving from perverted or morally unworthy sources are not good, not desirable, and it is possible to interpret this as meaning that a person who gains money or certain enjoyments through injustice or betrayal gains nothing good for himself, fails to have his well-being (even momentarily) enhanced. Sarah Broadie interprets the relevant passages in something like this manner,[9] and once one does so, there is an obvious way to treat Aristotle as an elevationist monist in ethics.

For if Aristotle is saying that pleasure and success count as elements in our well-being only if and when they can be obtained consistently with being virtuous, then his conception of well-being or the good life will at every point have to refer to virtue. The good or best life will then, roughly, be a life full of virtuous activity and of pleasures and successes that are consistent with virtue—and (largely) lacking in pains and failures that virtue might require. And on such a picture there are no purely natural personal goods or evils:

---

9. See her *Ethics with Aristotle*, Oxford: Oxford University Press, 1991, p. 376.

that is, everything that adds to or subtracts from our well-being must do so *in relation to higher moral or ethical values*.[10] We have ended up with a form of elevationist monism, but one that is less extreme and less implausible than Stoicism because it allows many ordinary pleasures and achievements a role in constituting/enhancing human well-being and allows many ordinary pains and failures a similar role in making lives worse than they otherwise could or would be.

However, as I indicated earlier, this is not the only way one could interpret Aristotle's views about the good of pleasure and achievement. In book X, Aristotle also says, for example, that the good man is the measure of what is truly pleasurable, so that what appears pleasant only to a spoiled or perverted taste is not really pleasant. Perhaps he is here making the quasi-linguistic point that what is pleasant only to a perverted taste cannot properly be called pleasant *tout court*, while at the same time being willing to grant that such things can be pleasant to—and perhaps even good for—the perverted individual. On such a reading, a vicious person can get something good-for-himself, something that enhances *his* well-being at least, from vicious actions, and this then leaves some natural or lower human good(s) outside the orbit of (specification in terms of) virtue. It makes Aristotle into a dualist about virtue and well-being.

But, following Broadie, I actually think the first interpretation is closer to Aristotle; and so I think we have uncovered an important historical example of (what can plausibly be interpreted as) ethical elevationism that doesn't entail the unpalatable Stoic view that virtue and well-being coincide. (The unpalatability is only in regard to the view's wildly unintuitive implications—for example, that pain is never a bad thing in one's life—but of course some of us may believe it would be very nice if individual virtue and well-being *did* or *could* coincide. That is, after all, some of the motive for believing or trying to believe in heaven and hell.) What we need now to do is consider whether what we can call "Aristotelian" elevatonist virtue ethics can allow us to unify virtue and well-being in a way that can rival or surpass the unification that utilitarianism has achieved in the opposite direction.

However, even if this new view claims no coincidence between individual virtue and individual well-being, and so avoids what I take to be the most

---

10. I stress this last phrase because it may be useful to us in answering the following objection due to Thomas Hurka. Aristotelian elevationism allows two people to be equally virtuous yet differ in well-being; but how, the objection goes, can this be possible if all distinctions in well-being are to be understood or explained in terms of distinctions in virtue? There is a difference, however, between distinctions in virtue (in one obvious sense) and distinctions having to do with, or having reference to, virtue. Remember that Aristotelian elevationism treats differences of pleasure, for example, as creating (immediate) differences of well-being only if the pleasures are consistent with virtue (not ignoble). In the case, then, where two individuals differ in well-being because one has more virtue-consistent pleasure than the other, the two don't perhaps differ in virtue, that is, in how virtuous they are; but there is still a distinction between them having to do with, or having reference to (or bringing in facts about), virtue, namely, the fact that one of them has more *virtue-consistent* pleasure than the other.

implausible implications of Stoicism, it has other implications that ought to bother us. It entails that the pleasures (or achievements) that a vicious person obtains only through being vicious are no part of her good, so that, for example, the pleasure of eating food she has stolen is no sort of personal good for the thief. But intuitively, and here I am following Kant as well, one wants to say that though it is not a good thing *that* someone should benefit from wrongdoing, what is bad here is precisely that a person does indeed *benefit* from acting wrongly or viciously.

Aristotelian elevationism will also seem implausible for what it has to say about personal evils. To maintain a thoroughgoing and essential connection to virtue in each aspect of its account of human well-being, the view has to maintain that the pain that virtue requires an individual to suffer involves no diminution of her well-being. If virtue requires someone to remain silent under torture, then the pain and suffering that occur during and result from such an episode will count as in no way making the individual's life worse, and, if anything, this seems even more implausible than what Aristotelian elevationism has to say about the well-being irrelevance of pleasures gained through vicious actions. In the end, I think this form of elevationism is seriously counterintuitive, though certainly less extreme and counterintuitive than Stoic elevationism. (Here I ignore what these views have to say about the content of virtue and refer only to how they connect virtue with well-being.)

But the possibilities of elevationistic ethical monism are not yet exhausted, and if we take the proper lesson from the assumed failure of Aristotelian elevationism, we may yet learn how to construct a (more) plausible form of elevationistic virtue ethics and, in addition, how to recognize an inchoate version of such a view in the historical past. At this point, I would like to see if we can avoid the unwelcome consequences of Stoic and Aristotelian elevationism by *weakening our assumptions about the connection between well-being and virtue*. Stoicism says that virtue and well-being coincide in the individual, Aristotelian elevationism says, in effect, that all elements of personal well-being must be compatible with *virtue taken as a whole*, and we have reason to criticize both these assumptions/conclusions. But what if we say, instead, that every element of human well-being must be compatible with or involve at least some *part* of virtue or one or another *particular* virtue? Such a claim might be entirely in keeping with the goal of elevationism and yet enable us to avoid the untoward implications of the Stoic and Aristotelian versions. For it allows us to deny that virtue and well-being coincide and to hold that a pleasure that a virtuous individual wouldn't desire, choose, or obtain, a pleasure incompatible with *virtue as a whole* might still count as part of someone's well-being *as long as it bore an appropriate relation to some particular virtue or part of virtue*. Better still, I believe that the beginnings of a theory that actually fulfills these requirements can be found in Plato's *Gorgias*.

1.3 Platonic Elevationism

Plato notably holds that all good things possess a common element or exemplify a common property or pattern, and Aristotle famously criticizes this fundamental view in the *Nicomachean Ethics*. But Plato makes a somewhat more specific claim about the things that are good in a rather neglected passage in the *Gorgias* (S. 506), where he says that "all good things whatever are good when some virtue is present in…them." (I use the Jowett translation here and in later quotations.) Leaving aside judgments about functional goodness (but remembering that good knives and good doctors are commonly spoken of as having their "virtues") and focusing solely on judgments about intrinsic personal good or well-being, Plato's claim implies that all personal good or well-being contains an element of virtue and thus has something in common with the virtues themselves. And notice too that the claim is consistent with saying that different kinds of goods contain *different virtues*. Clearly, if Plato's thesis were correct, then we would be able to defend a form of virtue-ethical elevationism, but what Plato is saying clearly sounds odd or undermotivated, to say the least, so let us at this point see what can be said in its defense.[11]

To defend Plato's idea here, we would need in particular to show that even common pleasures and enjoyments, in order to count as an intrinsic part of our well-being, must contain or be accompanied by some form or instance of (one of the) virtue(s). And at this point, such a view seems perilously close to the idea, previously rejected, that pleasure is a good thing in someone's life only if it is achieved compatibly with the dictates of (moral) virtue. However, the Platonic view we are considering in fact allows that a person who viciously steals food and then enjoys it may, contrary to Stoic and Aristotelian elevationism, have his well-being enhanced *as long as he exemplifies and exhibits one (particular) virtue in the course of that enjoyment*; and what I want to argue in what follows is that appetitive pleasures and enjoyments must be accompanied by at least some degree of moderation, a quality we admire and think of as a virtue, in order to count toward a person's well-being. (Actually, I shall only argue that appetitive goods require that one not be *totally immoderate*, but for simplicity's sake I shall continue to speak of virtue rather than of the absence of vice.) The idea that appetitive goods demand some sort of virtue is far from obvious and represents, I believe, the largest stumbling block to any acceptance of the Platonic approach I am

---

11. Julia Annas has pointed out to me that *arête* (excellence or virtue) is the noun that normally corresponds to the Greek adjective *agathos* (good). But she agrees that "slippage" between the two is possible in Greek the way it isn't possible, in English, between "goodness" and "good." My view, then, is that in the passage cited from the *Gorgias*, Plato is moving to deny or cut off the possibility of such slippage. That is a substantive (nontrivial) ethical move or thesis, and my acceptance of it as the basis for the kind of elevationist view of well-being, I shall be proposing here, is also substantive.

proposing. But before we consider more closely what can be said about the relations between appetitive satisfactions and the virtue of moderation and before I then go on to show in greater detail how such ideas were anticipated by Plato, let me say a bit more about other sorts of personal good or well-being whose connection to one or another virtue seems far less problematic. (I shall also later on say something about how Platonic elevationism treats personal ills or evils.)

Most accounts of human well-being that don't reduce such well-being to pleasure or desire satisfaction and that seek some sort of intuitive account or understanding of the kinds of things that are (intrinsically) good for people regard not only appetitive enjoyments, but also certain kinds of wisdom or knowledge, certain kinds of friendly or loving relationships, and certain kinds of achievement or accomplishment as (fundamental) human goods.[12] And in each of the last three intuitive categories of human (personal) good, it is not difficult to find a (different) particular virtue that is essential to constituting them *as goods*.

For example, the connection between the personal good that one gains from (but that is also inherent in) certain kinds of relationships and a certain kind of virtue is fairly evident. Love and friendship essentially depend on loving or (at least) caring about the welfare of one's friend or loved one; for, intuitively, a relationship doesn't count as love or friendship if its participants are entirely selfish in their relations with one another. Even some of the less intimate social ties we might regard as elements of an individual's well-being—for example, (participating in) "civic friendship"—seem to require some connection to virtue, some degree of intrinsic concern, for example, for the well-being of (other members of) a community, association, or nation. Where there is no concern for others, we simply have people using one another, and though, arguably, various personal goods can *come from* such interaction, the interaction itself is not commonly regarded as an independent and substantial personal good on its own, the way friendship, love, and membership in a genuine community, etc., tend to be. (What I have just said holds *a fortiori* of relationships involving abuse or enmity.)

---

12. Views that regard these sorts of things as elements of our well-being often include other kinds of personal good as well, and this sort of approach is often called the "objective list" view of personal good or well-being. I find the "objective" part of this appellation helpful because it indicates that one isn't trying to reduce human good to facts about what we *desire* (under appropriate circumstances)—but then one can also say (as I believe Shelly Kagan somewhere has said) that hedonism, the view that only pleasure is an intrinsic part of our good, is also an objective theory or view about human good. But in any event, I do object to the "list" part of the above name because that word suggests a mere hodge-podge with no underlying unity. If the Platonic elevationism I shall be describing and to some extent defending in what follows is correct, then every element of human good will contain or be accompanied by a virtue. And even though it will be different virtues in the case of different (kinds of) goods, there will still be enough unity to make it inappropriate or misleading to apply the term "objective list account" to what we shall have said about the relation(s) between human good and human virtue.

The goods of personal interaction or relationship—goods like love and civic friendship—thus seem to require a certain virtue,[13] and it shouldn't be surprising that that virtue is focused on other people. But the other "objective" goods we mentioned above are not essentially (or in every instance) interpersonal and, therefore, not surprisingly, involve only virtues that are typically or often self-regarding. Thus almost anyone who thinks there are elements of personal well-being other than pleasure would mention achievement or accomplishment as a good thing in life, and if one regards achievement and accomplishment in this way, one will presumably want to hold that despite all the suffering and sacrifice that may be involved, a life can be made good or better through the achieving of the goals that required all the suffering and sacrifice. This talk of suffering and, especially, sacrifice will help to pinpoint the virtue that the good of achievement depends upon.

A certain degree of talent or aptitude is certainly necessary to most achievements, but talent and aptitude are arguably not virtues, whereas strength of purpose or perseverance pretty clearly is a virtue, and I think any genuine achievement will essentially depend on the presence of some degree of perseverance. Even Mozart, in whom musical invention seems to have arisen spontaneously, had to write down the tunes that occurred to him, and develop and orchestrate them, in order to produce his actual compositions. But talent itself doesn't depend on effort and perseverance; indeed, one needn't at all develop a talent one knows one has, but, interestingly, most of us are much less inclined to treat the presence of raw talent as in itself a personal good in someone's life. If the talent isn't developed, is left fallow, then it doesn't seem to represent any sort of life good for the individual who has it, and so the case of talents contrasts intuitively with what we think about achievements, about successfully making something out of and with a talent or ability. Achievements seem to qualify a life as better in a way that mere unused talents do not, and I think part of what leads us to such a distinction is our sense of the effort and perseverance that go into actual achievements. Talent doesn't require any application or exemplification of virtue, but achievement always requires some degree of perseverance, and the latter fact influences, I think, our willingness to treat achievement, but not sheer talent, as a genuine life good somewhat independent of pleasure and enjoyment and despite the hardship and sacrifice that are likely to be involved.

But what about knowledge or wisdom? Do these putative personal goods also require the presence of virtue? Now knowledge, at least of deep or important facts, and wisdom may themselves be thought to be virtues, intellectual virtues, so once again, and fairly straightforwardly, there is a connection between what we tend to think of as personal goods and certain possible virtues, in this

---

13. I may have been speaking a bit loosely. Perhaps one shouldn't say that one person's *friendship* with another person counts as a personal good for each of them, but should claim, more accurately, that *being* in the (two-person relation of) friendship is inherently good for each. Or one could talk of the good of *having* a certain friend. Similar points apply to "the good of love."

case a relation of absolute identity. But more can be said about the connection between wisdom or deep knowledge and at least one familiar *ethical* virtue: courage.

Nowadays we tend to think that some of the deepest and most important facts about the universe and our relation to it are frightening or at least highly unpalatable. In consequence, we also think that it takes a certain kind of courage to face those facts rather than deceive ourselves or think wishfully about them (or avoid thinking at all about certain topics). I say nowadays because (for reasons it would be very interesting to pursue on another occasion) very little of this attitude is to be found in ancient thinkers like Plato and Aristotle, despite all their emphasis on the virtue of wisdom.[14]

Consider one famous example of the courage it takes to face facts about the universe. In the nineteenth century (though not merely then), accumulating evidence of the age of the earth and cosmos and of the evolutionary origin of plants and animals led many people to doubt the Biblical account of things and reexamine their religious beliefs. But it took some courage to face and "take in" this evidence against the Biblical account of human life and human destiny. It is much easier and more comfortable, in the main, to believe that there is a God who has a plan for human beings, and one (Whiggish, I admit) way to interpret the struggle that occurred in the nineteenth century (and is far from over yet) between secular science and religious tradition is to see it as a test of the courage of human beings.

But the test of courage versus self-deception and wishful thinking occurs in a host of other areas. It takes courage to face some of one's own deepest fears and desires, and to the extent wisdom as a life good requires facing one's inner demons, the important connection between wisdom and courage is further underscored. Finally, it can take courage to face the results of philosophical argument. What we initially hope for from philosophy, philosophy in many instances proves itself incapable of providing: Hume, Goodman, Quine, and Wittgenstein all show us that philosophy can run out of justifications more quickly and more irrecusably than we hope or desire. And it is interesting that Wittgenstein himself seems to be noticing the connection between

---

14. In the *Meno* (S. 86), Plato's Socrates urges us to have the courage to seek philosophical wisdom despite all the disagreement and skepticism that exist about philosophical questions. But none of this has anything to do with how frightening or daunting the facts of the universe or our place in it are. There is nothing I have seen in Plato or, for that matter, in Aristotle to indicate such a "modern" view of things. Interestingly too, though we moderns also place enormous emphasis on creativity and would want to say that Plato's and Aristotle's philosophies were great creative achievements, this too is not something Plato or Aristotle would likely have said or believed. And the reason isn't modesty. I think, rather, that Plato and Aristotle both saw themselves as philosophically able enough to just report or record how things are in the universe. We might in fact, then, see this as far from modest; but, if I am correct, their view of what they were accomplishing—and they would certainly have each thought that they were accomplishing something of importance— would in any event have to downplay the creative element in (their) philosophical thinking and achievements.

philosophical understanding or wisdom and moral virtue when he says: "You could attach prices to thoughts. Some cost a lot, some a little. And how does one pay for thoughts? The answer, I think, is: with courage."[15] I believe that Wittgenstein is basically right here. Many of the conclusions philosophy tends toward are unsettling and uncomfortable, and it requires courage rather than wishful thinking to accept them. More generally, Platonic elevationism will say that knowledge constitutes a distinctive form of personal good, and counts as wisdom, only when it takes courage to acquire it.[16]

It would seem, then, that some of our best candidates for status as (intrinsic) personal goods have an intimate connection to one or another virtue or set of virtues—and, in the light of what we have just said, a Platonic elevationist could also say that the various goods or elements in human well-being that we have discussed are distinguished by *which* virtue (or, possibly, virtues) they require. But there are other plausible candidates for status as personal goods that we haven't mentioned and that we really don't have time to discuss. So let me just say at this point that most or all of them do seem to require a tight connection to some virtue—different virtues for different ones of them; and let us then turn and return to the chief challenge facing any Platonic elevationist treatment of human goods, the question whether it is or can be made plausible to suppose that appetitive goods have to be tied to, accompanied by, some virtue. This challenge can, I think, be met if we can show, or show that it isn't implausible to hold, that someone totally lacking in the virtue of moderation, someone insatiably immoderate in their desires, gains no personal good from the pleasures she frenetically or restlessly pursues and obtains.

A moderate individual who is enjoying food or drink will at a certain point decide that she has had enough (enjoyment) and stop pursuing, perhaps even turn down further gustatory enjoyment(s). But the totally insatiable person will never feel she has (had) enough and will remain thoroughly unsatisfied no matter how much she has had or enjoyed, and it is not counterintuitive to suppose that such an individual gains nothing good (at least noninstrumentally) from her pursuit of pleasure or power or whatever. We feel sorry for someone who is never even partially satisfied with what she has or has obtained, and in feeling thus, I don't think we are necessarily assuming that the insatiable pursuit of power, gustatory sensations, sexual pleasure, or whatever is automatically frustrating and painful; rather, it seems somewhat plausible to suppose that we feel sorry for such people because their frenetic pleasure and desire for pleasure are never "rounded off" by any sense of satisfaction with what they have

15. See Ludwig Wittgenstein, *Culture and Value*, Oxford: Blackwell, 1980, p. 52e.

16. Elevationism is then committed to saying that sheer information, however instrumentally valuable, is not intrinsically good for people. Note, however, that where knowledge doesn't require courage *but is difficult to attain*, the elevationist can still regard (attaining) it as a personally beneficial *achievement*. (Something similar may even be true of the insatiable person who gains more and more power or pleasure through persistent efforts—see our forthcoming discussion of appetitive personal goods.)

or have had. When people gain something good for themselves from pleasure, it is, I am arguing (and the elevationist can say), because the pleasure is part of a "package" containing both pleasure and some degree of satisfaction with that pleasure. (We will say more just below about how, according to a Platonic elevationist, the elements in this package may metaphysically relate to one another and to the personal good that requires them.)

Moreover, I am assuming that there is nothing *unintuitive* about the supposition that (some substantial degree of) satisfaction with pleasure is necessary for an appetitive (or any other pleasure-related) good to occur in someone's life.[17] The Platonic elevationist is saying, in effect, that the pleasure or enjoyment we take from an activity in some (perhaps metaphorical or analogical) sense *anticipates* some measure of satisfaction and that where the satisfaction, the sense of having had enough, never comes, the pleasure seems empty, the activity not worth it (except perhaps instrumentally). There is something pitiable about insatiability that reminds us of Sisyphus and also of Tantalus. (Everyone knows about Sisyphus, but Tantalus, according to mythology, was condemned by the gods to stand under luscious grapes that always eluded his reach and in water that always receded when he tried to drink it.) For surely we can say that the totally insatiable individual wishes to have or obtain something good in her life, yet, on the Platonic view I am exploring and in some measure defending, personal good seems always to recede from the insatiable individual as she seeks to approach and attain it. So the appetitively insatiable individual may not only fail to be admirable, because of her immoderate, indeed unlimited, need for and dependence on appetitive (or other) pleasures, but, in addition and as a result of that lack of virtue, also act self-defeatingly in regard to her own good.

But why not say, rather, that the insatiable individual does get something good out of his restless and insatiable pursuit of more and more pleasure, namely, whatever pleasure he obtains along the way? Is this view really so contrary to common sense? I think not; but neither, as I have been saying, is the claim that the appetitively insatiable individual gets nothing good from his appetitive pursuit. I don't think common sense is really decisive on this issue, and so a Platonic elevationist can propose letting theoretical considerations resolve the issue for us. If we say that pleasure needs to be accompanied by some measure of satisfaction with it in order for an appetitive good to occur in someone's life, then Platonic elevationism has a chance

---

17. Georges Rey has pointed out to me that sexual pleasure can seem like a good thing even in the absence of (eventual) orgasm. However, that might simply mean that one can be to some extent satisfied with sexual pleasure even without "achieving" an orgasm. And this point won't be disturbed by the additional assumption that a failure to achieve orgasm might lead to later painful sensations (of frustration). Those sensations may be (momentarily) a bad thing for the individual, but such an individual might still see the earlier pleasure as a strongly counterbalancing good. The nonorgasmic pleasure might personally *outweigh* the painfulness (and let's not exaggerate that painfulness) of the later sensations.

of succeeding.[18] Such an account unifies our understanding of (the relations between) human good and virtue in a presumably desirable way, and in the name of such unity, one might wish to make assumptions which, though not counterintuitive, are also not overwhelmingly obvious apart from such theoretical considerations. (Compare the way linguists like Chomsky have allowed considerations of theory, sometimes in different directions depending on the theory then being espoused, to decide the syntactic status—that is, the grammaticality or ungrammaticality—of "don't care" sentences like "Colorless green ideas sleep furiously.") If we assume that virtue needs to accompany personal good in appetitive cases, then since it is much easier also to make such an assumption for the other personal goods that common sense tends to acknowledge, we end up with a more satisfactory elevationist account of human well-being than Stoicism or Aristotle provides. In that case, accepting the idea that pleasure is not a sufficient condition of personal good might seem a small price to pay for an elevationist view that achieves so much theoretical/ethical unification and that can plausibly stand up against the kind of reductive ethical unification utilitarianism entails.[19]

What we have seen thus far is that the Platonic claim in the *Gorgias* that all goods require (their) virtues is or may well be borne out in what would naturally seem to many to be its most problematic instance. However, what would really show Plato to have anticipated the elevationism I have been describing would be evidence that Plato regarded appetitive good in particular as requiring a virtue

---

18. Of course, someone might claim that nothing *counts as pleasure* unless the individual is in some degree satisfied with it. But this assumption clearly makes it easier for Platonic elevationism to hold that appetitive goods require some degree of virtue; and it is in any event very questionable. The French use the term "*alumette*" (literally "match") to refer to hors-d'oeuvres that are supposed to inflame one's appetite, and this more than suggests that such appetizers are pleasurable yet the very opposite of satisfying.

19. Platonic elevationism as developed in these pages entails not only that pleasure may not give rise to an appetitive (or other) good, but also that appetitive desire fulfillment may also fail to result in any good for the individual. Someone insatiably seeking a certain kind of pleasure may have an open-ended desire that is never fulfilled, but will certainly have particular desires along the way: the desire for a given piece of pâté de foie gras, for example. That desire may certainly be fulfilled, but on the account being worked out here, the insatiable person gains nothing good thereby. (We also speak of the desire being "satisfied," but if the *individual* is in no way satisfied with her resultant state, then she has, in Platonic elevationist terms, gained nothing good from the fulfillment or satisfaction of the particular desire. I am indebted here to discussion with Richard Wollheim.) Let me finally mention an intermediate case that was brought to my attention by Richard Kraut. It is conceivable that someone might be somewhat satisfied with the gustatory (or other) pleasure they have been enjoying and still *prefer* to continue enjoying (new instances of) such pleasure—even though they also wouldn't be *unhappy* or *miserable* if that turned out to be impossible. This constitutes a kind of insatiability, but not what I have been calling *total* insatiability or a *total* lack of moderation, and I am inclined to say that such a person gets something good from the pleasures they are somewhat satisfied with. Still, a different person who could more easily become totally satisfied might get more personal good from less pleasure than the kind of person I have just been describing would get from more pleasure. This is a delicate matter that would need to be explored further.

like moderation. It is one thing for Plato to make a general statement, as he does in the *Gorgias*, connecting all good with virtue. It is quite another for him to have realized the implications of that general claim for our understanding of appetitive goods and to have indicated the connection between such good and a virtue like moderation in such a way that this particular instance of his generalization doesn't seem like a counterexample to it. I want to claim now that Plato does in fact take such an additional step—though, as we shall also see, he does so somewhat obscurely and in somewhat metaphorical language.

I think we can see this best by looking at Plato's *Philebus*.[20] When we examine that dialogue, I think we see Plato working on (or struggling with) the idea that appetitive personal good has to be constituted out of two elements that correspond pretty well to the two elements Platonic elevationism (as we have described it) says need to exist in order for an appetitive good to occur: namely, appetitive pleasure and some degree of satisfaction with it. But in order to make this plausible, we need to take a look at some of the more general themes of that dialogue. (I am going to be brief and rather selective.)

The *Philebus* raises some general issues about how things are constituted—what makes them be what they are—in terms of a contrast between the infinite and the finite. Everything in the world and even the world itself can be seen as a mixture or coming together of finite with infinite, and Plato illustrates this idea with respect to music, language, and a number of other areas. Both linguistic and musical sound are, he says, infinite in their potential, but something definite (and good) is achieved through language and music only if infinity is ordered or circumscribed in finite ways (S. 17).

Plato also discusses pleasure in relation to the issue of finite versus infinite. He says that "pleasure is infinite and belongs to the class which neither has, nor ever will have in itself, a beginning, middle, or end of its own." (S. 31). He seems to think that pleasure is not in itself good (S. 32 and 66), and the issue of when and how pleasure is or becomes good then naturally arises. Plato's answer seems to be that pleasure can be good only if it is ordered or constrained by measure or harmony that partakes of the finite rather than of the infinite. The infinite, he thinks, cannot make pleasure good (after all, pleasure is by its very nature infinite, but not all pleasure is good), so it can be or become good in relation to the infinite only by being *limited* (see S. 28).

Now Plato does talk at various points in the *Philebus* about the (for him) problematic status of "mixed" pleasures, pleasures admixed with pain (including the pain of desire itself). But his view that not all pleasure is good and that it is or becomes good only by being limited or subject to measure in some way isn't, I think, (exclusively) based on the problem of mixed pleasures. What he

20. Let me just say in advance, though, that I haven't found any other commentators (and among them is Donald Davidson in his Harvard doctoral dissertation) who interpret the *Philebus* in the way I am going to suggest. But I can't claim to have read all the commentaries there are on the *Philebus*.

says about the finite versus the infinite suggests to me at least that he holds the logically independent thesis that pleasure is good only when it is taken *in measure* and only when there are *limits* to one's desire or appetite for pleasure. And because Plato takes measure in the soul to be a constitutive element of the psychic harmony that constitutes virtue (see, e.g., S. 64 and 65), he is saying that we gain something really good from pleasure only if our desire is measured, limited, non-insatiable, moderate, and *virtuous* (see especially S. 52).

In that case, Plato seems to accept the idea that appetitive goods require virtue in the soul that enjoys them, and given the general claim he makes in the *Gorgias* and the fact that the virtue requirement is much more obvious with respect to non-appetitive goods than with respect to appetitive ones, he seems to be committed to elevationism as a general thesis about the relation between virtue and human well-being. Thus Plato says that "from a[n]...admixture of the finite and the infinite come the seasons and all the delights of life..." (S. 26); and because Plato, on the present interpretation, so thoroughly anticipates the ways in which I have here been developing an elevationist account of human good (that is more plausible than what Stoicism and Aristotle offer us), my choice of the name "Platonic elevationism" will now, I hope, make sense (if it didn't earlier).

But before we close the present, brief discussion of this, as I take it, most plausible form of elevationism, I would like to address some issues in the metaphysics of ethics that help us (even) more deeply recognize *or nurture* the Platonic roots of Platonic elevationism. We have been saying that appetitive goods (or pleasure-related goods like those we get from listening to music) require both pleasure and a measure of satisfaction with pleasure, but that doesn't yet tell us whether the satisfaction with pleasure that is necessary to the emergence/ existence of an appetitive good is part of that good or merely its necessary accompaniment. One might hold, in other words, that when appetitive goods occur, they consist merely in a certain kind of pleasure or enjoyment, but that such an enjoyment doesn't constitute a personal good for someone unless it possesses the relational property of being accompanied by satisfaction with it on the part of the person in question. But there is also the alternative of saying that appetitive goods *contain* both pleasure and satisfaction with pleasure. Similarly, with regard to the personal good of achievement, one can say that it consists merely in the attaining of the goal one has sought, but that attaining doesn't count as a personal good unless its way is paved by a virtuous perseverance or persistency that makes it possible. Or one can say that both the attaining of one's goal and the persistence one shows in doing so are elements in (the good of) any achievement. (There are also issues I won't address about whether achievement occurs only at the end of a certain process or occurs throughout that process.)

However, if we say that satisfaction with pleasure is part of any appetitive good and likewise say that persistence is part of (the good of) achievement and so on for the other goods we have spoken of, then Plato may turn out to have been right in claiming that for something to be good, there must be virtue *in* it. Wouldn't it be interesting and lovely if, in such an unexpected way, Plato turned out to be correct on this issue? Yes—but are there good philosophical reasons for agreeing with him?

Consider, for example, the possibility that appetitive pleasure and satisfaction with it don't merely accompany one another, but *interpenetrate* one another, so that the character or quality of pleasure differs to the extent one is satisfied with it (or the pleasure one has already had). If this were the case, then it wouldn't make much sense to separate the two phenomena and say that the pleasure constitutes an appetitive good, when one is satisfied with it, but the satisfaction lies outside the good thus constituted. However, the "interpenetration thesis" is hardly obvious, and I don't think this argument is enough to persuade us that we should regard "satisfaction with" as part of the appetitive goods that require it.

But what about the widespread assumption that pleasure, wisdom, and the like are *intrinsically good*? Doesn't this require us to hold that such goods can't depend, for their constitution or existence, on entities outside themselves? Not necessarily. A number of philosophers have in recent years defended the view that various good things may be *noninstrumentally* valuable (to us) even if that value exists *only in relation* to certain other facts or entities. So the idea that wisdom, pleasure, etc. are more than (mere) means to our well-being (are ends sought for their own sake) can arguably be accommodated without insisting that such goods depend on nothing external to themselves. In addition, it has been plausibly maintained that noninstrumental goods or ends that are constituted in relation to external facts or objects can naturally be regarded as having (a certain kind of) intrinsic goodness.[21] So I don't think we really have to regard the personal goods that require certain virtues as containing those virtues as part of themselves. It would be very nice if Plato were right, but nothing really requires us to assume that he is. So Platonic elevationism can plausibly remain agnostic on this issue, though we can also say that it may have a motive of *methodological conservatism* to hold onto Plato's view that goods contain virtues until and unless there is a better argument against it than anything we have unearthed so far.

But having focused almost exclusively on personal well-being, it is time we said something about how Platonic elevationism might account for personal ills or evils. What it can say in fact works symmetrically with what we have been saying about (its views about) personal goods. It can hold that nothing counts as intrinsically bad for a person unless it involves (and contains) some measure of vice (or an absence of total virtue). Thus on such a view, pain is a (constituent of) personal evil only if there is something less than fully virtuous or admirable about how a person takes or reacts to a pain, and just as it is best to be in some degree *satisfied* with substantial pleasure, so too does it seem appropriate and

---

21. See, for example, Christine Korsgaard, "Two Distinctions in Virtue," *Philosophical Review* 92: 169–85, 1983; my *Goods and Virtues*, Oxford: Clarendon Press, 1983, ch. 3; Shelly Kagan, "Rethinking Intrinsic Value," *Journal of Ethics* 2: 277–97, 1998; and Thomas Hurka, "Two Kinds of Organic Unity," *Journal of Ethics* 2: 299–320, 1998. The last two articles make a fairly persuasive case for saying that noninstrumental, but relational, goods can make some claim to being regarded as intrinsically good.

admirable—a kind of strength—not to be totally *dissatisfied* with, but, rather, (in some measure) to *accept* unavoidable, and perhaps also even (some) avoidable, pain.[22] For that reason, the Platonic elevationist may claim that where (a) pain is totally accepted, it doesn't constitute anything intrinsically bad for a person. Only when someone *minds* his pain or is (to some extent) *bothered* by it, does the pain enter into or count as something intrinsically bad for the individual. (Of course, there may be kinds of pain that no human is capable of accepting, and Platonic elevationism will regard such pains as entailing personal evils.)

Thus, the Platonic elevationist can say that it takes a "package" of pain (or discomfort) and the vice or non-virtue of nonacceptance for there to be a personal evil, and this implication of the theory strikes me as by no means implausible. Certainly, it is far less implausible than saying, with the Stoics, that pain is never (part of) a personal evil, but it also seems somewhat intuitive to suppose that a person who so totally accepts (a state of) pain that he doesn't (any longer) at all mind it is suffering no intrinsic ill. (Of course, if one wants to claim that something can't count as a pain if it is totally accepted, that makes things easier, not harder, for the view that every personal ill requires some measure of vice.)

Moreover, when one applies Platonic elevationism to more spiritual forms of human ill, one arrives at a view with some obvious attractions. Given its assumptions, failure to succeed in one's goals doesn't amount to an independent personal ill (an ill independent of painful feelings of frustration and possibly lesser income) *unless some vice was involved in the failure.* But this means that if someone fails, despite valiant efforts and through no fault of her own, that failure merely constitutes the absence of something good rather than a "positive" personal evil; whereas if someone fails through a total lack of virtuous effort and perseverance, the failure really does amount to a personal evil. And this distinction has some intuitive force, since it is natural to think there is something far more pathetic and unfortunate about a life where failure results from fecklessness than about one where it is due to bad luck. By the same token, it seems acceptable to suppose that a lack of wisdom that results from sheer cowardice is to that extent more unenviable and pathetic than a lack of wisdom that results, say, from the cultural unavailability of certain kinds of knowledge, and this is precisely what Platonic elevationism claims.

If the above discussion is on the right track, then intra-ethical elevationism in a form inspired by Plato is capable of avoiding the problems that beset the

---

22. Could one totally accept a pain and yet wish/want it not to continue into the future and, knowing that its future continuation is avoidable, take steps to end it? Well, of course, one might want to end it if one knew it would distract one from reaching certain practical goals, but I am asking about what one could want/do if such (other) instrumental considerations were not at issue. The answer may depend on whether one knows one would (without too much difficulty) totally accept the future pain as well. If one does, then, on the view I am advocating, one who totally accepts present pain won't make an effort to avoid the continuation of the pain. Indeed, under the conditions mentioned, such an effort would show that one *didn't* totally accept the present pain. I am grateful to Richard Kraut for initially raising these interesting issues.

Stoic and Aristotelian version of elevationism, while at the same time offering us an account of the relation between virtue (or vice) and well-being (or ill-being) that has some of the unifying power we find in reductive utilitarian (and Epicurean) accounts of that relationship. I say "some" because Platonic elevationism leaves virtue in a more pluralistic condition than the utilitarian account leaves the notion of well-being. (Again, let us leave ill-being to one side.) If well-being is understood as pleasure or desire satisfaction, then utilitarianism is capable of reducing all virtue (as well as rationality and morality) to well-being conceived in unitary fashion, whereas Platonic elevationism relates different goods to different virtues and offers no immediate prospect of treating all those virtues—moderation, benevolence/caring, perseverance, and courage—as forms of some underlying "master virtue." But still, Platonic elevationism does allow one to see all common-accepted forms of well-being as dependent on (and possibly containing) commonly accepted forms of virtue, and we have seen that such a conception of well-being substantially unifies our ideas about what well-being is without (it has seemed) having any really implausible ethical or metaphysical implications. That gives us reason to hope that a (one) form of ethics that is *opposed* to utilitarian reductionism, and *very different* from Kantian dualism, may offer the most plausible way to think about the relationship between human virtue and human well-being.[23]

23. It is probably worth noting that Platonic elevationism, as I have been defending it, involves one in rejecting an assumption that Plato and all ancient virtue ethicists seem to have accepted, the "eudaimonistic" assumption that virtue, if it is to count as virtue, must pay, that is, must be to the advantage of the virtuous individual. We moderns tend to reject such eudaimonism and to find it inherently implausible; we think that virtue and morality—and especially the moral virtue of caring/concern about others—can and often do involve individual self-sacrifice. So the defense I have given of Platonic elevationism isn't something that Plato would have accepted in its entirety; and I think and have in effect argued that such elevationism is plausible in contemporary terms because it *rejects* the tight connection between individual virtue and well-being that Plato, Aristotle, and other ancient virtue ethicists attempted to demonstrate. Even modern-day *virtue ethicists* like James Martineau, Rosalind Hursthouse (in her later work), and myself reject eudaimonism; and it is perhaps worth noting that modern *hedonism* also cuts across the major schools of ethical thought (in a way that ancient hedonism did not). Utilitarians in most cases are hedonists about human well-being, but so too, essentially, is Kant; and James Martineau accepts a hedonist conception of personal in his *Types of Ethical Theory* (2 vols., Oxford: Clarendon Press, 1891). Let me also now make one small reversal of engine. In the essay "Ancient Ethics and Modern Moral Philosophy," later in this book, I mention—approvingly—Nicholas White's argument in various places that Plato isn't entirely a eudaimonist because he thinks that the *virtue* of a philosopher/king leads him/her to abandon philosophy and sacrifice his/her own greater well-being for the sake of the state and its inhabitants. If such a view of Plato is correct, then the non-eudaimonistic character of (my version of) Platonic elevationism doesn't have to render it (to that extent) un-Platonic. In any event, the view defended here says nothing about the Forms, and is certainly to *that* extent un-Platonic. (I am indebted here and elsewhere in this essay to discussion with Julia Annas.) Finally, I should mention that the somewhat unified theory I have offered of the basic kinds of human good doesn't (yet) amount to a view of how such goods fit together to make an overall happy or good life. This is a large topic and best left to other occasions.

2

THE END OF TELEOLOGICAL ETHICS

The term "teleological" comes from the Greek word *telos* for goal, aim, or end. The idea of teleological ethics in recent usage has been understood, most fundamentally, as standing in contrast with "deontological" approaches to ethics. Deontological moralities require people or societies sometimes to act in disregard of or even against good consequences, for example, by forbidding the killing of an innocent person even if that is the only way one can prevent a greater loss of human life. Teleological theories, by contrast, are all supposed to accept some version of the idea that the end (always) justifies the means.

In addition, the notion of a teleological ethics is generally thought to embrace two rather different kinds of approaches to morality or ethics: ancient virtue ethics and modern-day consequentialism (including utilitarianism). However, the widespread assumption that these two forms of ethics have something in common that distinguishes them from deontological theories is subject to great, if not insuperable, difficulties that threaten the very idea of a fundamental distinction between teleology and deontology.

In the first place, the idea that (act-)utilitarianism and (act-)consquentialism are teleological is something of a stretch. True, utilitarians like Henry Sidgwick often speak of happiness or pleasure as a/the rational (final) end of human action and also hold that the morality of any action is determined by how much (of a net balance of) happiness or pleasure it yields. But none of this entails that the agent who acts rightly must *aim* at the general happiness or indeed at happiness at all. If the best consequences for human happiness will actually be achieved by an agent's concerning herself only with her own family or by her refusing even to think about using deontologically forbidden means to certain good ends, then it will be permissible and even obligatory for her to disregard the "goal" of universal happiness. In that case, utilitarianism is more properly regarded as a consequentialist view than as a teleological one; and indeed the modern-day tendency, initiated by Elizabeth Anscombe, to dwell on the consequentialist, rather than on the teleological, character of utilitarianism, perfectionism, and the like, shows, I think, an implicit recognition of the inaccuracy of regarding these views as necessarily prescribing that people should have universal happiness or any other particular good as their goal, aim, or end in life.[1]

By the same token, the indiscriminate application of the term "teleological" to all ancient forms of virtue ethics is also problematic. To be sure, Aristotle not only begins the *Nicomachean Ethics* by saying that happiness, or eudaimonia, is a reasonable ultimate end of all human action, but also subscribes to a metaphysical form of teleology according to which all (living) things aim for ends or goals that are dictated by their natures. This might then understandably lead one to suppose that Aristotle thinks of the human virtue(s) he describes in books II through V of the *Ethics* as *character traits required for individual human happiness*, and that he is perhaps even an ethical egoist who holds that the virtuous, rational individual aims for her own happiness in all her (deliberate) actions. But in fact this gives a distorted picture of Aristotle's view in the *Ethics*, and we can take the first step toward seeing this if we recognize that Aristotle conceives of happiness or eudaimonia as consisting mainly in acting virtuously (over a long life).

If eudaimonia is to be understood in terms of living virtuously, then, upon pain of circularity, virtue cannot also be understood as what contributes to or is required for eudaimonia. And indeed there is a great deal of evidence in the *Ethics* that Aristotle rejects the latter idea and instead understands virtue in intuitionist terms. The virtuous individual, on that reading, is someone who, without the benefit of formulas or rules, "sees" what is just or courageous and, therefore, noble in various situations and, without a struggle or mental reservations, (habitually) acts accordingly. Situational facts about what is just or courageous would then function as the ground floor of Aristotelian ethics, with happiness being understood in terms of virtue, rather than vice versa.

Moreover, Aristotle often describes the virtuous person (e.g., the soldier who risks his life for his country) as someone who acts "for the sake of the noble," and this seems to rule out or at least move away from the idea that (rational) virtue consists in seeking one's own happiness. Certainly, in a fashion rather typical of ancient virtue ethics, Aristotle sometimes argues that, in doing what is noble (for its own sake), we invariably are better off than if we had been the sort of person able or likely to do otherwise (accordingly, even a young man who dies bravely in battle will have had a better life than a coward who lives a long life). But, again, this only means that virtuous actions contribute to or are requisite to our happiness, not that our happiness is their goal. (Aristotle is a eudaimonist, but it seems a mistake to think of him as an ethical *egoist*.)

In that case, the idea that Aristotelian ethics is unambiguously teleological is mistaken or at least dubious, and this conclusion is further strengthened by considering the seemingly deontological character of Aristotle's thinking.

1. See G. E. M. Anscombe, "Modern Moral Philosophy," *Philosophy* 33: 1–19, 1958.

Aristotle says, for example, that the just individual will distribute goods in accordance with virtue or merit, and there is no suggestion here that this injunction might sometimes be ethically suspended or superseded in the name of overall good consequences. Moreover, certain sorts of actions—for example, adultery and matricide—are said to be always wrong, and such absolute prohibitions seem to place Aristotle with the deontologists and against the consequentialists, once again, therefore, calling the whole teleological/deontological distinction into question.

Does this mean that we have no use for the idea of a teleological ethics? Not quite. The problems we have encountered come from the assumption that ancient virtue ethics and modern consequentialism are (most) usefully classified together and the assumption that teleology and deontology together exhaust the possibilities for ethics. But if, in line with etymology, we were to conceive teleological ethics more narrowly as the sort of ethics that prescribes certain goals, purposes, or ends for agents, then we could avoid the just-mentioned assumptions and still have a useful distinction. After all, some forms of ethics—for example, various forms of the "self-realization" ethics so characteristic of British neo-Hegelianism—do seem to tell the agent consciously to strive for or seek certain goals, and it might be useful to be able to distinguish such views from approaches to morality that don't require particular purposes in agents (even if they do require the agent somehow to produce good results or consequences).

Alternatively, we might reserve the term "teleological" for forms of ethics that derive from or accompany a teleological metaphysics or (philosophy of) science; and this narrow usage would also, I think, escape the difficulties that a more overarching construal of teleology appears to create. But such more specific or narrower usages do render the idea of teleological ethics less important as a classificatory notion, and it may even be possible that future philosophical/ethical encyclopedias will not feel the same need to explain the notion that they certainly have felt up till now.

3

ANCIENT ETHICS AND MODERN
MORAL PHILOSOPHY

3.1 Some Contrasts

The idea that there is a vast difference between ancient ethics and modern moral philosophy is a philosophical commonplace, but philosophers have various different ideas about where the difference lies, and many of those ideas are true. I want to review, briefly, some of the differences that have been mentioned and then go on to mention another difference between ancient and modern that I think is more important than people have realized and that in fact is generally ignored. By ancient ethics I shall mean, exclusively, the ethics of classical antiquity in the West, the ethics of Greece and Rome—so I shall be excluding not only Jewish thought, but also the philosophy that flourished before the Common Era in India and China as well. But let me now mention *seriatim* some of the distinctions others have used to characterize the divide between ancient ethics and modern moral thought.

First and foremost, I suppose, is the idea that the (Greek and Roman) ancients lacked our concept and phenomenon of morality—an assumption which lends itself to the title of this essay. It has been said that Greek culture was a shame culture, not a guilt culture like our own in modern times, with the result that one can only properly speak of ancient ethics, not of ancient moral philosophy. Now some part of this undoubtedly is true—though it would take a person with better scholarly credentials than I have to make the best case for this assumption and I don't propose to get into the textual details of either the primary or the secondary literature that is relevant here. Still, and as I said, the notion of guilt and, commensurately, of conscience seems absent in Plato, Aristotle, the Epicureans, and the Stoics, and this may mark an important difference between the ancient and the modern. Some philosophers have inferred from this difference that the Greeks altogether lacked moral concepts, and the title of this essay seems to imply this further thesis. It is easier for us to distinguish the moral and the ethical than it would have been for the Greeks and Romans, and the Greeks and Romans seemed to lack a word that means what we now mean by "morally"—though of course that very term comes from Latin. Still, we can have concepts that we lack a specific distinguishing word for, and the way Plato and Aristotle in particular speak about (what we would call) moral phenomena makes me hesitate—and more than hesitate—to say that they lacked moral concepts, even that they lacked *our* moral concepts. When Plato says that the philosopher should sacrifice his interest in philosophy to the larger needs of the state, the way he is thinking does seem distinctively, particularly, moral; and the fact that neither Plato nor Aristotle seems to be an ethical egoist (even if they are ethical eudaimonists) and the fact that they both have so much to say about *justice* also lend support to the idea that they were (sometimes) thinking morally without, perhaps, having fully expressed or articulated moral *language*. We are certainly talking about important differences here—not having specific or completely articulated moral language is certainly different from having it, lacking (ideas of) conscience and guilt is certainly different from having them. But if the Greeks did in important instances think morally, and not just ethically, then the differences we have just been speaking of may not mark the philosophically deepest kind of distinction one can make between ancient ethics and modern moral philosophy.[1]

However, I just above mentioned (without clarifying) the notion of eudaimonism, and if, as I believe, all the positive ethical doctrines of the ancient world are eudaimonistic, then that may well mark a very important distinction between the ancient and modern. For most modern moral philosophy is distinctly non-eudaimonistic. By eudaimonism I mean, roughly, the idea that no character trait counts as a virtue (or as ethically justified) unless it serves the interests of, is profitable to, those who possess it. (Alternatively, as Julia Annas puts it, eudaimonism holds that the entry point for ethical thought and speculation is the interests, the well-being, of the person doing the thinking and speculating.)[2] Relatively few important modern philosophers count as eudaimonists—with Hobbes being, perhaps, the most notable modern exemplar of eudaimonism. But certainly utilitarianism and Kantian ethics are far from eudaimonistic, and perhaps the main reason why I feel so comfortable saying this is that both views think morality allows for and sometimes requires the sacrifice of self-interest. Now Plato's idea in the *Republic* that the philosopher should sacrifice himself for the greater good of society seems to be neither egoistic nor eudaimonistic, and given what I have just been suggesting, this means that Plato, at least in this one place, is espousing a distinctively modern view of how the individual, or some individuals, should act.[3] But Aristotle, on the other hand, never (as far as I know) strays from his espousal of eudaimonism, and, for example, when he talks of the soldier who gives up his life

---

1. For trenchant criticism of the idea that the Greeks paid no heed to moral considerations, see John McDowell's "The Role of Eudaimonia in Aristotle's Ethics," reprinted in his *Mind, Value, and Reality*, Cambridge, MA: Harvard University Press, 1998, especially pp. 15–16.

2. See Julia Annas, *The Morality of Happiness*, Oxford: Oxford University Press, 1993, pp. 27ff. Incidentally, I am assuming that eudaimonism doesn't entail egoism, because one trait that might actually benefit an individual is an intrinsic altruistic concern for the well-being of certain others. Our example, just below, of the courageous soldier who dies defending his polis may very well (at least given Aristotelian assumptions) illustrate this distinction.

3. My thinking here has been influenced by Nicholas White, "The Ruler's Choice," *Archiv fuer Geschichte der Philosophie* 68: 24–46, 1986.

for the good of the polis, he nonetheless insists that such a person does better within his short life span than he would have done if he had been cowardly and, as a result, had lived a longer but unvirtuous life. (*Nicomachean Ethics* 1169a 12–30). And I also know of no instance or place where either Epicureanism or Stoicism clearly rejects or criticizes eudaimonism, so the fact that ancient ethics is almost exclusively eudaimonistic and that the most important modern ethical thought is definitely *not* indicates something very importantly different between the ancient and modern world.

If I may be allowed to speculate, it seems to me that this major shift in emphasis is in considerable measure due to the influence of Christianity (and of Judaism operating through its influence on Christian ideals). Christianity teaches us to honor and admire Jesus's self-sacrifice on behalf of humankind, and no one ever said that Jesus was himself (or that God as identical with him was) better off as a result of Jesus's suffering and dying on the cross than would have been the case if that self-sacrifice had never occurred. So Christianity emphasizes the value and virtue of self-sacrifice in a way that goes against classical eudaimonism, and the fact is, too, that ancient Judaism, and not just Christianity, idealized kindness and compassion in a way that seems to take us beyond Greek and Roman eudaimonism toward distinctly modern moral views. The Christian ideal of agapic love, which is to some extent embodied in the Jewish injunction to love one's neighbor as oneself, also anticipates modern moral thought. And none of this should come as any sort of surprise. Judeo-Christianity anticipates modern thought because it *shaped* that thought, and it is widely recognized that even such predominantly secular moral philosophers as Hutcheson, Hume, Kant, Bentham, and Mill were influenced by the Christian moral/religious milieu in which they were raised, lived, and did their thinking.

So the rejection of eudaimonism is one of the most important differences between modern moral philosophy and ancient ethics, and for the longest time I was convinced that it represented *the* most important difference between the two. However, I now think that the eudaimonism/anti-eudaimonism distinction relates to another distinction that is just as, or perhaps more, important, but before I say more about this, I want to briefly discuss two other possible ways of distinguishing between ancient and modern., both suggested by what we have been saying about the prevalence of ideals of compassion and kindness in Judeo-Christianity.

First, Plato, Aristotle, the Stoics, and the Epicureans say very little about (the value of) kindness and compassion, and the reason may be that the Greeks were all intent on giving a *rational basis* to their ethical thinking. It is not at all clear how one could show kindness or compassion to be dictates of reason/ Reason, and certainly Christianity and Judaism never attempt such a thing. To that extent, Christianity and Judaism implicitly espouse or favor a more sentimentalist approach to morality/ethics than anything one finds in ancient Greece and Rome. When Christianity praises and idealizes God's love, and God *as* love, it doesn't offer any rational basis for that love or for admiring it, and to that extent Christianity anticipates and shaped eighteenth-century

British moral sentimentalism and the sentimentalism both of present-day care ethics and of contemporary versions of virtue ethics that follow Hutcheson and Hume more than Plato, Aristotle, or the Stoics.

For one very obvious reason, however, I don't think one can use this distinction to mark the main difference between ancient and modern; for even if there wasn't any sentimentalism in the philosophical thought of classical antiquity, there is plenty of rationalism in modern moral philosophy. Kant and Sidgwick in their very different ways are both rationalists about morality, and it would be absurd to suggest that they aren't typical of modern thought. Modern thought is *divided between* moral rationalists and moral sentimentalists—with the preponderance, if anything, favoring the rationalist side. Thus rationalism has been the predominant trend in both ancient and modern thought, but the distinction between sentimentalism and rationalism also suggests another possible major difference between ancient and modern thought.

In ancient times, the individual was seen as unproblematically connected to or immersed in his or her community (though putting things this way is perhaps too suggestive of self-consciousness about this issue that didn't exist in ancient times).[4] The idea that the individual is autonomous from others and has rights *against* his or her community never clearly occurs to Plato, Aristotle, et al.; but this idea has great prevalence in modern times, and one might conceivably want to hold that the most important difference between ancient and modern lies in this direction. Now certainly the emergence of ideals of autonomy and of the idea of rights of autonomy against other people or one's larger community is a major development of modern thought—though I don't think I know enough to usefully say anything about how or why all of this happened in modern times but not before. But in modern times and especially very recently, there has been a considerable backlash against the ethical individualism (as it seems reasonable to call it) that one finds in the modern but not the ancient world.

Recent communitarians and care ethicists argue strenuously against the ethically atomistic rationalism that is perhaps most paradigmatically exemplified in Kant's philosophy, with its focus on autonomy as the basis for all morality. They oppose rationalism in general and in particular oppose the idea that the individual is metaphysically or morally conceivable independently of his or her community or circle of intimates. Morality, rather than being due to hypothetical or actual autonomous choice, is said to be something largely pre-given and not dependent on individual choice, and this is more than a little reminiscent of the kind of thinking that went on (or was presupposed, but not self-conscious) in the world of classical antiquity. So one can't just say that the

---

4. This way of seeing Greek thought and social life can be found in Hegel's *Philosophy of Right* and in his *The Philosophy of History*; also, more recently, in Alasdair MacIntyre, *Whose Justice? Which Rationality?*, Notre Dame, IN: University of Notre Dame Press, 1988, pp. 33–34. But the view is widespread and familiar. For sustained criticism of it, however, see Nicholas White, *Individual and Conflict in Greek Ethics*, Oxford: Clarendon Press, 2002, ch. 4.

ancient world treated the individual as an integral part of her society while the modern regards the individual as autonomously standing out from society. The modern world is divided on this issue, just as it is divided on the issue of rationalism versus sentimentalism, though one difference between the two cases is that ancient rationalism agrees with the "majority opinion" of modern times, whereas ancient communitarianism or collectivism (if I may put it this way) agrees only with the "minority opinion" of the modern world. And, stating things this way, the divide between ancient and modern thought with respect to rationalism seems less important than the divide that exists with respect to individualism. So the axis of individualism/collectivism is an important way of characterizing what in most cases distinguishes ancient and modern ethical/ moral thought, but I now want to discuss an important distinction that I think has been somewhat neglected (at least during the past century), but that also marks a major difference in intellectual tendency between the ancient and the modern world.

3.2 The Dualism of the Ethical

The difference or divide I have in mind centers around what I shall argue is a certain dualism (or set of related dualisms) that characterizes modern moral thought, but not ancient ethics. Rationality, virtue, and well-being all come together in the ancient world in a way that they characteristically do not in modern times, and my defense of this "hypothesis" will begin with Sidgwick's idea of the "dualism of practical reason." It was Sidgwick's discussion of this (supposed) dualism that actually launched my own thinking in this area.

The notion that practical reason or rationality is subject to a duality or dualism is a major (concluding) theme in *The Methods of Ethics*, and, precisely enough for our purposes, what that theme amounts to is the view that there are strong and seemingly conclusive reasons for regarding both utilitarianism and ethical egoism as universal requirements of practical rationality, even though the two are capable in principle of making incompatible demands on individuals.[5] Sidgwick reaches this conclusion in part because he assumes that utilitarianism is a view about what practical reason requires of us. If the principle of utility tells us that it is wrong to perform an act that fails to maximize human

5. Seventh edition, London: Macmillan, 1907. In his *Outlines of the History of Ethics* (6th edition, Boston, MA: Beacon Press, 1931), Sidgwick claims that Butler was the first person to be explicitly aware of the dualism. After I had written the first draft of the present essay, I found that its discussion of the difference between ancient and modern thought is in important ways anticipated by Nicholas White's treatment of the dualism of modern thought (and non-dualism of the ancient) in his *Individual and Conflict in Greek Ethics*. But there are important differences of interpretation and emphasis between our treatments, and in particular I focus on the conceptual connections between and among different views much more than White does. I believe and hope it is worth having both discussions.

welfare, happiness, or utility, then, the assumption goes, it tells us that we always *ought* to maximize (one of) these things, and that appears to be tantamount to claiming that practical rationality or reason(ableness) dictates such maximization.

But this line of thinking is based, at least in Sidgwick, on one further fundamental assumption. Sidgwick holds that there is basically only one concept for expressing ethical requirements and that (therefore) rightness, rationality, and reasonableness are all ultimately one notion. Now I don't at this point and in this context want to harp on the distinction between the rational and the reasonable, a distinction that contractualists or contractarians have very notably insisted upon. Rather, I'd like to focus on Sidgwick's assumption that the rational and the morally right are basically the same notion. There is much to worry about in that assumption, and I have long been more than a little perplexed that Sidgwick pays no attention to those reasons for worry. Sidgwick is a tremendously meticulous and sensitive recorder of commonsense moral/ethical distinctions, but, as far as I can tell, he never takes note of the way in which, commonsensically at least, actions can seem stupid, crazy, or irrational, without seeming immoral, wrong, or vicious. For example, we can harm ourselves through stupid or irrational inattention to what we are doing, but we aren't inclined to call such acts or actions (morally) wrong.

I assume this would have been apparent to Sidgwick too, and what these considerations amount to is some sort of argument for distinguishing the concept of the rational from the concept of the moral. To be sure, a utilitarian might want to claim that harming oneself through irrational inadvertence is morally wrong, but this would be a substantive claim of ethical theory, not something dictated by mere concepts or terminological meanings, so it is difficult to see how Sidgwick could have been right to assume that there is only one basic normative concept in ethics and that in particular the notion of rightness and the notion of rationality are one and the same. However, once these assumptions are discarded, one is left having to *show* that utilitarian morality represents a requirement of practical rationality as well, and Sidgwick does make efforts to show this. And, of course, the idea that valid moral requirements constitute dictates of practical reason as well is a fairly widespread and familiar one, both historically and nowadays.

I have no intention here of reviewing and critiquing the vast literature that is devoted to developing and justifying this idea. The assumption or belief that moral requirements are requirements of rationality is a distinctive or defining assumption of rationalist approaches to morality, and, historically speaking, most philosophical attempts to define, justify, or understand the nature of morality have been couched in rationalist terms. But even if one thinks morality is or can be based in reason, even if (a slightly different matter) one thinks that moral requirements are also rational requirements, it doesn't follow that there aren't also rational requirements, say, of self-interest that are somewhat independent of the dictates or ideals of morality. Most of us think of egoism as more plausible as a theory of rationality than as a theory of morality, but the rational considerations that egoism exclusively emphasizes can be seen as having a certain amount of force against the rational or reason-derived require-ments (or ideals) of morality. In which case, there is still some sort of dualism within practical reason or the rational, but it has a somewhat different character from the dualism Sidgwick assumed existed.

Sidgwick's dualism is a dualism of two total ethical theories, and it involves the idea that two such theories may clash and yet both be (entirely) plausi-ble and even compelling. His dilemma, if I can put it this way, is a dilemma between theories, not between the choice of actions relative to a given rich univocal theory or understanding of morality like that embedded in common sense; and since these theories, according to Sidgwick, are theories of what it is rational to do, of what practical reason requires, he calls the seemingly irrecusable clash between them a/the dualism of practical reason. By contrast, the dualism I have just been speaking of is a dualism that seems or can seem to hold when one abandons the Sidgwickian ideas that there is only one nor-mative notion in ethics and that egoism is a moral view. It is a dualism within or for our ordinary thinking if we add in the assumption, which is not neces-sarily part of *ordinary* ethical thought, that moral requirements are rational ones, are based in reason. If we make that assumption and take an otherwise commonsense view of both morality and rationality, it will seem as if moral requirements can clash with what are naturally regarded as the rational dictates of self-interest. But then, since we *are* assuming that morality has a rational basis, the clash we are speaking of will still appear to occur within the sphere of reason or rationality. In effect, it will be the dualism of practical reason that remains, or emerges, when we discard some obviously problematic assump-tions that Sidgwick made.

But, of course, the assumption that morality is based in practical reason or that moral requirements are rational requirements is not an assumption every approach to ethics is willing to make. Sidgwick made the assumption and many rationalist philosophers before and since have agreed with this and/or attempted to support the idea. But we also know that (the) moral sentimental-ists *don't* believe that morality is based in reason or required by being rational, and I would like now to say something about what happens to the idea of a dualism of practical reason once one starts thinking in sentimentalist terms. It turns out that if one does so, the original dualism is transformed or transmuted, but doesn't at all go away.

The early sentimentalists, and most notably Hume, were inclined to deny the very existence of such a thing as practical reason. They not only thought that morality wasn't based in reason, but also that there was no such thing as practical rationality *outside* the moral domain. For Hume, at least, there was no such thing as (extra-moral) reasons of self-interest and also (though this is slightly controversial) no distinctively practical rational requirement of taking means to one's ends. (Failure to do so could, of course, involve irrationality or at least ignorance of an intellectual/theoretical kind.) Now this means that Hume himself doesn't see any rational or ethical tension between the dictates or advice or morality and those of practical reason. There can't be a conflict if one side won't or can't fight.

But it does seem very odd and implausible to suppose that there is no such thing as practical reason or rationality, for example, that the taking of means to ends isn't a genuine requirement of being practically rational—and Hume's defense of this conclusion does in fact seem very weak. It seems in particular to beg a number of issues: for example, to assume what it seeks to establish, namely, that theoretical reason is the only sort of reason it makes sense to suppose there is. But (again) I don't want to go into details here. My purpose in making the last point is to indicate how, from a less tendentious standpoint that assumes that there is such a thing as practical reason, Hume's views amount to a kind of dualism, what one might call dualism via truncation.

Hume is saying that (what many of us call and believe in as) practical reason is actually impotent to influence or justify human action, but that morality does and should influence us, and this therefore involves two very different attitudes, on Hume's part, to what we consider to be two main (or the two most important) parts of our ethical thought. That's a *kind* of dualism, a dualism of how the different departments of ethics are *treated*. But some of you may find this extension of the notion of an ethical dualism somewhat stretched or far-fetched. However, if the claim of Humean dualism *does* seem forced or stretched, that is only, I think, because Hume's actual views are so stretched or forced in a seemingly unreasonable and unmotivated direction. The contrast in what Hume says about practical rationality and what he says about morality is so extreme that the dualism that he assumes (if one wants to call it that) can also seem far-fetched or extreme as a form of dualism. Moreover, Hume does (please, let us assume) believe in theoretical reason, and by denying practical reason, he ends up with a dualism between (theoretical) reason, which can't motivate action, and morality, which can. This isn't a dualism *within* ethics, but it is the kind of dualism one ends up with if one empties the notion of reason of all practical content and leaves it entirely in the hands of theoretical/intellectual thought. So I think it makes sense to think of Hume as a dualist regarding practical *motivation*, and in any event his view stands in very marked contrast with what the ancients saw as the deep and tight connections existing among the ethical notions of rationality, (moral) virtue, and human good (or well-being).

But a sentimentalist doesn't have to agree with (what we have said is) the Humean assumption that there is no such thing as practical reason either inside or outside morality. Contemporary sentimentalists like Nel Noddings, Carol Gilligan, Virginia Held, and myself—and we are all devotees of what is nowadays called the ethics of care—tend to believe that morality can't and doesn't need to be based in reason or rationality, but that doesn't mean we think there is no such thing as practical rationality. The sentimentalist can hold that practical reason has a/its distinctive place outside of morality and the sentiments, can hold, for example and in particular, that means-end, or instrumental, rationality has a validity that is quite independent of any moral and any sentimentalist considerations. However, it is also possible for a sentimentalist about morality to argue for a sentimentalist conception of practical reason as well, and this is something I have tried to do in a recent book. Of course, the sentiments I mentioned as grounding practical rationality were very different from those I or others have seen as underlying morality. Care ethicists and virtue ethicists who focus on caring stress, of course, the importance and centrality of caring about others to the moral life; but in my *The Ethics of Care and Empathy*, I argued that a different sentiment, concern/desire for one's own long-term well-being, constitutes the basis of or for practical rationality, though, if one says this, the real trick is to show (as I attempted to do) that and how instrumental rationality and non-weakness of will can be subsumed under this sentiment.[6]

But whichever way the sentimentalist conceives practical reason in positive terms—either seeing it as having a life of its own apart from the sentiments or conceiving of it in terms of certain sentiments/desires/feelings—the sentimentalist who accepts practical reason is likely to end up accepting a form of ethical dualism as well. For there are times when morality moves us in one direction and rational concerns like self-interest move us in another, though if this amounts to a dualism, it is not a dualism within the rational or within practical reason, but a dualism that exists *between* practical reason and morality. I think that sentimentalism and common sense as regards issues both of rationality and of morality can lead us toward or into an ethical dualism that exists, as I say, not *within* the realm of the rational, but *between* the important ethical realms or spheres of the rational and the moral, and I think it may be easier to see how this does or can develop, if I bring in an approach that harks back to ancient virtue ethics and that effectively denies such a dualism.

I am thinking here of Philippa Foot's *Natural Goodness*, and I believe the best way to clarify matters at this point is by reference to an example that is quite crucial to Foot's argument and that illustrates the character both of her approach to virtue ethics and of ancient (virtue) ethics more generally.[7] Foot's view is neo-Aristotelian, and one of its many features is the assumption (roughly) that in situations of choice, there is one and only one virtuous choice, only one choice that is ethically acceptable. In illustration of this point (p. 79), Foot mentions the example (ultimately due to John Taurek) of the choice facing someone who would have to give up one of her limbs (or a foot?) in order to save another person from an even worse bodily injury. Foot implies that there is a right and virtuous choice in such a situation and indicates that that choice would involve the agent's refusing to make the sacrifice. On her view, it is both virtuous and rational not to make the sacrifice, and anyone who gave up a limb to save another person, say a stranger, from a worse injury would (other things being equal) show herself to be irrational and lacking in virtue.

6. London: Routledge, 2007.
7. Oxford: Clarendon Press, 2001.

But are things that unambiguous and/or unproblematic? What Foot is saying here is certainly in keeping with the Aristotelian view that there is only one rationally acceptable or virtuous thing to do in any circumstance of serious ethical choice, and for Aristotle, though not for Foot, this view emerges from or is tied to the further view that virtuous rational choice is medial, lies in a mean (though not necessarily the exact midpoint) between vicious and irrational extremes. However, one consequence of Aristotle's and Foot's common position is that moral/ethical supererogation becomes impossible, for the possibility of supererogation depends on there being at least two ethically acceptable choices in a given situation of choice, something denied by both Aristotle and Foot. However, in the case Foot describes most of us would, intuitively, think that sacrificing a limb and not sacrificing a limb are both morally acceptable; and there is no reason why a sentimentalist shouldn't think so as well. And there would be a strong tendency both for common sense and for the sentimentalist to hold that the act of sacrifice would be morally meritorious, beyond the call of duty, supererogataory.[8] That is, most of us would see why a person might not be willing to sacrifice a limb for the sake of preventing even worse injury to a stranger, and we wouldn't want to criticize someone who refused to make such a sacrifice (and stood by that decision after the fact). But we would also feel that there is something especially praiseworthy or admirable about someone who *would* be willing to make that sacrifice for the greater good of another person, and that is why the idea of moral supererogation makes sense to us in such a case (and others).

So Foot and Aristotle deny something that seems strongly entrenched in our thinking (and that many or most sentimentalists would also want to accept), but at the same time, it is clear that their approach has a certain kind of advantage over what most of us intuitively think and feel. When we contemplate Foot's case, we are typically tugged in opposite directions. If we imagine ourselves in such a situation, most of us will feel that we would be justified in not parting with a limb; and yet we would consider someone who *was* willing to do so (to that extent) morally superior to ourselves. We are ethically and emotionally split in a certain kind of way, whereas the Aristotelian offers what one might call a seamless univocal picture of the values at stake in the situation Foot describes. On Foot's view, self-interest both rationally and virtuously overrides concern for others without "remainder" in the situation she describes—in effect, the values of self-interest (agential well-being), rationality, and virtue *line up together* in, or with respect to, that situation. And both from a theoretical standpoint and from the standpoint of a perhaps understandable practical desire for unencumbered, uncomplicated decision-making and action, such a

8. In *The Ethics of Care and Empathy*, I attempt to show that sentimentalist views about both rationality and morality needn't be at variance with commonsense thinking. In particular, I argue (ch. 7) that common sense doesn't commit us to thinking of moral requirements as based in reason or to holding that it is irrational (as opposed to immoral) to be indifferent to the welfare of other people.

more unifying interpretation would seem to have its advantages. But as I have indicated, those advantages are purchased at the expense of some very strong modern-day moral/ethical intuitions, intuitions that moral sentimentalism may be in a particularly good position to account for and justify (though I won't say any more about that here).

Yes, we are pulled in two directions with regard to a case like the one Foot describes. We feel (that we would be) justified in not sacrificing a limb, feel moral admiration, nonetheless, for someone who is willing to make and actually makes such a sacrifice, and—a new point—also feel it would be somewhat unwise of us to give up a limb in the circumstance mentioned. It's not that we are reluctant to sacrifice a limb but recognize that we would be more rational if we were willing to do so—like someone who is unwilling to go to the dentist's but recognizes the irrationality of her own attitude. Rather, many of us feel it would be unwise and irrational of us to give up a limb to prevent worse injury to a stranger. And so when we contemplate some possible other person who makes such a sacrifice, we have some tendency to regard what they do as irrational (or rationally inexplicable) even while we at the same time admire and praise their action(s). We are genuinely tugged two ways about such persons, and I think that the main reason for this is that we understand practical rationality as having a large self-interested component, but have an other-regarding, other-benefiting conception of what is involved in morality. If the situation Foot describes really is evaluatively wrenching or ambiguous for us, I think that is because we think morality and practical rationality are both ethically significant, but conceive these two major elements of the ethical in ways that allow them, at the most fundamental level, to oppose or contradict one another. And that is the ethical dualism that, once we discard some unwarranted assumptions Sidgwick makes and leave moral rationalism out of the picture, common sense leads us to.

So we are stuck or fated with one or another form of ethical dualism, whether we accept Sidgwick or not, as long as we don't move in the direction of Aristotelian (or ancient) ethics. And I want to say that ethical dualism, whether *within* practical reason (or the rational) or *between* important parts of practical reason, on the one hand, and morality, on the other, is characteristic of much modern moral thinking and characteristically absent in ancient ethics. But I say "much" rather than all, not only because of Foot and others who recently have looked to ancient ethical models, not only because of Hume's rather quirky stance on practical reason and morality, but also because of what one finds when one looks at Kantian ethics. Kant doesn't subscribe to the sort of ethical dualism we have just described, but he is an ethical dualist in a larger sense that I think I now need to describe. Ethical dualism in a larger sense *is* characteristic of all or almost all characteristically modern (e.g., non-Aristotelian) moral philosophies, and what I propose to do now is consider Kant's views, explain why they amount to a kind of (properly generalized) ethical dualism, and then show how and why the kind of virtue ethics one finds both in classical antiquity and, by way of revival, in contemporary thought isn't dualistic in any of the ways that characterize almost all modern views that don't hark back to ancient ethics. I will also say something to clarify those two "almost"s in the last sentence.

3.3 Kant, Some Forms of Virtue Ethics, and One Form of Utilitarianism

Kant believes that morality is grounded in pure practical reason and seems to hold that it is irrational to act in a way that runs counter to morality, irrational, that is, to act immorally. And Kant doesn't think there are other, fully dignified kinds of rationality to be found outside or independently of morality. Imperatives of prudence or self-interest represent hypothetical (or assertoric) rational requirements, rather than strict, unavoidable, categorical ones, and Kant sees the rationale or focus of virtue as connected with categorical reasons or rationality, rather than with the objects or aims of hypothetical reason(s), and so as relatively disconnected from (or only indirectly and by derivation related to) human well-being. Moreover, and unlike so many philosophers in the ancient world, Kant's ideas about what serves self-interest, what makes for human well-being, are fairly hedonistic or subjective. So if a complete ethics contains views about rationality, about morality or virtue (I won't make distinctions between them at this point) and about personal good or well-being, then Kant's ethics contains a strong or deep dichotomy between well-being ("das Wohl"), on the one hand, and virtue, morality, and reason or rationality (all of which intimately connect with what Kant calls "das Gute"), on the other.[9]

So even if Kant sees rationality and morality as aligned with one another (more than sentimentalism or, as I have argued, commonsense thinking does), he assumes and defends a disconnect between these aspects of ethical thought and practice and considerations of sheer well-being or its (rational) pursuit. Thus Kant subscribes to a form of ethical dualism, but its point of demarcation is different from what Sidgwick, common sense, sentimentalism, and various other modern views conceive it to be. We can therefore articulate an important sense of dualism that is more general than anything we have seen illustrated up to this point: we can say that ancient ethics aligned (considerations of) virtue/ morality, rationality or good reasons, and (the pursuit, promotion, or achievement of) well-being or the good life with one another, saw them as tightly connected, and this is as much true of Epicureanism and Stoicism as it is true of Plato and Aristotle. But modern views deny this alignment in one or another deep way and this fact, we can now say, constitutes their ethical dualism in the most general terms available to us.

---

9. See the *Critique of Practical Reason*; but for more particular references and further discussion, see "The Opposite of Reductionism," earlier in this volume. In that paper, I use the term "dualism" of Kant in a sense somewhat different from and, in particular, more ontological than the sense I have given it in the present essay.

Now in speaking this way, I am making an exception of modern approaches that deliberately anchor themselves in ancient theories or approaches. I earlier mentioned Philippa Foot in this connection, and what I have just said seems also to be true of Rosalind Hursthouse's earlier (Aristotelian) ethical views as articulated in her influential paper "Virtue Theory and Abortion."[10] More recently, too, Kieran Setiya has articulated an ethics that (in a way that resembles Aristotelianism) claims that what is most virtuous is also what we have the most reason to do and that avoids all modern forms of dualism.[11] But the reader may now wonder how I can say this, given my earlier claims about the deep dualism implicit in commonsense ethical thought. Isn't it commonsensical to suppose that what is most virtuous is what we have most reason to do? So if Setiya, who says this sort of thing, avoids ethical dualism, we may well ask how common sense can then *fall into* such dualism.

The answer lies in the connection between (good) reasons and rationality. Speaking intuitively or commonsensically, it can't be rational to act against what one has the most (good) reason, that is, the best reason, to do. But then consider the case of giving up a limb. We don't think it is irrational not to do so, but we think it is more virtuous, more admirable, *to* do so. However, given the intuitive assumption just made, it can't be said that the person who chooses not to act (more) virtuously in this way acts against what he or she has most reason to do (or acts against the balance of good reasons). And, again speaking commonsensically, it doesn't seem right to say that such a person does what he or she has less (good) reason to do, even though the person clearly doesn't do what it would be most admirable to do in the circumstances. So, given the rather weak and intuitive connection between reasons and rationality I have been assuming, what is most virtuous is not necessarily at all what one has most or the best reason to do. Common sense therefore disagrees with Setiya, even though Setiya's own discussion pretty much ignores the notion of rationality and in fact therefore also ignores (and certainly doesn't make) the point I have just made. Because common sense allows a difference between what one has most reason (or it is rational) to do and what is most admirable or virtuous, it entails ethical dualism in a way Setiya's views, like the ancient ethical theories that inspire or resemble his approach, do not.

So we have seen that ancient virtue ethics and some Aristotle-inspired (or Aristotelian-like) contemporary forms of ethics don't entail or involve the ethical dualism that is so characteristic of modern views. Some of these views are

10. In *Philosophy and Public Affairs* 20: 223–46, 1991. In her later book, *On Virtue Ethics* (Oxford: Oxford University Press, 1999), Hursthouse no longer accepts a form of eudaimonism, but arguably accepts or should accept a connection between rationality/morality/virtue and human well-being *generally* (as opposed to exclusively agential well-being). So it is not obvious to me that even the later Hursthouse counts as any sort of ethical dualist. On this point, see what follows in the main text.

11. See Kieran Setiya, *Reasons without Rationalism*, Princeton, NJ: Princeton University Press, 2007, especially pp. 116ff.

clearly eudaimonistic, but I don't want to insist that the acceptance of eudaimonism is a necessary condition of avoiding ethical dualism. A virtue-ethical view that tightly connects rationality and virtue and conceives both as relating, not to the agent's well-being, but to human well-being generally avoids eudaimonism, but also aligns rationality, virtue, and (human) well-being in a very strict way. So in the terms I have been employing here, such a view (and Hursthouse's approach in *On Virtue Ethics* comes very close to this) avoids ethical dualism.[12] On the other hand, other versions of virtue ethics—like Hume's and my own—don't look to ancient models or subscribe to any form of eudaimonism, and they turn out to be just as capable of ethical dualism as the other, non-virtue-ethical modern approaches we have been speaking of.[13] Indeed everything we have seen thus far fits quite well into the scheme of division or differentiation between ancient (inspiration) and modern (inspiration) that I have offered. But things are a little bit messier than that, because I can think of one modern theory that doesn't involve the characteristic dualism(s) I have described, and, ironically, that exception can be found within the very same intellectual tradition or ism where the idea of ethical dualism was first articulated and defended: within utilitarianism (understood very broadly).

Sidgwick's approach, we have seen, leads to a sense of dualism concerning the rational and thus within ethics overall. And other utilitarian views also entail ethical dualism. Peter Railton, for example, holds a utilitarian view of right action, but defends a conception of rational choice that ties it to the agent's pursuit of her own ends, or her own well-being.[14] This differs from the view Sidgwick thinks the utilitarian holds or should hold about individual rationality—Sidgwick thinks the utilitarian needs the same criterion for rational choice/action as he or she has for morally right choice/action. But in that measure, Railton's ideas about individual rationality come much closer to (what I have been saying about) common sense than Sidgwick's utilitarian views, and that aspect of Railton's total view means that he too allows of a dualism of the ethical: not one like Sidgwick's within rationality, but rather one that (very commonsensically) entails a dualism *between* acting rationally and action rightly. For on Railton's theory, there will be many times when we have to choose between acting rationally and acting morally rightly or virtuously, and this stands in marked contrast with ancient virtue ethics, which argues that we aren't faced with such an ethically dire choice.

12. To the extent Plato in the *Republic* moves away from the idea that justice is always advantageous to(ward) the idea that philosopher rulers should sacrifice their own well-being for that of the larger group, his view is no longer eudaimonistic but is still ethically non-dualistic. Rationality/virtue still is aligned with well-being, even if the well-being isn't that of the virtuous individual. Hursthouse's transition from her earlier views to those she defends in her *On Virtue Ethics* interestingly resembles the Platonic transition I have just mentioned.

13. See Hume's *A Treatise of Human Nature*, ed. L. A. Selby-Bigge, Oxford: Clarendon Press, 1958. For my own dualism-involving, eudaimonism-denying, sentimentalist-inspired version of virtue ethics, see *Morals from Motives*, New York: Oxford University Press, 2001.

14. Peter Railton, "Moral Realism," *Philosophical Review* 95: 163–207, 1986.

But I have found one utilitarian theory that allows morality and rationality to line up in a way that also avoids the necessity of such a dire choice, and that is Shelly Kagan's view in *The Limits of Morality*.[15] (I am not saying there aren't others either within utilitarianism or elsewhere, but I haven't found them yet.) Kagan argues against egoism both as a theory of rationality/reasons and as a theory of morality, and when he advocates utilitarianism, it is also as a theory both of rationality/reasons and of moral right and wrong. So Kagan isn't at all ambivalent about the choice between utilitarianism and egoism as theories of rationality or good reasons and doesn't, therefore, see any dualism within practical reason of the kind that so much worried Sidgwick. But neither does he offer fundamentally different criteria of rational and moral choice in the manner of Peter Railton, so he avoids the larger ethical dualism that the latter is committed to, and in fact his view that reasons and moral virtue/right action march, or line up, together is not only in line with ancient ethics but (for the current reader, though not chronologically or historically) also reminiscent of, or similar to, what we have seen Kieran Setiya say about virtue(s) and reason(s). So Kagan doesn't subscribe to any form of dualism I am aware of, and his example spoils the neatness of the little scheme of division/differentiation I have proposed. But neat or not, the scheme does articulate a distinction between ancient and modern that holds in most, or almost all, cases. For that reason, I think it is important to add the distinction I have been making to the others that I mentioned earlier and that also hold only for the most part. We can't understand the difference between ancient and modern neatly, but that doesn't mean that we can't understand it deeply; and the present account of the distinctions that yield or fail to yield ethical dualism can, I think, help deepen our understanding of that difference and of the history of ethics more generally.

---

15. Oxford: Oxford University Press, 1989 (see especially pp. 321–30). Kagan (pp. 6–7) allows for the possibility that factors other than well-being should enter into a valid theory of good consequences and a valid theory of morality/rationality/good reasons that uses good consequences as the sole basis of its evaluations; so he is not explicitly committed to *utilitarian* consequentialism, even though he seems quite favorably disposed to it. In that case, and to the extent that factors other than (amount of) human well-being would enter into his conception of good consequences, his view doesn't align rationality, morality, and well-being *perfectly* with one another; but by the same token, Kagan doesn't *deny* that these notions are in perfect alignment and so *makes room* for an overall view that decisively denies ethical dualism. I am indebted here to discussion with Scott Gelfand.

4

COMMENTS ON BRYAN VAN NORDEN'S *VIRTUE ETHICS AND CONSEQUENTIALISM IN EARLY CHINESE PHILOSOPHY*

I have learned a great deal from Bryan Van Norden's new book. I am not a scholar of Chinese philosophy, and so, of course, I had and have a lot to learn from what scholars in that field have to say, and much of it is very interesting to a philosopher like myself, someone who has long been a virtue ethicist and who has also had a long-standing interest in and theoretical preoccupation with consequentialism. The Chinese anticipated much of what we later learned and developed in the West and have, perhaps more importantly, their own distinctive take or perspective on the issues that contemporary Western consequentialists and virtue ethicists are so focused upon. As I say, we have a lot to learn.

But today I would like to see whether I can be somewhat useful to the scholars. In emphasizing the very valid comparisons that can be made between Ruism, or Confucianism, and Aristotelian virtue ethics, Van Norden has, I think, downplayed and even ignored the comparisons that can be made between early Chinese thought and another historically important and presently visible kind of virtue ethics, the kind inaugurated by Hume and the other British moral sentimentalists. I think Van Norden missed an opportunity to make these latter sorts of comparisons in his book, and I want to say a bit about what this would or could have amounted to. Secondly, though, I want to comment on and add a bit to his discussion of Mo Tzu's consequentialism. Here too I think there may have been some missed opportunities of comparison with Western views, and in particular I want to show you that much of Bryan Van Norden's and, indeed, also, of Mo Tzu's discussion ignores the possibility of a way of basing ethics on impartial caring or concern for others that actually amounts to a consequentialism-rejecting form of *virtue ethics*.

4.1 Mengzi and Sentimentalist Virtue Ethics

Although, during the recent revival of virtue ethics in the West, Aristotelian or neo-Aristotelian ideas have led the way, other ways of pursuing virtue ethics in plausible contemporary terms have also come to light during the last few years. There is some interest nowadays in reviving Stoicism—Julia Annas has moved in this direction, for example; and, as I and others have recently been urging, it is also possible to conceive virtue ethics in Humean or moral sentimentalist terms, rather than working along relatively Aristotelian lines. (I don't know of any serious recent attempts to revive Plato or Epicureanism.) And I should also at this point mention the ethics of care, which is also a form of sentimentalism and which is very close to sentimentalist virtue ethics, even if not exactly the same thing.

Sentimentalist virtue ethics—whether in its earlier or in more recent embodiments—bears some striking resemblances to aspects or parts of early Chinese philosophy, but before I say more about this, let me just give a couple of very general characterizations of the difference between the Humean/sentimentalist and Aristotelian approaches to virtue ethics. The largest difference concerns the split between ethical or moral rationalism and sentimentalism. Aristotle regards ethical thought, attitudes, and behavior as issuing from the rational side of our nature, and Hume certainly thought just the opposite. But, further, it is also possible to see Aristotle's account of the virtues as resting on a theory of eudaimonia, of what it is lead a good individual life. On this interpretation, Aristotle regards traits of character as virtues only if they promote or constitute part of the good life for those who have those traits, and some contemporary Aristotelian virtue ethicists—for example, Rosalind Hursthouse at least in her earlier work—also accept this form of "eudaimonism." By contrast, Hume seems to want to anchor the virtues in a more general contribution to human welfare, and in that measure he anticipated and influenced utilitarian ethics. But lest one imagine that Hume is best regarded as a proto-utilitarian rather than any sort of virtue ethicist, remember that Hume asserts that actions have moral merit only insofar as they express or evince attitudes and motives we think well of. In this respect, Hume's views resemble those commonly attributed to Aristotle as the basis for considering the latter to be pursuing a distinctively virtue-ethical approach to moral questions.

Finally, though, and by way of drawing a further deep contrast between Aristotle and Hume (or sentimentalism), consider the enormous emphasis Hume places on compassion, sympathy, and benevolence as the basis for moral thought and action. These feelings or motives play at best only a minor role in Aristotle's thought, and that isn't surprising in or for someone who takes a predominantly rationalist position about the moral life. This is a major difference between Aristotle and Hume and likewise, though less extremely, between their contemporary representatives. So we have (at least) two very different ways of developing or articulating an ethics of virtue, and we have to ask, therefore, whether both ways are represented within early Chinese philosophy or whether one can only find analogies or similarities with Aristotle inside the Confucian or Ruist tradition(s).

In his book, Bryan Van Norden stresses the similarities between Confucian ethics and Aristotle. Hume is mentioned, but not as having developed a form of virtue ethics that might be similar to what we find in any part of the Ruist tradition. And, as I said before, I think this represents a missed opportunity. Van Norden makes an excellent case, as far as I can tell, for seeing Confucius or Kongzi as advancing and anticipating something like an Aristotelian form of virtue ethics. The emphasis on human good and the good life and on tying ideas about virtue to notions about what is good for the virtuous individual certainly seems common to Confucius and Aristotle, if one accepts Van Norden's readings and interpretations of the ancient Chinese texts. I am certainly in no position to quarrel with any of that, but also want to say, by way of a compliment to his book, that Van Norden makes his interpretation of Kongzi's thought seem compelling to a reader like myself who comes from outside the field of Chinese philosophy and is armed only with a knowledge of Aristotle or Western virtue ethics. However, his discussion of Mencius, Mengzi, gave me pause, because what he said about Mengzi seemed to me at least more reminiscent of Hume than of Aristotle. Let me explain why.

I am not all that well acquainted with the classics of Chinese philosophy, but in recent months I have been reading Mengzi and also Mo Tzu or Mozi. And in what I am about to say I rely on Bryan Van Norden's account of Mengzi's philosophy—even though, and as we shall see later on, I have a few bones to pick with how he presents Mozi's consequentialism. The picture he gives us of Mengzi should be fairly familiar to most of you, and again I want to focus on what seem to me the principal points that affect how one might best characterize his virtue-ethical approach.

Mengzi places "ren" at the center of ethics, and, as I am told, "ren" can be translated as benevolence, sympathy, or humaneness. Van Norden also points out or argues—I don't know how controversial this is or would be among scholars of Chinese philosophy—that "ren" has a wider or larger sense in which it is equivalent, roughly, to the whole of morality, to being moral or righteous. This latter sense, Van Norden says, can be found in Kongzi, but Mengzi appears to use "ren" more frequently to mean just benevolence, compassion, etc., and Mengzi's ethics centers around benevolence and/or these other motives/sentiments much more than Kongzi's does. Given what I said above and what most philosophers know about Hume, this makes Mengzi's ideas appear to resemble Hume's to a certain extent more than Aristotle's. These warm sentiments just aren't central for Aristotle, and Mengzi's emphasis on *ren* makes his philosophy seem more naturally classified as a form of sentimentalism than of rationalism. If he is doing virtue ethics, which Van Norden would agree he is, then it is sentimentalist Hume-like virtue ethics rather than the Aristotelian variety. But Van Norden doesn't at all point this out.

In keeping with what I have just been saying, Van Norden's account of Kongzi stresses the role of the virtues in assuring the individual a good or prosperous life, and he doesn't place a similar emphasis on this Aristotelian idea when he discusses Mengzi. Once again, this makes Mengzi seem less Aristotelian than Kongzi. But consider too the partialism that is built into Mengzi's view of morality (of course, Kongzi is also a partialist). Mengzi makes a great deal of the fact that we have stronger obligations to people we know than to those we don't know, and though the emphasis, for example, placed on feelings for and obligations to one's older brother has no parallel in anything Hume says or any Westerner is likely to say, the main outline is fairly Humean.

Hume sees and says that our obligations to those who are near to us either spatiotemporally or in family or amicable relationship are stronger than to those we don't relate to in those ways, and he makes use of associationist/ empiricist ideas to explain how and why (we feel that) this is so. That discussion makes use of the idea of empathy, even though the term "empathy" wasn't invented till the twentieth century and the term Hume actually uses is "sympathy." But as Bryan Van Norden wisely tells us, we can't assume that an idea is absent or inoperative in people's thinking just because we have no (single or unambiguous) word for it, and in the little section called "Of the love of fame" as well as later in the *Treatise of Human Nature*, Hume speaks of the mechanisms of empathy/sympathy, of the "infusion" of one person's feeling into another, as depending on issues of proximity and resemblance.[1] Hume is actually, then, more explicit about or aware of empathy as a mechanism than Mengzi ever is, though in just a moment I want to say something about where I think the specific idea of empathy *is* anticipated, to some extent, within Chinese philosophy. But here my point is that both Hume and Mengzi believe that a gradated, partialistic concern for others that depends, roughly, on how close they are to us, is absolutely at the heart—forgive the pun—of morality. And Aristotle's picture of virtue and the virtues as habits of medial choice is not at all like this. Aristotle doesn't focus on our gradated obligations toward others or treat sympathetic concern for others as the main basis of morality, and for all these reasons I think it makes sense to compare Mengzi's virtue ethics to Hume's, or to other, more recent, forms of sentimentalist virtue ethics (e.g., my own previous approach to these issues) than to highlight the comparison with Aristotle. To be sure there are resemblances to or with Aristotle. But that is in great part, I think, because both Mengzi and Aristotle are virtue ethicists rather than consequentialists or proto-Kantians. However, when it comes to the *kind* of virtue ethics one finds in Mengzi, I think it is *more* accurate to call it Humean or sentimentalist than to characterize it as Aristotelian.

There are some other important facts or factors that serve strongly to reinforce this conclusion. For example, Hume speaks of benevolence as an original tendency of the human mind (in a way that malevolence isn't), and this is very much like Mengzi's view that humans are basically, or in tendency, morally good. By contrast, both Kongzi and Aristotle see human nature as morally neutral, though also (to different extents and in different ways) as morally malleable. Furthermore, and I wish I had the time to say more about this, Mengzi's account of the nature of human shame and human approval is surprisingly, or perhaps *not* so surprisingly, similar to what Hume says about these topics. (Hume uses the word "humility" to refer to shame.) Some scholars have noted

1. See Hume's *A Treatise of Human Nature*, ed. L. A. Selby-Bigge, Oxford: Clarendon Press, 1958.

the resemblance between Mengzi and Hume without calling them virtue ethicists, but I agree with Bryan Van Norden that it makes sense to view Mengzi as
a virtue ethicist and simply disagree with him about the *kind* of virtue ethicist
Mengzi is. And I should also note at this point that I am far from the first person
to argue that Mengzi is a sentimentalist virtue ethicist. In a dissertation that
I supervised and that P. J. Ivanhoe served as external examiner for, Shirong Luo
has defended that very point—though Luo sees Kongzi as more of a sentimentalist than I do. (That disagreement is a subject for another occasion.)

Finally, let me just mention briefly one further resemblance between Mengzi
and Hume and difference between him and Aristotle that David Nivison helps
us to see. In "Motivation and Moral Action in Mencius," Nivison says there is a
"sharp contrast between Mencius and Aristotle on the 'internality' of virtuous
acts. For Mencius, one cannot perform a (genuinely) virtuous act unless one
acts out of the appropriate motivation. In contrast, for Aristotle, a virtuous act
need be only the sort of act that a virtuous person would perform."[2] Nivison
goes on to say that a person who lacks virtue and virtuous motivation can perform an action that a virtuous person *would* perform; but then Mengzi is much
closer to Hume than he is to Aristotle in this respect, because Hume *does* say
that virtuous actions require virtuous motives. Unfortunately, Nivison doesn't
mention Hume in this connection and loses what seems to me a golden opportunity to point out the similarity between Mengzi and *a virtue ethicist other
than Aristotle*. The resemblance between various Chinese views and British
moral sentimentalism has all too often, I think, been lost in the shuffle.

Now if, having reached all these conclusions, I can get back to the subject of
empathy, let me just mention, as I earlier promised to do, the one place I have
learned about (and I have learned about it from Van Norden's book) where
something very explicit is said about empathy or at least about a phenomenon
that is tied to empathy more than, say, to the ideas of benevolence, sympathy,
compassion, and commiseration taken on their own. In contemporary usage,
we distinguish all these latter from empathy, and let me very briefly explain
how I think we do it. Take the difference between the Bill-Clintonesque "I feel
your pain" and "I feel sorry about the fact you are in pain and want to do what
I can to help." Most ordinary English speakers, if called upon to say which
of these two statements they associate with empathy and which with sympathy, would treat the first statement as referring to empathy and the second as
referring to sympathy, benevolence, commiseration, or compassion. When
Van Norden discusses Mengzi's treatment of *ren*, he doesn't refer to any facts
or phenomena that explicitly call forth the idea of empathy rather than compassion, benevolence, and the like; and although we nowadays (the psychology literature on moral development makes much of this) think benevolence
and compassion *depend* on empathy, Mengzi doesn't make that point and, at

---

2. This essay can be found in Nivison's *The Ways of Confucianism: Investigations in Chinese
Philosophy*, ed. Bryan Van Norden, Chicago: Open Court, 1996. See especially p. 116.

least as Van Norden presents his ideas, says nothing that to me at least speaks directly to or of empathy.

However, late in his discussion of Mengzi, Van Norden mentions a much later Chinese ethicist, Wang Yangming, who says something about benevolence that goes beyond anything one finds clearly in Mengzi. Wang says that when we are benevolent toward animals or other persons, our benevolence "forms one body" with those others. (He also speaks of forming one body with plants and mere things, but I won't go into that here.) Now those who nowadays speak about empathy sometimes point out that when we empathize with someone, we feel an identity or identify with that person. (They don't say this about benevolence or sympathy as such.) But to share an identity with someone is very much like the even-less-literal idea of forming one body with them, so I am inclined to think that Wang is homing in on the notion of empathy more than two hundred years before Hume did. This is the first philosophical (or literary) reference or allusion to the phenomenon of empathy that I am aware of. (Malebranche to some degree anticipates Hume on empathy, but, again, this is much later than Wang.)

Some support for this interpretation of Wang comes from David Nivison's essay "Golden Rule Arguments in Chinese Moral Philosophy." Nivison thinks that Wang's notion of forming one body with others involves the idea of a "sympathetic identification with others that leads one to see others fully as individuals, in their own situations and with their own viewpoints."[3] This description doesn't use the term "empathy" but it pretty well embodies what those who like to speak in terms of empathy think of empathy as (distinctively) involving. If Nivison's interpretation is on the right track, therefore, it supports the idea that Wang anticipates Hume's discussion of empathy and has something very important in common with Hume. However, I now think it is time for me to say something about Van Norden's discussion of Mohist cosequentialism.

4.2 Mo Tzu and Consequentialism

First off, let me mention that some commentators regard Mo Tzu as a utilitarian, not just as a consequentialist, but I propose to set that issue aside for the duration of the present talk. What I do want to talk about is the distinction between a commitment to impartial caring or universal benevolence, on the one hand, and a commitment to direct consequentialism, on the other. Mo Tzu

---

3. This essay can also be found in *Ways of Confucianism*. See especially p. 70. Nivison's piece mentions Kant in connection with Golden Rule arguments, but doesn't see or at least say that the idea of forming or having one body with others points us toward Hume much more than toward Kant. In fact, despite the essay's title, and its Kantian/reciprocalist implications, Nivison's discussion of "ren," of having humane feelings toward and being sensitive to others (see p. 70), also points much more in the direction of Humean sentimentalism than toward Kant or any other rationalist.

accepts both as part of his philosophy, and during his discussion of Mohism, Van Norden acknowledges that one can advocate impartial caring without necessarily advocating consequentialism. But he doesn't make very much out of this point, and I think that leads him to underestimate the difficulties involved in justifying the Mohist position. To be sure, he argues that the latter is inferior to Ruism because it fails to recognize the varying strength of our moral obligations to people depending on how they relate or are related to us. And I don't disagree with him here. But once one sees that a commitment to impartial caring is even compatible with taking a virtue ethical approach to morality and moral theory, it becomes clear that Mohism is even more questionable, and certainly more underdetermined, than Van Norden shows us.

But how, you ask, could impartialism lead us toward virtue ethics? Well, not every virtue ethics need stress or accept partiality. It is possible to anchor right action in an ideal of impartial motivation and, in particular, caring, and this idea may already be somewhat familiar to you, though in a less than familiar guise. Hare and others have regarded agapic, universal Christian love as an ethical ideal very much akin to utilitarianism, and indeed it is. But an ethics of universal love needn't evaluate actions in terms of consequences; it can stress, and most plausibly would be regarded as stressing, the motivation behind actions— it can say that actions are right to the extent they exemplify and express universal love, rather than to the extent they actually or expectably achieve the goals of such love. This would be an impartialist form of virtue ethics, and if you allow me to switch from speaking of love to speaking of benevolence or caring, then I am saying that it is possible to speak of and defend a virtue ethics that evaluates actions in terms of how well or closely they exhibit or reflect impartial benevolence or caring.

In my book *Morals from Motives*, I mentioned the possibility of advocating this sort of virtue ethics and pointed out the difficulties of showing it to be inferior to utilitarian consequentialism.[4] And what I said there is relevant to Van Norden's discussion, for many of the things Van Norden says by way of characterizing Mohist consequentialism don't actually entail Mohism. For example, he says (p. 139) that "Mozi offers us a general algorithm for determining what is right: aim at maximizing benefits impartially." But this description also applies to the kind of virtue ethics that *Morals from Motives* called morality as universal benevolence (one could, in the light of Van Norden's terminology, just as easily call it morality as impartial caring). Morality as universal benevolence also requires one to aim at maximizing benefits impartially, but it differs from Mohist or contemporary consequentialism by tying its moral evaluations of actions to their underlying motivation rather than to their consequences. An act will be wrong if it was motivated, say, by indifference to or malice toward humanity, even if it somehow, surprisingly or accidentally,

---

4. New York: Oxford University Press, 2001.

produces optimal consequences. Van Norden also says (p. 146) that Mohism seems to "regard impartial benevolence as the fundamental standard of rightness," but, once again, this is *neutral* as between consequentialism and morality as universal benevolence or impartial caring.

Now I am not saying that a virtue-ethical morality as impartial caring is superior to consequentialism, only that it is difficult to show that it isn't. To be sure, and as Van Norden notes, the Mohists thought their doctrine possessed the advantage over other views of offering a clear criterion of rightness; and one might say that by substituting good motives for good consequences, morality as impartial caring *doesn't* offer us a clear way to assess actions. After all, motives may be more difficult to assess than (the goodness of) consequences. But it is not at all clear that a Mohist is entitled to say such a thing. After all, Van Norden points out that the Mohist characterization of good consequences is rather vague because it mentions three different factors that are relevant to the assessment of consequences and doesn't offer a clear, or in fact any, method of balancing those factors. More importantly, perhaps, from a dialectical standpoint, the Mohist himself stresses the need to teach or develop impartial benevolence, and it would be more than odd if they complained about the clarity of the very sort of talk of motives that they themselves make use of.

As far as I have been able to determine, none of Van Norden's characterizations of Mohism in his book and none of the quotations he offers entail Mohism as a consequentialist doctrine. They are all neutral between that doctrine and the virtue ethics of impartial caring/universal benevolence. But in fact there are passages in Mo Tzu that *do* commit him to consequentialism rather than virtue ethics. He says that since partiality causes calamities, it is wrong; and this precisely avoids saying that there is something inherently wrong with partiality as a motive or set of motives, which is what a virtue ethics of universal benevolence would presumably say. Mo Tzu also says that what is praiseworthy is what is helpful or useful, and, finally, he says that since universal love causes the major benefits of the world, it is right.

All these statements (and I am here using Yi-Pao Mei's edition of Mo Tzu's writings) seem pretty clearly to entail consequentialism or at least to favor a consequentialistic interpretation over an impartialist virtue-ethical one. But then one also has to consider whether Mo Tzu says anything that justifies him in advocating (impartialistic) consequentialism in preference to virtue-ethical impartialism. I don't think he does, and even if he himself wasn't perhaps aware of morality as universal benevolence as a distinct possibility, once we are aware of it, we have reason beyond anything Bryan Van Norden says, to question Mo Tzu's advocacy of consequentialism.

Before concluding, let me make one point of general comparison that is independent of any issue about the merits of various doctrines or theories. At the considerable risk of being accused of chauvinistic Eurocentrism, I want to say that I find it quite impressive that Mo Tzu anticipated later Western utilitarianism and that Mengzi anticipated later Western moral sentimentalism each by over two thousand years. By contrast, Kongzi's virtue ethics didn't appear very long before Aristotle's, so although his ideas have had a greater influence in China than perhaps anyone else's have, their historical appearance doesn't seem quite so remarkable a fact.

The upshot of what I have been saying in this talk is that Bryan Van Norden takes us only part of the way toward the comparative understanding of Chinese and Western thought that his book does so much to advance. Comparisons with Aristotle and Aristotelian virtue ethics are important, very important, because, for one thing, recent discussions of virtue ethics in the West have owed more to Aristotle than to any other philosopher. But Humean and sentimentalist virtue ethics more generally are now increasingly regarded as promising and relevant theoretical possibilities, so we need to have more discussion, I think, of the ways Ruism, and, as it turns out, even Mohism, resemble this kind of moral approach. As Christine Swanton has so nicely put the point about the recent emergence and development of virtue-ethical moral sentimentalism, virtue ethics turns out to be a genus, not a species. Aristotle is only one way to do virtue ethics, and any attempt to consider the similarities between Western virtue ethics and Chinese must therefore take in both Aristotle and Hume and those who have been influenced by them.

5

HUME ON APPROVAL

I am going to be talking about Hume's sentimentalist view of approval and disapproval, but arguing that sentimentalism can and should offer us a more plausible theory of approval (and disapproval) than Hume did. Still, Hume was, I think, the first to identify the mechanisms that *any* sentimentalist theory of approval must operate by, and I shall be attempting to show—and this is no easy matter—that Hume's views on approval may at least have been on the right track. Most philosophers nowadays, and not just rationalists, would find it implausible to suppose, with Hume, that moral approval and disapproval can occur prior to, and form the basis of, moral judgment. But this is what a sentimentalist in metaethics has to say, and though I shall be rejecting Hume's particular theory of approval and disapproval, and his varying, mutually incompatible accounts of the way (moral) approval enters into moral judgment(s), I will be defending an account of approval and disapproval that doesn't presuppose moral judgment. And if we can use this account to help us toward a better understanding of the nature of moral claims or judgments, that would be some sort of vindication of (a major part of) what Hume was trying to accomplish in book III of the *Treatise*.

5.1 Moral Approval and Disapproval

As sentimentalists, Francis Hutcheson, David Hume, and Adam Smith all offered theories of approval that didn't rest on or presuppose (the making of) moral judgments and that didn't treat approval as based in—as any sort of form or expression of—rationality or reason. I am not going to talk much about Smith here, because, although his ideas are very interesting in themselves, I don't think they are particularly useful in helping us to develop a plausible contemporary form of sentimentalism vis-à-vis approval and moral judgment. At least, they don't help *me* to go in the direction *I* find most plausible.[1] But

1. Although (the Third Earl of) Shaftesbury is usually regarded as the first of the moral sentimentalists, the first in a line that proceeds through Hutcheson and on to Hume and Smith, he is a very incomplete or imperfect exemplar of the tradition he is thought of as inaugurating. In particular, his conception of moral sense is rather rationalistic, so I prefer to begin my discussion with Hutcheson, who has a genuinely sentimentalist notion of moral sense.

a brief consideration of Hutcheson will help us, I think, to see how Hume's discussion of approval represents an advance over what Hutcheson said about it, and the particular nature of that advance—namely, that it specifies a mechanism of approval in a way that Hutcheson never did—is very helpful in moving us toward the kind of view that I do want to defend and that I believe is more plausible than what Hume tells us about approval. The kind of approach I want to argue for relies on a mechanism or mechanisms of approval and disapproval—just not the particular ones that Hume relies on in his account of moral judgment. And the view of approval and its mechanisms that I shall be advocating naturally leads toward a certain interesting, and I hope plausible, way of understanding moral judgments.

Francis Hutcheson regards the most extensive, that is, universal, benevolence as the morally best of motives and treats that status as independent of the consequences of that motive.[2] Utilitarianism à la Bentham evaluates all motives (and of course all acts) by reference to their consequences, and Bentham leaves open the possibility that universal benevolence might turn out to be a less than morally good motive if it led to overall less good results than (acting from) other motives did. But Hutcheson is not a utilitarian or consequentialist about motives, even if he was the first, at least in English, to introduce a version of the principle of utility with regard to human *actions*. He considers motives to carry their moral value intrinsically and is to that extent a virtue ethicist.

In addition, however, he holds that we apprehend the value of motives via a moral sense analogous to the senses of sight, smell, etc. Benevolence is morally good, and we know or detect that goodness via a moral sense. So just as sensations of red are the way our sense of sight allows us to apprehend or register the redness of objects outside us, the moral sense allows us to apprehend the moral goodness of benevolent motives via pleasurable feelings of approval—and the moral badness of other motives via disagreeable feelings of disapproval.

Now the Hutchesonian idea of a distinct moral sense was rejected by subsequent sentimentalists. To be sure, Hume sometimes speaks of a moral sense or sense of morals, but he also makes it clear that he doesn't understand this, in literal Hutchesonian terms, as a distinct mode of perception on all fives with the other human senses. Because there is no distinct organ or psychological mechanism for moral sense, Hutcheson's idea has widely been regarded as a nonstarter. The idea of a moral sense clearly does rule out reason/rationality as the basis for moral approval and judgment, but it is difficult to take it literally and it is certainly also vague, because the metaphor involved here doesn't tell us (enough about) how moral knowledge actually occurs. But at the very least the concept of a moral sense can function as a placeholder for a fuller

2. For fuller discussion of both Hutcheson and Shaftesbury, see Stephen Darwall, *The British Moralists and the Internal "Ought": 1640–1740*, Cambridge: Cambridge University Press, 1995, chs. 7 and 8. The present discussion of Hutcheson draws on his *An Essay on the Nature and Conduct of the Passions, with Illustrations on the Moral Sense*, 3rd edition, Introduction by Paul McReynolds, Gainesville, FL: Scholars' Facsimiles and Reprints, 1969.

sentimentalist account of the mechanisms of moral knowledge, and Hume certainly rises to this challenge. So however implausible it may be in itself as an account of what approval is, Hutcheson's theory (if that is the right word for it) performs the useful, the important, task of staking out a claim for further sentimentalist exploration and elaboration.

Hume, responding immediately to Hutcheson's view, sought precisely to supply what Hutcheson's theory seems mainly to lack, namely, a theory of the mechanism or mechanisms of moral approval and judgment—rather than relying on the metaphor/hypothesis of a moral sense. Hume held that our capacity for moral approbation/approval and moral judgment depends on our "propensity" or tendency to sympathize with others, but the sympathy at issue here is not the kind of sympathetic concern for others that we nowadays readily designate by using the term "sympathy," but is rather, for Hume, a mechanism of psychological influence.[3] Sympathy is involved when the passion or feeling of another is mirrored in us, when we receive "by communication" the passions and feelings of others and thus feel something analogous to what those others feel. Hume says a good deal about how such communication or psychological "contagion" works, but we don't, I think, need to go into all the details of his account here. However, it is worth noting (though it *may* at this point be obvious) that the sort of "sympathy" Hume is talking about is or involves what we nowadays usually refer to as empathy (rather than as sympathy)—the kind of phenomenon Bill Clinton was invoking or referring to when he said: "I feel your pain." (The term "empathy" didn't exist in Hume's time, and it is, in fact, not very surprising that he uses the term "sympathy" sometimes to refer to what we call empathy and sometimes to what we call sympathy.[4])

In any event, what is most important at this point is the fact that Hume views moral approval and disapproval as based in or involving the mechanism(s) of "sympathy"—what I am going from now on to refer to as empathy. For Hume (as, essentially, for Hutcheson), approval is a feeling, not a judgment to the effect that something or someone is morally right or good. (That is one reason why Hume says that morality is "more properly felt than judg'd of."[5]) And

---

3. See especially the *Treatise of Human Nature*, ed. L. A. Selby-Bigge, Oxford: Clarendon Press, 1958, p. 473. The present discussion of Hume draws mainly on the *Treatise* book II, part I, s. XI, and part II; and book III, part III, s. I and III. Note that I shall for the most part be ignoring Hume's *Enquiry Concerning the Principles of Morals*, where the term "sympathy" is more often used in the present-day sense that is equivalent to sympathetic concern for (the welfare of) others. (See Selby-Bigge, ed., *Hume's Enquiries*, Oxford: Clarendon Press, 2nd edition, 1961, for example, pp. 298n, 303.)

4. For a fairly comprehensive contemporary treatment of (the mechanisms of) empathy, see Martin Hoffman, *Empathy and Moral Development: Implications for Caring and Justice*, Cambridge: Cambridge University Press, 2000.

5. See *Treatise*, p. 470. On the next page, Hume says: "To have the sense of virtue, is nothing but to *feel* a satisfaction of a particular kind from the contemplation of a character. The very *feeling* constitutes our praise or admiration...Our approbation is imply'd in the immediate pleasure [character traits] convey to us."

Hume holds that that feeling can be aroused via mechanisms of empathy: when we become aware of the pleasures that other people have experienced as a result of their own or others' prudence or benevolence, for example, we feel pleasure at their having been given pleasures in that way, and that received, mirroring, or (as Hume himself sometimes puts it) "infused" pleasure, roughly, constitutes our approval of the prudence or benevolence that caused the pleasures. (Notice that no moral *judgment* is involved here.) In similar fashion, the disapproval of malice, selfishness, or indolence results through pained empathic awareness of (awareness that reflects) the pains that people (both those who have the traits and others) have experienced as a result of such traits.[6]

However, apart from such considerations of traits' utility, Hume also thinks that moral approval and disapproval occur when (we believe that) a trait or motive is "immediately agreeable or disagreeable" to ourselves or others; but here too he seems to want to say that the approval and disapproval occur via some sort of empathic mechanism.[7] In addition, according to Hume, our pain and pleasure at the pain and pleasure of others varies with and is influenced by how closely we are related to them in space, time, consanguinity, etc. Thus Hume thinks that some of the same associative mechanisms that influence our willingness to ascribe causal influence also mediate how much empathic pleasure (and approval) we feel at or because of the pleasures others feel. But, according to Hume, moral judgment seeks or is supposed to abstract from such differences. We judge the murder of a spatially and temporally distant person with whom we are personally unacquainted to be no less blameworthy than the murder of one of our kin. And Hume certainly attempts to explain this phenomenon.

In order to arrive at a general and stable basis for communicating with one another, Hume argues, we need to "correct" our tendencies toward greater empathy with those best known to us, and for that reason we set up a more impartial standard or rule for making moral judgments that depends not on our variable and often mutually contradictory empathetic relations to those affected by different actions or motives, but rather on the point of view of those "who have any immediate connexion or intercourse" with the person we are judging.[8] So (at least in "calm" moments) we are equally critical of child abuse involving people we don't know and of child abuse involving a person or people we do know and even love. But Hume also thinks that the actual

6. I am stating Hume's view very roughly at this point, but the criticisms I shall be making of his view don't, I think, depend on any finer discriminations. For a more nuanced account of Hume on approval and disapproval, see, for example, S. Darwall, "Hume and the Invention of Utilitarianism," in eds. M. A. Stewart and J. P. Wright, *Hume and Hume's Connexions*, University Park, PA: Pennsylvania State University Press, 1994, pp. 58–82.

7. See, for example, *Treatise*, p. 590.

8. See *Treatise*, pp. 602–03. For interesting discussion of the need to "regularize" moral judgment in the way Hume suggests, see, for example, Geoffrey Sayre-McCord, "On Why Hume's 'General Point of View' Isn't Ideal—and Shouldn't Be," *Social Philosophy and Policy* 11 (*Cultural Pluralism and Moral Knowledge*): 202–28, 1994.

consequences of various traits or kinds of action are more variable and irregular than their causal tendencies, so he goes on to argue that moral judgment is reasonably grounded in the *tendency* to cause harm (or good) rather than in actually caused harm (or good).

Thus according to Hume, moral judgments are or should be made in a (relatively) impartial way that abstracts from the judger's relation to those who are or tend to be benefited or harmed by given traits or actions, and the same point can be made regarding those who are or tend to be immediately pleased or displeased by certain traits or actions. But judgment is not the same thing as approval or disapproval, and Hume never says that the latter requires, or exists only when subjected to, the above-mentioned corrections. He does, however, seem to think (though he isn't very clear about the point) that approval and disapproval only count as *moral* approval and disapproval, when the particular relationships of the person registering approval or disapproval have been substantially discounted or set aside in the process of arriving at the approval and disapproval. So although Hume thinks that both moral approval and moral judgment can involve mechanisms of empathy, that empathy is or is supposed to be corrected or regularized in the direction of an impartiality that, according to Hume, natural virtues like benevolence don't require and even rule out.

However, if we for the moment set aside the differences between approval and judgment and the question of partiality versus impartiality, we can see that Hume allows two different routes to virtue status and to moral approval and judgment as well: what immediately pleases and what is useful (in Hume's empiricist hedonic terms). But there is a problem with this view that Adam Smith (and others) early on pointed out.[9] If moral approval and judgment can be based on how certain traits or actions affect or tend to affect (certain) people's welfare, it is unclear why inanimate objects or events cannot be the subject of moral approval and disapproval: for example, why we shouldn't and don't morally criticize hurricanes for tending to cause harm and misery. And if approval and judgment can be based on whether something immediately pleases or displeases, there likewise seems to be no reason why we can't morally disapprove of an ugly sunset or unpleasant non-human noise(maker).

Hume seeks to answer that objection (which it is thought he originally received directly from Smith himself) in a long footnote in *An Enquiry Concerning the Principles of Morals*.[10] That reply appeals to the (assumed) fact

9. See Smith's *The Theory of Moral Sentiments*, eds. D. D. Raphael and A. L. Macfie, Oxford: Oxford University Press, 1976, part IV, ch. II. For discussion of similar early criticisms of Hume, see James Fieser, "Hume's Wide View of the Virtues: An Analysis of His Early Critics," *Hume Studies* XXIV: 295–311, 1998.

10. *An Enquiry Concerning the Principles of Morals*, in ed. L. A. Selby-Bigge, *Hume's Enquiries*, 2nd edition, Oxford: Clarendon Press, 1961, s. V, p. 213n. See also the *Treatise*, pp. 471–73. Hume's view also allows for approval and disapproval of animals, and for animals to possess certain virtues and vices, but Hume doesn't seem to have thought this would be problematic. See, for example, Tom Beauchamp, "Hume on the Nonhuman Animal," *Journal of Medicine and Philosophy* 24: 322–35, 1999. I won't take up this issue in its own right here.

that the pleasure we feel regarding inanimate things is simply (phenomeno-logically) different from that we feel in respect to human beings. Even if the mechanism of empathy/sympathy can operate to make us feel pain at the pain caused by a hurricane, that second-order pain is not of the right kind to qualify our attitude toward its cause as one of disapproval, and similarly when we feel pleasure at the pleasure (that we know or see) nonhuman things or entities cause.

This reply seems rather tendentious or question-begging (a point that Hume comes very close to making against his own future self near the end of the *Treatise*, p. 617). Aside from the desire to shore up a particular account of human approval and disapproval, is there really any reason to think that the pleasure we feel at the pleasure caused by humans is phenomenologically different from what we feel in regard to pleasure caused by inanimate entities? And, more generally, is Hume really right to assume moral approval is (always) pleasant and disapproval unpleasant or disagreeable? On the face of it, there are many occasions when approval doesn't seem pleasant and can even seem unpleasant. Thus, as Pall Ardal has pointed out, one can feel *begrudging* approval of the decent or noble acts of someone one strongly dislikes; and, similarly, it can feel good and even be enjoyable to disapprove (and criticize) other people.[11] And surely such an appeal to phenomenology is a dialectically fair form of criti-cism to direct at someone like Hume who places such importance on phenom-enological considerations. Still, one might hold that approval and disapproval have a distinctive feel, even if that feel isn't apparent or realized on every occasion when they occur, and so I prefer to argue against Hume's account at least partly on the grounds that the difference in phenomenology between approval and disapproval (and between those phenomena and other phenom-ena) is *better* captured in terms other than pleasure and pain. But in order to see why, I believe we need an account of approval and disapproval that focuses on agential traits and the standpoint of those who possess them, rather than on (empathy with) the effects such traits have on the welfare of others.[12]

That is precisely what Hutcheson does in holding that the moral sense of approval or disapproval is primarily directed toward the greater or lesser benev-olence of moral agents, rather than toward any results of such motivation. (This is also true of Adam Smith's account of approval and disapproval.) But we also want a theory that goes beyond the implausible (or purely metaphorical) idea of a distinct moral sense, one that spells out an understandable *mechanism* for moral approval and disapproval, but that also, as I have just been suggesting,

11. See his *Passion and Value in Hume's Treatise*, Edinburgh: Edinburgh University Press, 1966, pp. 114ff.

12. Elizabeth Radcliffe has pointed out to me that Hume himself moves to some extent in this direction when he allows that we can sometimes evaluate actions and settled traits favorably even when they don't produce their usual good effects. But even here Hume thinks our approval depends on our imagining the usual effects, and this seems to me to place too much emphasis on effects rather than agents. See *Treatise*, pp. 584–85.

allows our approval and disapproval to focus on moral agents rather than on the consequences of their actions. And what I want now to argue is that we may be able to find what we are looking for in a certain way of using or understanding the notion of empathy. Empathy focused on agents will not only offer us a mechanism for approval and disapproval, but also allow us to understand the phenomenology of approval and disapproval more accurately and intuitively than Hume's theory enables us to do. (Unlike Hutcheson, Adam Smith in fact makes use of what we would call empathy in his account of agent-directed approval; but, as I indicated earlier, I believe a reliance on his views would take us in an ultimately less satisfactory and in fact less *sentimentalist* direction than I and other sentimentalists would like. So I will not discuss his views further.)

Now the most familiar form or instance of empathy is not directed at agents, but felt *by* agents for those who need help or are suffering. Empathically sensitive and caring agents will act on behalf of (some of) those who need their help, etc.; and I have recently written a book, *The Ethics of Care and Empathy* (henceforth, *ECE*), that spells out (many of) the ways in which our helpfulness toward those in pain or need is mediated by empathic mechanisms— mechanisms, for example, that make us more concerned about our intimates and about people we see than about people we only casually know or merely hear *about*.[13] But agential empathy or empathic concern for others is itself a psychological state that may be the subject or object of empathy. We sometimes see that someone else feels empathic concern for another and/or see that empathy reflected or expressed in their actions toward that other person, but our ability to see or notice such things may itself partly or wholly depend on our ability to empathize with such an empathic agential point of view, with the empathy of agents.

When we empathize with agential empathy, what we are doing is very different from what the agent herself is doing. The empathically concerned agent wants and seeks to do what is helpful to some person or persons (leaving aside animals for simplicity's sake). The empathic agent feels empathy, for example, *with* (the point of view of) certain people her actions may affect and is concerned *for* or *about* (the welfare or wishes of) those people. But when we feel empathy with an empathically concerned agent (as an agent), we empathize with *them*, not with the people they are empathizing with or focused on. We empathize, in other words, *with what they as (potential) agents are feeling and/ or desiring*; and such empathy is, I believe, the core or basis of moral approval and disapproval. If moral goodness consists or is embodied in certain sorts (or a certain pattern) of empathic concern for or about (the well-being of) those who may be *affected* by given actions or traits, then, I believe, moral approval may involve a different sort or direction of empathy, empathy with (the standpoint of) *agents*.

---

13. London: Routledge, 2007.

People whose capacity for empathy is fully developed will, I believe, have a different empathic reaction to (the characteristic actions of) agents whose empathy is also fully developed from that which they will have to (the characteristic actions of) agents who have less-developed empathy. In particular, if an agent's actions reflect empathic concern for (the well-being or wishes of) others, empathic beings will feel warmly or tenderly toward her, and such warmth and tenderness empathically reflect the empathic warmth or tenderness of the agent. I want to say that such (in one sense) reflective feeling, such empathy with empathy, also constitutes moral approval and admiration for the agent and/or her actions.

This view is interestingly similar to things that Hume and Shaftesbury say about approval. (We will be speaking about disapproval in just a moment.) On pp. 604 and 605 of the *Treatise*, for example, Hume points out that our approval of love has an origin different from the prospect of utility to oneself or others and depends, rather, on our being moved to tears or "infinitely touched" by tender sentiments and those who have or exhibit them. This at the very least implies that we feel tenderly toward those who themselves are tender, and Hume then goes on to say that: "Where friendship appears in very signal instances, my heart catches the same passion, and is warm'd by those warm sentiments, that display themselves before me."

If one were to regard *all* approval as having such a basis (and so deny that approval can be grounded in the utility of motives or traits), one would be very close to my suggestion that we empathically warm to empathic agential warmth toward others and that approval consists in our having such a reaction. And notice too how Hume's image of our being moved to tears (his actual words are "[t]he tears naturally start in our eyes") works against his general view that (all) approval is phenomenologically pleasant or pleasurable in an unambiguous way. Similarly, Shaftesbury explicitly treats moral approval as involving a kind of affection (and also liking) for certain agential affections (and disapproval as involving an aversion to negative feelings and actions on the part of agents), and this too is very much like the view I want to defend here.[14]

Disapproval can then be understood on analogy with approval. If a person's actions toward others exhibit a basic lack of empathy, then empathic people will tend to be chilled or repelled by her actions, and I want to say that those (reflective) feelings toward the agent constitute moral disapproval. Thus empathy with an agent's lack of empathy or empathic concern for others, with their coldness toward others, yields a similar feeling in the person who *has* empathy, and that feeling, which I have just said amounts to a feeling of disapproval, is very different from the warmth or tenderness that is characteristically expressed in what an empathic person does as an agent.

14. See Shaftesbury's *Characteristicks of Men, Manners, Opinion, and Times*, ed. J. Robertson, 2 vols., Indianapolis: Bobbs-Merrill, 1964, Vol. I, p. 251. I am indebted here to Darwall's discussion in *British Moralists*, pp. 233–34.

We are clearly, then, talking about two different points of view here: that of agents and that of someone who approves or disapproves of a given agent or agents. The latter is not exactly the point of view of a judge, because we are speaking here only of moral approval and disapproval and are understanding these as feelings that aren't as such tantamount to any kind of moral claim or judgment. Perhaps the point of view of approval and disapproval is best characterized at this point as *third-personal*, since, like the notion of a judge, this allows us to draw the contrast between the first-person standpoint of agents deciding what to do or choose and what happens when we react to agents and their actions with approval or disapproval without ourselves being (immediately or as such) in the position of having to decide what to do or choose.

These distinctions are very important, if we are not to slip into the mistaken belief that a theory like the one we are proposing regards empathic concern for others and the moral approval or disapproval of an empathic person as the very same thing—which we could simply call empathy. First of all, and most obviously, I am not treating approval as being the same as disapproval, because the latter involves feeling a chill or repulsion in contemplating (the actions of) some agent, whereas approval involves the/an *opposed* or *contrary* feeling of warmth or tenderness. To be sure, it takes empathy for someone to arrive at either or both of these opposed feelings, but the empathy and/or the capacity for it isn't the feelings and isn't the approval or disapproval. But then too, and as I indicated earlier, the empathic warmth that constitutes approval most immediately reflects what is going on in some agent as an agent, and this clearly differentiates it from the warmth that an agent concerned about (the welfare or wishes of) others feels about or toward those others. The feelings of warmth may or may not be phenomenologically similar, but (as we shall see more clearly just below) they are in any case different with respect to their source.

But note that our account also explains why (or yields the conclusion that) people incapable of empathy are not only lacking in virtue, but also incapable of genuinely approving or disapproving the virtues and vices of others. (They may be able to use language that is typically used to express approval and disapproval, but, as we have known at least since Hare's discussion of "inverted commas" value judgments, this may be compatible with saying they aren't really capable of moral approval and disapproval.)[15] So the unvirtuous or immoral agent who is coldly indifferent or unempathic toward others doesn't have the empathic capacity to *feel* the indifference or cold that *other* immoral agents feel and exert in the direction of others, and to that extent, ironically but not implausibly, a morally good person can momentarily, through empathy, take in (or

15. Someone who is partly or occasionally immoral may be capable of empathy and thus, according to the present view, of moral approval and disapproval (of herself and others). Note too that Hume allows that some people are more capable of empathy and warm feeling than others. In fact, he seems to think that there can be people who are completely devoid and incapable of such feeling.

"pick up") something from a bad person that another bad person will not be able to take in (or "pick up") despite his or her *similarity* to the first bad person.

But I think we need to say a bit more at this point about some of the feelings that I have said are involved in moral disapproval. We can presumably understand the way in which virtuously feeling empathic concern for other people involves feeling warmly toward them, and the idea that empathy with such warmth involves warm feeling makes a good deal of sense. But what about the idea that disapproval involves empathically reflecting the cold/indifferent attitudes of those whom we consider unvirtuous and (according to the view defended in *ECE*) lacking in empathy? Do unvirtuous unempathic people really have such attitudes?

What the unvirtuous, morally bad, unempathic person feels toward others may be indifference or may be malice, but both of those feelings contrast with warmth and show a lack or absence of warmth. Comparatively speaking, then, such a person is cold (or very cool) in his attitudes or feelings toward other people, and someone who empathically registers that coldness will thus be *chilled* by the attitudes or desires of a morally bad person (as expressed in certain actions). Such a person will, in effect, "catch (or pick up) a chill" from agents who lack a warm concern for others, and the chill thus caught will constitute disapproval of such agents (or their actions). On the present theory, then, the familiar phrase "the chill of disapproval" applies much more literally than (I suspect) philosophers and others who use that phrase ever imagine.[16]

Furthermore, the present approach also avoids the difficulties that Adam Smith attributed to the Humean approach to moral approval and disapproval.[17] If approval and disapproval involve empathy with (the point of view of) agents, then there is no danger that we will morally approve or disapprove of boulders, houses, storms, or other things that can be useful or harmful to people. If we feel chilled or, possibly, repelled by certain people and that constitutes a disapproval of them, that is because those people lack warm concern for others and our being chilled or repelled empathically reflects that (immoral) motivation

16. However, one must be careful in saying this, because the phrase "the chill of disapproval" typically applies to how someone feels when she is *disapproved of* rather than to how the disapprover feels. But if one feels the chill of someone's disapproval (of oneself or possibly of another), there presumably has to be something chilly in (and emanating from) the attitude of the disapprover, and *that* chill, according to the present theory, both reflects the chill*ing* attitudes/motives/actions of the person disapproved of and constitutes disapproval of them. So the chill or cold at issue here can go full circle: the agential coldness or lack of warmth of certain individuals can be reflected, as disapproval, in those who behold or learn about it; but that chilly disapproval can in turn be felt as "the chill of disapproval" by someone (possibly the agent who is disapproved of) who comes into contact with the disapprover—though that person has to be capable of some empathy, not be a psychopath, for example, for this to happen.

17. Emotivism is sometimes criticized for making facts only causally, rather than logically, relevant to evaluative attitudes and utterances. (See, e.g., Richard Brandt, "The Emotive Theory of Ethics," *Philosophical Review* 59: 305–18, 1950.) But the present account of approval and disapproval and, eventually, of moral judgment asserts precisely such a tighter connection.

on their part.[18] But inanimate objects don't harm or hurt us as a result of having such motives. So there is nothing for empathy to latch on to in what inanimate objects do in their (quasi-)agential capacity, and our theory therefore allows us to make it understandable, as indeed it ought to be, that inanimate objects are not the targets of moral approval and disapproval.[19]

At this point, however, there are some further issues we need to consider. I have said that approval involves feeling warmth in empathic response to the agential warmth involved in morally good or approvable action and that disapproval involves a similar relation to the relative coldness or coolness underlying immoral behavior. But if these feelings are similar or analogous to what they reflect, then they may seem to lack the right intentionality to count as approval or disapproval. Warm agential concern for others focuses on those others, for example, and empathy with such concern may focus on the same people, rather than being (exclusively) directed toward the agent herself. But approval is primarily an attitude toward an agent, not toward those the agent is concerned about, so it may be wondered how empathically feeling (some of) the warmth the agent feels toward others can constitute approval *of the agent*; and the same point can, of course, be made about coldness and disapproval as well.

But here we must remember an important distinction we drew earlier between the empathy felt by an agent concerned with other people and the empathy felt by someone who empathically reacts to and approves of such empathy. The two kinds of empathy differ with respect to their *source*, and this not only distinguishes them, but also allows us, I think, to understand approval (and disapproval) in the terms sketched above. The source of agential empathy (or empathic concern) is the plight or state of certain individuals seen as potentially affected by her actions and not (in that respect) as agents themselves. But empathy felt in response to agential empathy has a somewhat different causal history, a different kind of source overall, precisely because it is responsive to what an agent feels. The source(s), in turn, of that agential feeling may also be included among the sources of empathy about empathy, but the difference between the empathy involved in approval and the empathy involved in agential concern is that the former has an agential source that the latter lacks.

I want to say that this difference in source helps to constitute empathy about empathy as approval of an agent. Even if the empathic warmth the approver

18. I take it that feeling repelled is (like) feeling a kind of chill. But I won't attempt to be more fine-grained about this here.

19. Disapproval may be an empathic response to the indifference to others of an immoral person, but indifference is a real attitude which disapproval conceived as empathy can latch on to. The so-called indifference of the Universe or of inanimate objects is not literally a psychological attitude, so our theory is not committed to (making sense of) disapproval of inanimate objects. The trouble with Hume's view that disapproval embodies a (corrected) sympathy with the point of view of those who receive certain benefits and harms is that it doesn't in and of itself rule out disapproval of inanimate causes of such harm. But if disapproval embodies empathy with something, and in particular with cold or cool attitudes, there is no way that we can disapprove of mere things.

feels for the warmth of someone concerned about others takes in that very concern and is to that extent focused on those others, its immediate source is the agent, not those the agent is concerned about, and what approval is approval *of* depends to a large extent, I think, on such causal matters rather than on pure phenomenology or seeming intentionality. After all, we have causal theories of reference and of memory that tell us that what we refer to or are remembering at a given time is more dependent on the causal source or origin of a putative reference or memory than on the phenomenology or seeming intentionality of what we are doing.[20] And although I think some such theories don't sufficiently acknowledge intentional or phenomenological factors that may also be involved in the phenomena they theorize about, they at least helped us (for the first time) see how important a role causality plays in our mentalistic vocabulary. There may be (and indeed I believe there are) limits to what, on grounds of intentionality or phenomenology, can constitute reference to an object, memory of an event, or empathic (dis)approval, but it is important to see how causality plays a role in constituting these psychological phenomena. Thus even if the empathic warmth felt third-personally in response to agential concern for others may be phenomenologically similar to that concern and share some of its focus and origins, its causal origin is different because that origin includes agential empathy itself, and so, on the theory I have been describing, moral approval is a kind of second-order empathy and to that extent differs from the empathy of an agent concerned simply with how other people may be affected by her actions.[21]

20. On causal theories of reference, see especially Saul Kripke, *Naming and Necessity*, Oxford: Blackwell, 1980. On causal theories of memory, see C. B. Martin and Max Deutscher, "Remembering," *Philosophical Review* LXXV: 161–96, 1966.

21. I have simplified matters by speaking of approval and disapproval causally reflecting the actual warm or cold attitudes of actual agents. But one can also approve or disapprove of actions and individuals that one merely hears about and that may not actually exist or have existed (in the way they are depicted to one). But just as one may have empathy for the plight of a group that one merely hears about and that may in fact not actually exist, so too may one empathically respond to what, on the basis of false accounts or misleading perceptions, one takes to be the warm concern (or cold/cool indifference) embodied in the actions or character of some (perceived or imagined) agent. In such cases, there is a causal connection between what one thinks one knows or can tell about an agent and one's own empathic *response to it*; and so although the causal picture has to be a bit more complicated for situations where one is misinformed or even hallucinating, I don't think this issue casts doubt on our account of approval and disapproval. However, it does show that the present account of approval is somewhat different from causal theories of reference, memory, and knowledge. Does this put our account out in left field and undercut its plausibility? Not at all. Even if empathy/(dis)approval doesn't work entirely the way memory, etc. do, we have reason to believe that many mental phenomena work similarly to the way I have said it works. Thus anger doesn't require the existence of what one is angry with or at, but causal factors are involved in determining what one is angry with/at, and, at the same time, there may be phenomenological/intentional limits on what such causal factors can qualify as anger. If this seems plausible for concepts like anger, the present view that things work similarly for empathic (dis)approval is given some plausibility as well.

Now the present sentimentalist approach also treats moral disapproval as *discordant* in a way that approval isn't. For those it regards as empathic enough to be capable of approval and disapproval generally feel warmly toward other people. Yet when they disapprove of someone's motives, character, or actions, they empathically register that agent's coldness or coolness, and this at the very least will be disharmonious with their general warmth or tenderness (though it is not obvious that such disharmony has to be felt as unpleasant or disagreeable). By contrast, approval is a matter of warm feeling that harmonizes with an empathic person's overall warm concern about others (though, again, such harmony may not need to be felt as positively pleasant or agreeable).

Hume typically speaks of moral disapproval as involving a feeling of uneasiness, rather than of unpleasantness, and the use of that term at the very least suggests, though it doesn't actually say, that disapproval is discordant or inharmonious with the usual feelings of the person who disapproves. But, in any event, I think there is nothing implausible in the idea that disapproval involves disharmony in a way that approval does not. (The person who is totally inhumane and unempathic in his actions toward others presumably lacks the empathy that is necessary to register either approval or disapproval of other agents.)

In addition, however, both Hume and Hutcheson hold that approval is a pleasant and agreeable feeling, and although we have seen how an empiricist/associationist psychology operating via pleasure/pain mechanisms might want to say such things, present-day sentimentalism needn't rely on such a narrowly empiricist psychology. The present theory of approval and disapproval doesn't have to say that approval is (automatically) pleasant or disapproval (automatically) unpleasant, and this seems truer to experience than what Hume says about approval and disapproval. Phenomenologically speaking, the difference between approval and disapproval seems more a matter of warmth versus coldness than of pleasantness versus unpleasantness, but at the same time, our account doesn't want or have to say that all warmth constitutes approval and all feelings of chill or coldness disapproval. Differences of causation can distinguish phenomenologically similar feelings, and we now need to consider some important further issues about the causation of approval and disapproval.

As we have described them, approval and disapproval are feelings, roughly, of warm tenderness and coldness or chill that are part of an empathic, but to that extent also a causal, response to the motives/attitudes/feelings of agents.[22]

---

22. This is a bit of (useful, but inessential) oversimplification, because we needn't regard those who hate as likely to do things to others, when we disapprove of their hatred. People can be ashamed of the hatred they feel and perhaps have no tendency to act on that hatred, so when we, like them, disapprove of how they feel, we are not necessarily viewing them as agents rather than, simply, as people with morally criticizable feelings. (I shall take up issues of self-approval and self-disapproval further on.) Let me at this point, however, also mention how idiomatic or natural it is to think of someone who warms to another's attitudes or actions as approving of them and to think of someone who is chilled by another's attitudes or actions as disapproving of them. The present complex theory of moral approval and disapproval thus rests on some very intuitive ideas, and that very fact stands somewhat in its favor.

But feelings can be disrupted or prevented by other factors, and especially by other feelings, and Hume famously noted the various ways in which our personal relations to a given person may alter or affect our approval or disapproval of what they have done. Thus a mother whose son is on death row for the murder of a baby may be so concerned about saving him from death that she fails to experience the feelings of disapproval she would feel about another killer, but, by the same token, the baby's parents may be too angry as a result their personal loss for their disapproval of the killer to register as a distinct or separate phenomenon. Such facts support Hume's contention that we need a more neutral or impartial perspective from which to make open and public moral judgments, but they are also consonant with what I have been saying above and have interesting implications that it is worth dwelling on.

We can get angry when someone frustrates our purposes or the purposes of those we love, but, if we keep our moral heads about us, we can sometimes recognize the difference between the targets of such anger and what we morally disapprove of. We may become angry with a person who gets a job we would have liked for ourselves or for someone in our family, but there may be nothing immoral, cold, or lacking in empathy in that other person's actions, and we may know both that our frustrated anger isn't an empathic response to the coldness and anger of an agent and that it isn't tantamount to disapproval. On the other hand, there are times when we or others may *not* be able to tell whether our feeling of chill toward another represents genuine disapproval or a phenomenologically similar feeling that has arisen in reaction to the frustration of personal desires and purposes. This is a familiar fact of the moral life (though it tends to be obscured when one is oneself angry with another person), and our present approach has no problem accommodating it, because it understands disapproval (and approval too) in substantially (though not exclusively) causal terms and because it is often so difficult to know the origins of a feeling like being chilled.

So certain personal feelings or reactions can interfere with approval or disapproval and/or make it unclear whether someone's feelings really are feelings of approval or disapproval, but the influence can also work in the reverse direction. Seeing someone one is concerned to help do something hurtful to a third party may arouse feelings of disapproval that disrupt or weaken one's original desire to help. In any event, what seems to follow from the above discussion is that disapproval and approval are more likely to occur and to be recognizable as such in cases where we are not closely involved with the people whose motives or actions are being considered. Hutcheson says that our tendency to approve and disapprove of actions in the remote past that we have nothing to gain or lose from is a very good argument for the non-selfish character of (some) human motivation, but in the terms of the present discussion we can also say that such cases are the ones in which it is easiest to know that any seeming approval/disapproval that has been elicited really is approval/disapproval. If someone is empathically concerned with other people and more concerned with certain people, those near and dear to her, than with others, then it may be easier for her empathy to glom on to what is morally bad or good if it doesn't have to compete with her other emotions, and perhaps the clearest case where this happens is when we are told in some evocative way about the motives and actions of some person in the remote past, since what this person has done or failed to do will have presumably had no practical bearing on ourselves or those we love (or dislike). (I am indebted here to discussion with Elizabeth Radcliffe.)

As I mentioned earlier, Hume can be interpreted as saying that moral judgment and perhaps even moral approval and disapproval make it desirable for us to take a disinterested or impartial standpoint, and he cites our need for common terms of communication as the basis for that desideratum. However, leaving aside issues of moral judgment till a bit later, the present account of approval and disapproval lays stress on impartiality for somewhat different reasons. The present causal-sentimentalist theory of approval and disapproval treats impartiality, rather, as epistemically desirable for the way it helps to clarify whether given warmth or coldness really constitutes approval or disapproval and (whether this is a desirable thing or not) as providing the best conditions for these moral reactions actually to occur.[23] So the present theory makes impartiality into an important factor in moral approval and disapproval (and moral judgment), but the importance it places on it is to some extent independent of the considerations that the eighteenth-century sentimentalists treat as favoring or requiring impartiality.

At this point, it would also be interesting to consider to what extent disapproval and approval can be self-directed. When one is practically engaged in action, approval, etc. of others and of oneself, may be drowned out or inhibited by other feelings and the sheer complexity of practical decision making and activity. But after we have acted, we may well feel disapproval or approval of what we have done, and according to the present account, these attitudes will empathically (and nonpractically) reflect (what the agents knows or believes was) the motivational basis of what the agent has done. Someone who is weak-willed, for example, and who hurts another person in a way that he would have hoped never to hurt anyone may thereby show himself to have a less empathically concerned attitude toward others than he would have hoped, but the same person may also have enough empathy to feel, after the fact, the deficient warmth of his own underlying character, and such a person may then disapprove his own earlier weakness of will in the same basic way that occurs in third-person cases. (Cases of after-the-fact approval and disapproval are more like third-person cases than like first-person cases, because a great deal of first-person thought is practical and action-oriented.)

Because we typically think of our own futures as open, empathy and approval/ disapproval regarding potential future actions is perhaps harder to come by, but where it can or does occur, there is no reason to think the mechanisms have to

---

23. However, compare Hume, *Treatise*, for example, p. 472.

be any different from those we have described as operating elsewhere. However, two further and related concluding points need to be made.

Approval is different from admiration, and I have so far have had almost nothing to say about the latter topic. Approval, as I have been describing it, doesn't have to involve so positive or praising an attitude as admiration, and when we approve of some action of our own or others, we may simply be viewing it as morally all right, rather than as good—or admirable. But then too admirability is a characteristic that is exemplified outside the moral realm— we admire sheer intelligence, great beauty, and great art. But our discussion of approval has been implicitly confined to the moral realm. We don't "approve" of intelligence, beauty, and art precisely because, or when, these subject matters don't touch on moral issues. The account I have offered of approval and disapproval is specifically geared toward the moral through its central focus on empathy concerning others. Someone who wants to prove a theorem needn't feel any such empathy, but the concern to help others (and, if *ECE* is correct, the concern not to break promises or kill the innocent) *is* moral, and the fact that it involves a responsive empathic concern for others helps to characterize it as moral. And similarly, for empathic approval of other people's concern for third parties.

To be sure, empathy is sometimes said to be necessary to understanding and properly responding to works of art, but the kind of empathy this requires doesn't seem to entail any empathic concern for anyone, and that is why it is natural not to regard it as particularly moral. So the theory of approval I have offered is *ipso facto* a theory of moral approval, and that makes it appropriate to use it, as I now propose to do, in understanding and (to some degree) explaining the character of explicit moral judgments or utterances.

5.2 Moral Judgments

Sentimentalist accounts of moral approval and disapproval have often been criticized for failing to allow for a judgmental aspect to or basis for these attitudes. The sentimentalists regard moral judgments as grounded in feelings of approval and disapproval, but many critics—starting with Richard Price in *A Review of the Principal Questions in Morals* (1758) and Thomas Reid in *Essays on the Active Powers of Man* (1788), but including many up to the present day—have argued that such an approach misses an essential element of approval and disapproval: the fact that they involve or are constituted by judgments about the rightness or wrongness (or goodness or badness) of certain (kinds of) acts, motives, or traits of character. In that case, the sentimentalist metaethical enterprise is doomed to a kind of circularity. Far from having the potential to help us understand the character of (or even define) moral judgments or moral "sentences", approval and disapproval presuppose, involve, or are equivalent to such judgments or sentences, and the sentimentalist attempt to base moral attitudes in judgment-free feelings of approval/disapproval (or more generally in nonrational elements in human psychology) is therefore doomed to failure.

The last section, however, offered an account of moral approval and disapproval that seems truer to the emotional quality or phenomenology of those attitudes than anything rationalists have to say about them. And the account was truly sentimentalist, because nothing that was said about empathy as the constituting basis of approval and disapproval presupposed the making of, or a commitment to, specific or general moral judgments. The idea that moral approval doesn't require a moral judgment about rightness may seem odd and implausible at first, but the empathic reaction of being warmed by someone's helpfulness toward others doesn't seem to involve any judgment and *does* seem to involve a positive emotional attitude toward the person('s helpfulness), one that contrasts with the empathic "chill" we take from seeing (learning about) someone else's cruelty or indifference toward others, a chill that it seems natural to describe as constituting or involving a negative feeling toward the cruel person ('s behavior).

However, things are a little more complicated than I have just implied. If, as I argued earlier, warm approval isn't always (unambiguously) pleasant, we can wonder what marks it as positive and cold disapproval as negative and what therefore marks particular moral judgments or properties as either positive or negative. This problem is raised in a slightly different form by Simon Blackburn in "Circles, Finks, Smells, and Biconditionals;" and we need to say something about it because a sentimentalist account of moral judgment needs to be able to make the distinction between positive and negative in sentimentalist terms, and that means being able somehow to say why the empathic chill of disapproval is negative and the (not necessarily pleasurable) empathic warmth of approval positive.[24]

Now, as I indicated earlier, someone whose empathy in regard to others is well-developed will (as an agent) empathize with and have some desire to help those who need his help; but such a person will also (as an observer of the actions of others or even of himself) empathize with other agents. It follows that someone with well-developed empathy who disapproves of the action of another person because it displays selfish indifference or malice toward some third party will have some motive/desire not to do that kind of action. (Similarly, if the disapproved action is a merely potential action of the agent herself.) But if to disapprove of some action is to be motivated *away* from doing actions of that kind, that gives us a sense in which chilly disapproval counts as a negative attitude; and if, as we could analogously show, warm approval of an action

---

24. *Philosophical Perspectives* 7: especially 275, 1993. In this article, Blackburn argues that metaethical accounts of moral terms that analogize such terms with color terms will have to explain and have a hard time explaining why moral terms are positive or negative, but color terms aren't. This is a powerful challenge to (the) metaethical sentimentalism (defended here), which at various points and in various ways *does* invoke an analogy with color terms.

motivates us toward doing actions of that kind, that means that approval is a positive attitude. This explanation doesn't presuppose or make use of moral judgments, but it does allow us to use our account of approval and disapproval to explain why judgments of rightness and moral goodness based in approval count as positive and judgments of wrongness or moral badness count as negative. And it also helps us understand why both classes of judgments motivate as they do.[25]

Moreover, the fact that certain nonjudgmental empathy-derived attitudes or feelings toward (the ways) agents (treat others) can be characterized as positive and negative lends definite support to the view that they *are*, respectively, attitudes of approval and disapproval. If what we are talking about here isn't full-blown moral approval or disapproval, then at the very least it can be plausibly viewed as the ur-phenomenon of moral approval and disapproval; and if we can now use what we have said about these (ur-)attitudes to clarify moral judgments and the kind of (full-blown) moral approval and disapproval that spring from or require moral judgment, then the sentimentalist approach will be largely vindicated or at least made to seem somewhat plausible as a way of doing metaethics.

Now Hume attempts to clarify—some would even say offer definitions of— moral judgments/claims/sentences on the basis of his views about approval and disapproval as nonjudgment-presupposing attitudes or feelings, but we earlier rejected the Humean consequence-oriented account of these attitudes in favor of one that focuses on empathic reactions to the agents who bring about certain consequences.[26] But that might still allow us to use what Hume says about the link between feelings of approval and the moral judgments we actually make (or, so as not to presuppose cognitivism, the moral sentences we actually utter) to illuminate, or define, the latter. But if we go this route, we should recognize that it loads us with an embarrassment of riches. Hume scholars and others have found a variety of different theories of the meaning of moral judgments/sentences (and of

25. Incidentally, on the basis of the studies that have been done on empathy, Hoffman (*Empathy and Moral Development*) and many other psychologists hold an "empathy-altruism" hypothesis according to which empathy is necessary to and helps to sustain altruistic concern for other people. But Hoffman doesn't hold that empathy is necessary to the making of moral judgments and (so) is not a metaethical sentimentalist. Let me also just mention that I am for now sweeping under the rug questions (raised by Elizabeth Radcliffe) about the difference different agential capacities for empathy might make to reactions of approval or actual behavior.

26. One might also criticize Hume for regarding pleasure felt at the good someone does to others as a form of *approval*, but that criticism wouldn't be so telling against Hume's overall enterprise if he could show how that pleasure can ground and/or clarify the making of positive moral judgments. If he could accomplish *that*, then it wouldn't be so important whether we called the pleasure in question approval or ur-approval or even something else. Certainly, any pleasure tends to be regarded as positive and therefore resembles the "feel" of approval in most cases, but whatever we might say about these issues, the criticisms of Hume made in the text, if valid, undermine his overall metaethical approach or at least make it seem somewhat unsatisfactory. I am indebted here to discussions with Charles Pigden.

their relation to feelings of approval) within the *Treatise*, and many of these were original with Hume. But the theories are also all inconsistent with one another, and if one wants to be more consistent than Hume seems to have been, then one has to decide among these theories or advocate some different sentimentalist account of (the relation between approval and) moral judgment. (I'll drop the qualification about moral sentences, because the reader who prefers that formulation will know how to adjust what I say about "judgments" accordingly.)

Hume has been (not so unreasonably) viewed as a subjectivist ("x is right" means "I like x" and describes one's approval of x), as an emotivist ("x is right" means something like "hurrah for x!" and *expresses* one's approval of x), as an ideal observer theorist about moral judgment ("x is right" means something like "an impartially benevolent well-informed calm spectator would feel corrected warm feelings of approval toward x"), or as a projectivist/expressivist error theorist about moral judgments (they project our feelings of approval *onto* the world but always speak falsely about what they purport to characterize). And it is also possible for a sentimentalist to maintain a Kripkean reference-fixer view of moral judgments that sees "benevolence is morally good" on analogy with a posteriori claims about sensible qualities like "red is what reflects such and such light frequencies." On such a view, which I myself have developed and defended in past work, warm empathic feelings of approval noncircularly fix the reference of "morally right" the way the experience of red(ness) fixes the reference of "red" for us.

If one wants to offer a specific definition of "morally right," one certainly has to choose among these (or possibly other) theories of the meaning of moral sentences/predicates, and some of the theories mentioned just above seem implausible on their face and have seemed so to most recent metaethicists. Almost no one accepts subjectivism or (simple) emotivism these days, and as the only person who has explicitly promulgated a Kripke-type reference-fixing sentimentalist approach to moral predicates (though David Wiggins comes close in some of his work), I can assure you that I have found insuperable difficulties in defending this approach along strictly Kripkean lines.[27] Such a sentimentalist reference-fixer view has to treat judgments like "benevolence is good" and "malice toward others is wrong" as a posteriori, and the more I have thought about it, the more implausible this idea has seemed to me.

This leaves us still with Blackburn's projectivist error theory of moral judgment and with ideal observer theory, the first of which denies the truth of moral judgments generally and the second of which makes ample allowance for moral truth (and falsity).[28] For reasons that are on the whole too complex for me to enter into here, I think it makes sense to hold onto the pre-theoretical, common-

27. See Wiggins, "A Sensible Subjectivism," reprinted in eds. S. Darwall, A. Gibbard, and P. Railton, *Moral Discourse and Practice: Some Philosophical Approaches*, New York: Oxford University Press, pp.237–42; and also his "Truth, Invention, and the Meaning of Life," in his *Needs, Values, Truth: Essays in the Philosophy of Value*, Oxford: Blackwell, 1987.

28. See his *Spreading the Word*, Oxford: Clarendon Press, 1984.

sense idea that moral claims are at least occasionally true and objectively valid, so I think we have some reason to reject projectivism. But that doesn't mean we have to accept the ideal observer theory. We can leave open the question of whether ideal observer theory or some other very specific theory no one has yet articulated is correct about moral judgments/utterances; but *this needn't prevent us from using what was said in the previous section about moral approval (and disapproval) to illuminate the general character of moral judgments or utterances.* If some such, or a substantial amount of, illumination can be provided, then it may not matter so much that we cannot define moral sentences or give a *precise* account of what they involve—a sentimentalist approach that starts with approval and disapproval as feelings and uses what it says about them to explain or illuminate the character of explicit moral utterances and of approval or disapproval based on explicit moral opinions will have been given sufficient support to make it at least seem a viable, a not implausible option, within present-day metaethics. And that is all that I aspire to here, and *can* aspire to given my inability, at this point, to define or precisely explicate moral language.

Moreover, the position I as a sentimentalist am in here is no worse, and may in some respects be much better, than the position Kantians or intuitionists are in with respect to moral judgment. Kantians and intuitionists don't offer definitions or precise explications of moral predicates or sentences (in fact Moore explicitly argues that such definition is impossible), but that doesn't make them deny that moral claims can be true (or at least rationally compelling), nor does it prevent them from holding that such claims can be inherently motivating (and provide reasons for action). Mackie held that such "objective prescriptivity" is queer and defies genuine understanding.[29] But I think his view gives short shrift to the approach defended by Thomas Nagel in *The Possibility of Altruism* and developed further by John McDowell in various articles (published after Mackie's book).[30] When one considers, for example, what Nagel says about prudence, it does seem as if an ethical judgment can be both objective and inherently motivating (what Mackie calls "prescriptive"). For Nagel points out that the belief that one will in the future have reason to (want to) do something can quite naturally, or plausibly, be seen as giving one a reason, and motivating one, to do things now that will make it easier or possible to do what one knows one will want and have reason to do in the future. Yet the idea that we will have such a reason doesn't seem to be necessarily subjective (nonobjective) or merely emotional, so Nagel's account of prudence seems to allow of "objective prescriptivity" in that realm, and that example seems to undercut the claim that such prescriptivity is necessarily queer or unacceptable.

Of course, and famously, Nagel goes on to argue for the "objective prescriptivity" (not his terminology, but it will do) of moral claims, and this part of his

29. See his *Ethics: Inventing Right and Wrong*, Harmondsworth: Penguin, 1977.

30. Oxford: Oxford University Press, 1970. McDowell's arguably most important contribution, "Virtue and Reason," is reprinted in eds. R. Crisp and M. Slote, *(Oxford Readings in) Virtue Ethics*, Oxford: Oxford University Press, 1997.

argument is generally seen as less successful than what he says about prudence. John McDowell then enters the picture (as I reconstruct the history) and offers what some regard as a better defense of the idea of objective prescriptivity *within the moral realm*. But in any event, the non-implausibility of (or at least the difficulty of ruling out) objective prescriptivity gives sentimentalism a basis for some rather parallel claims about moral utterances or judgments. Nagel is a rationalist about morality, but McDowell, though a rationalist in some respects, makes considerable use of Hume-like ideas about our moral sensibility (e.g., he sometimes invokes comparisons between moral properties and sensory properties like redness); and so I want to claim that some of what Nagel and McDowell say can be transposed or applied to or within a senti- mentalist account of moral judgment that builds on what it has to say about approval as a nonjudgmental feeling or attitude.

I can't at this point offer you a definition of moral predicates any more than Nagel or McDowell can. But on the basis of the views I defended in *ECE* and shall be briefly summarizing in a moment, I think we can argue that empa- thy is involved in the making (and therefore in the understanding) of moral claims, and such a claim allows one to defend the objective prescriptivity of moral judgments from something other than a (Nagel-like) rationalist point of view. It is natural for ordinary folk to regard some moral claims as objectively true, and we naturally regard moral claims as also forceful, action-guiding, and motivating—that's why when Charles Stevenson spoke of the "magnetism" of moral utterances, what he was saying seemed at least initially plausible. Mackie thinks it queer if we try to combine these ordinary views about moral utterances, but the rationalist Nagel has, with McDowell's help, made this not seem so queer, has made it seem plausible at the very least in the prudential realm, and this means that this idea is not in itself inherently implausible. And what we have said about approval/disapproval and some ideas borrowed from *ECE* can then help us toward a sentimentalist understanding of these features (and others) of moral judgment. If we arrive at such a view, then it seems to me that the sentimentalist approach to metaethics will have been shown to be at least promising; and that will be my main aim in what follows.

In *ECE*, I defended a normative view of individual (and political) morality that based itself in ideas about empathic caring. I was there defending an ethics of care, and I argued that such an ethics, if it wants to account for or conform to the moral judgments we intuitively, or commonsensically, want to make, must make rather heavy use of the notion or phenomenon of empathy. If we talk just about caring, then it is not, simply on that basis, clear why it is worse to neglect one's children's health than that of strangers or why it is worse not to save a child drowning right in front of one than not to save a child by giv- ing five dollars to Oxfam. (This assumes that Peter Singer is mistaken about such cases, but *ECE* as a whole represents a reply to and critique of Singer.) However, if we introduce empathy into the mix, we end up with something that corresponds pretty well with intuitive moral judgment: for we (normal humans) generally feel more empathy, and more empathic concern (or caring), for those whose plight we witness than for those whose plight we merely know *about*, and for those who are related to (or intimately involved with) us than for strangers and people we know only by description.

In *ECE*, I also argued (what may seem initially hard to believe) that our deontological views also correlate well with distinctions that can be made in terms of normal empathic-caring responses, and, interestingly, some recent work on the neurophysiological underpinnings of moral behavior and judgment supports the idea that emotional-empathic factors enter into our willingness to make and act in accordance with deontological judgments/beliefs.[31] But although I also applied the idea of empathic caring/concern for others to questions of justice, let's leave such issues out of the picture and concentrate here on individual morality; and what I would like the reader to accept at least for purposes of the present discussion is the idea that distinctions of empathy correspond one-to-one with the moral distinctions we intuitively wish to make, a conclusion of *ECE*.

At the end of *ECE*, I speculated about this correspondence or correlation and argued that it gives us some reason to think that empathy enters into the making and understanding of moral judgments/utterances. For if this last hypothesis is correct, that would explain why there is a general correspondence between distinctions or differences in our empathic (caring) reactions and the moral distinctions we want, intuitively, to make. Thus (I argue in *ECE* that) empathy leads us to be more responsive to perceived pain or danger than to pain or danger we merely know about. But if our empathy and, in particular, our differential empathic tendencies also enter into our understanding of moral judgments/utterances, that would help to explain why we intuitively understand/judge an unwillingness, say, to relieve pain we perceive to be (at least other things being equal) morally worse than an unwillingness to relieve pain that is merely known about. And similarly, as *ECE* argues, for a host of other cases. Putting the matter another way, if the very same empathy that leads us (as agents) to respond differently to different kinds of situations enters into our understanding of (claims about) what is morally better and worse in those situations, it is no wonder that there is a correlation between our differential empathic tendencies and the moral distinctions we want to make.

So the idea that empathy enters into our understanding and making of genuine moral claims—what I call the empathy-understanding hypothesis—is supported by its ability to explain the correlation or correspondence just mentioned—at least if we assume that the arguments for that correspondence given in *ECE* are somewhat persuasive. Of course, that last assumption, in the present context, leaves a very large hostage to fortune, but perhaps the reader will be willing to live with this danger or threat to what I am saying here and allow me now to continue with the clearly conditional defense I am giving of metaethical sentimentalism.

A perceptive reader will already have noticed that what I am now saying (conditionally) about moral judgment and what I said earlier about moral

---

31. See Michael Koenigs et al., "Damage to the Prefrontal Cortex Increases Utilitarian Moral Judgments," *Nature*, online version, March 21, 2007.

approval and disapproval are similar in a very important respect: both discussions bring in empathy in a central way. And from the sentimentalist perspective that is (and had better be) no accident. For what I now want to claim is that the (in something, ironically, very much like the Kantian sense) schema, or schematism, that connects approval and moral judgment within a plausible ethical sentimentalism is the phenomenon or idea of empathy, understood both as giving rise to differing agential reactions to (other) people's situations and as a factor in our reactions to the ways agents react to or treat (other) people. The empathy-understanding hypothesis seems plausible at least given what I concluded in *ECE*; but what we said earlier about approval (and disapproval) together with the basic sentimentalist idea that (our understanding of) approval grounds (our understanding of) moral judgment allows us to further clarify the implications and nature of that hypothesis. For we have argued that empathy enters into approval and disapproval, and since sentimentalism holds that our attitudes of approval and disapproval enter into the making of moral judgments, we can conclude that empathy enters into our understanding of moral claims (which is what the empathy-understanding hypothesis asserts) *because attitudes/feelings of approval/disapproval enter into the making of moral judgments*. We thus end up with a strictly sentimentalist picture of the relation between approval and moral judgment and of the character of moral judgment "in itself," and, far from making sentimentalism seem unsupported, odd, or paradoxical, the picture we have painted seems plausible *as far as it goes*.

I say "as far as it goes" because I haven't offered a definition of moral predicates and because there is a lot more to be said (hopefully in sentimentalist terms) about moral approval and judgment than I have said here. Still, and for dialectical and other reasons mentioned earlier, it doesn't count against sentimentalism that it has a difficult time (as, I am assuming it does) defining moral predicates or sentences. As I mentioned earlier, Kantian rationalism and intuitionism have the same problem, and if there is safety in numbers, then perhaps this isn't really a problem, but a condition of our having and understanding morality, a condition that in no way seems to interfere with or undercut the possibility that moral judgment is or can be objective.

And the picture presented above has some distinct positive advantages, too. It can, for example, help explain how and why moral claims are inherently motivating, something that, other things being equal, it seems plausible, and we want, to say. For although there have been arguments against this view, none of them seems absolutely knockdown, and the preponderance of philosophical opinion, at least, is that allowing for the motivating force of moral claims or utterances is a desideratum for or within metaethical theory. And our particular explanation for why moral judgments inherently motivate those who make them is that the empathy inherently involved in the making of genuine moral judgments is precisely the empathy that inclines us to do what we think of as right and avoid what we think of as wrong. For example, and as I mentioned earlier, our being chilled by agential indifference toward others requires developed empathy, and such empathy also inclines us not to be indifferent ourselves (as agents) toward others. So when, on the basis of our disapproval of indifference, we (are able to) make an explicit moral condemnation of indifference, we are condemning something we are (to some extent) motivated to avoid in our own actions. It is no wonder, therefore, that we are inclined to *act in accordance with* negative moral judgments, and the same point can be made about positive judgments. Thus our view that approval and disapproval are based in empathy and themselves enter into the making of moral judgments helps explain why such judgments have motivating force for us, and this lends further support to the view being defended here. However, nothing we have said about the nature of empathy and/or the way it operates in moral contexts argues *against* the possibility, the antecedently plausible view, that moral judgments are objective or cognitive, and so the metaethical sentimentalism being defended here seems to *allow for* objective prescriptivity every bit as much as rationalist or quasi-rationalist views like Nagel's and McDowell's presumably do.[32] Moreover, the account we have given can also explain—what, again, intuitively and other things being equal it is desirable for us to be able to explain—how and why psychopaths cannot make or fully understand genuine moral judgments (but are confined, e.g., to "inverted commas" uses of moral predicates). If moral approval and disapproval essentially enter into the making of moral judgments, then if these attitudes involve empathy, psychopaths, who are usually said to lack empathy, will be unable to make or understand moral judgments.[33] If I may invoke the often-invoked parallel with judgments about color, a psychopath can't make or fully understand moral judgments for something like the same reason that congenitally blind people are supposed to be unable to make full-blown claims about (objective) color or fully understand what others who speak of color are saying to them: they both lack the right sorts of experiences.[34] (It

32. Wiggins in "A Sensible Subjectivism" comes closer to the kind of sentimentalist metaethics I have developed here than any other recent philosopher, and he clearly takes moral predicates/judgments to be both motivating and cognitive about the world or facts in it (see pp. 234–35). This is tantamount to accepting the objective prescriptivity of moral claims, and supports the idea that sentimentalist metaethics can allow for objective prescriptivity as easily or as well as moral rationalism does. My own commitment to objective prescriptivity is therefore not at all idiosyncratic.

33. Psychopathic sadists may be able to "get inside" people's heads and on that basis find apt and exquisite ways to torture or harm them; but the empathy by "contagion" that lets us "feel" another person's pain involves a motivating emotional reaction, and the psychopath doesn't have this kind of reaction to other people's mental states. On the inability of psychopaths to feel empathy, see, for example, Hoffman, *Empathy and Moral Development*, pp. 35–36.

34. I have been assuming that if an adult can't make moral claims, then he or she can't understand the moral claims of others. If moral judgments require empathy, then a person lacking empathy not only will lack the ability to make moral claims, but also won't fully understand the empathy involved in *other people's* making of genuine moral judgments. But this is parallel to what we think about the inability to see things as red: such inability makes it impossible for one to make full-blown claims about redness or to understand fully what others have in mind when *they* talk about redness. Note further what the present theory has to say, for example, about those whose (putative) moral judgments about someone are clouded or interfered with by anger with that person for, say, besting them in some competition. Hume thinks such angry people really aren't taking the moral point of view, and, in somewhat similar vein, I want to say that such people may not really be making moral judgments. For even if they are usually capable of empathy, empathy presumably doesn't enter into a supposed moral condemnation that is based solely in anger, and it doesn't

was this analogy that earlier persuaded me to develop a reference-fixer account of the meaning of moral terms along the lines that Kripke had offered for color terms and terms designating other natural kinds.[35])

Finally, the sentimentalist theory/view that empathy enters into the making and understanding of moral judgment via states of moral approval and disapproval that are themselves empathic attitudes is supported by what we know about the character and contours of normative moral judgment. Just to cite the most obvious instance, our commonsense moral judgments are self–other asymmetric in a way that has often been noted and never been explained. Thus we think it is wrong negligently to hurt another person in a way that it isn't thought morally wrong—as opposed to imprudently inattentive—if one merely negligently hurts oneself. But why, one might ask, should such a distinction be made? There are forms of moral theory like utilitarianism that aren't self–other asymmetric in the way common sense is, and since each typical moral agent has the same kind of dignity, freedom, and welfare interests as the individuals morality tells him/her to be concerned about, why should our moral duties be more abundant and/or stricter toward others than toward ourselves, the way common sense says they are? (Jerry Fodor once said to me that it is *analytic* that morality involves concern just for others.)

But if empathy enters into the making of moral judgments, we have an explanation and potentially even a justification for the asymmetry of commonsense moral thinking. For empathy itself is self–other asymmetric: empathy for others is a much more understandable idea than empathy for oneself—in fact the latter makes the most sense when one thinks of having empathy for one's much earlier unhappy childhood or adolescent self, and here there is something analogous to the distance or nonidentity that Hoffman (*Empathy and Moral Development*) and others who study empathy have said is essential to empathy. So if moral judgment is grounded in empathy via psychological states of moral approval and disapproval as we have described them, we have an explanation of why our moral judgments tend to be self–other asymmetric, and the justificatory force of common opinion thereby helps to (further) justify the

seem counterintuitive to hold that in such a case an angry person isn't really expressing a *moral* judgment, even if he or others mistakenly imagine that he is. According to the present theory, there are other cases too where, because a person's empathy is (largely) inoperative, putative moral judgments may not really be moral judgments, and I think such cases can be handled as plausibly as what we have just said about (putative) condemnations made in anger.

35. See Saul Kripke, *Naming and Necessity*, Oxford: Blackwell, 1980. Let me just add that I have recently been developing a reference-fixer account of moral terms that follows Kripke's treatment of color and other natural kind terms in certain respects, but nonetheless allows one to say that "cruelty is wrong" is a priori, and objectively, true. This work will appear in a book called *Moral Sentimentalism* (Oxford University Press, 2010); but I don't want to anticipate that discussion any further here.

sentimentalist metaethics offered above.[36] It is clear, then, that our sentimentalism allows us to explain a good many things we want to explain and doesn't seem to have any really implausible implications; and this, I hope, will make metaethical moral sentimentalism seem more promising than I think it recently has seemed to most philosophers. But *ECE* worked mainly with, or at the level of, normative ethics, and the fact that it used empathy (or empathic concern) as criterial for normative moral distinctions means that the same factor that works (if it does) within the sentimentalist normative context also features within a sentimentalist metaethical approach of the kind offered here. So the present essay takes us beyond the predominantly normative discussion of *ECE* and allows us to understand both the normative and the metaethical in sentimentalist terms. Sentimentalism in the larger sense that includes both metaethical and normative components, sentimentalism of the kind Hume was clearly committed to, can be redeployed or reworked in ways Hume didn't fully anticipate and is now, I believe, in a position to offer itself as a plausible, promising, and *fully systematic* alternative to rationalism and intuitionism about the moral. The things I have argued for here I certainly haven't *proved* to be correct, but I *am* asking you (as it were) to take on approval the Humean picture of morality I have been sketching.

36. On the nature of the self-other asymmetries of commonsense morality, see my *Commonsense Morality and Consequentialism*, London: Routledge and Kegan Paul, 1985, especially ch. 1. But at that point, I was far from recognizing the relevance of empathy to commonsense moral distinctions and to the ordinary making of moral judgments.

6

HUME ON THE ARTIFICIAL VIRTUES

Hume's theory of the artificial virtues is historically the first, and probably also the most philosophically significant, sentimentalist account of (a major part of) deontology. But that account has always struck philosophers as problematic, and Hume himself at various points expresses uncertainty about his own attempt to ground these virtues and the strict observance of rules that he considers essential to their operation. The familiar criticisms that Hume argues (or that artificial virtue itself requires us to argue) sophistically or in a circle, so that such virtue cannot coherently be explained in sentimentalist terms or in any others, are certainly worrisome, but here I shall be emphasizing somewhat different (though related) problems in or for Hume's theory. And even if Hume's "artificial virtues" approach is problematic for the reasons I shall be mentioning in what follows, I don't think sentimentalism has to give up on the project of accounting for deontology. The "natural virtues" approach to deontology that I have advocated elsewhere may represent a *second chance* for sentimentalism to show that it can cope with deontology (and offer a plausible alternative to rationalist attempts to account for deontology).[1] But I don't want to talk about that any further here; the focus will be on Hume.

Hume argues that the virtues of fidelity and justice/honesty (and other artificial virtues as well) require an attitude of respect for rules and a fairly strict obedience to those rules in one's actions; and the moral force of the rules governing promises, property, etc. is conceived as tied to certain social conventions that have been arrived at or contrived by human artifice, human cleverness. Hume also believed in a need to justify (what we nowadays call) deontology in a way that his predecessor, Francis Hutcheson, did not. Hutcheson realized that (what is called) justice and (universal) benevolence can conflict—that is, dictate incompatible actions—in a given situation, but Hutcheson held that we should always choose benevolence over justice if and when they clash,[2] and to that extent he seems to have failed to see the attractions, the intuitive moral

---

1. See my *The Ethics of Care and Empathy*, New York: Routledge, 2007, especially ch. 3.
2. See Hutcheson's *An Inquiry into the Original of Our Ideas of Beauty and Virtue*, Treatise II: *Concerning Moral Good and Evil*, s. II, art. 1, in *Complete Works of Francis Hutcheson*, Vol. I, Hildesheim: Olms, 1969–71.

force, that deontology has for most of us. Hume, by contrast, sees that we ordinarily think of justice as having overriding force against considerations of public (or universal) benevolence, and his account of justice and the other artificial virtues seeks to justify, or at least explain, such an attitude. Hume also differs from Hutcheson in appreciating the partiality of human virtue outside the sphere of artificial virtue. Hutcheson's master virtue is universal, that is, impartial, benevolence, and although he makes room for partiality toward near and dear, he doesn't consider such partiality to be essential to virtue. Instead, he seems to think it is or would be morally better and more virtuous to be universally benevolent than to be partial toward near and dear (while still being substantially concerned with the welfare of those outside that circle).

Hume, on the other hand, thinks that total agential impartiality can never seem morally attractive and regards (our notions of) virtue and vice as following our natural tendencies toward partiality outside the deontological sphere.[3] So here, as with deontology, Hutcheson's views seem closer to act-utilitarianism than Hume's and Hume's closer to commonsense moral intuition than Hutcheson's. However, it is easier to make the sentimentalist case for extra-deontological partiality toward family and friends than to do so for deontology. Hume's discussion of natural sympathy offers a possible explanation and justification of our greater concern for near and dear; but deontology is a much trickier matter, and Hutcheson's (arguable) denial of deontology may be tempting for the sentimentalist who has a high regard for benevolence (as it is for the utilitarian who also makes a moral appeal to benevolence).[4]

But to give up on deontology is to give up on or reject something that has great force with us and that most of us would find extremely difficult to eliminate from our own psychology. Hume deserves great credit for trying to account for this important feature of the human moral landscape in sentimentalist terms—and also for noticing some of the tension that exists between his own empiricist sentimentalism and a rule-based approach to deontology that seems to capture the (benevolence-overriding) *force* that deontology has for many or most of us (including, apparently, Hume).

Hume thinks that both our mental and, more specifically, our moral capacities and tendencies can be understood in empiricist terms. He tends to see human moral sentiment as based in our human capacity for sympathy with the suffering and joy of others, a capacity that depends on associations of ideas that can be charted in empiricist psychological terms. However, in his attempt to account for the whole of morality, he defends a distinction between two kinds of virtues, what he calls the natural virtues and what he calls the artificial virtues. (This language suggests that Hume is a virtue ethicist, but although he makes some distinctively

---

3. See Hume's *A Treatise of Human Nature*, ed. L. A. Selby-Bigge, Oxford: Clarendon Press, 1958, pp. 488–89. (See also pp. 439, 441, 518–19.)

4. On the comparison between Hume and Hutcheson, see Stephen Darwall's *The British Moralists and the Internal "Ought": 1640–1740*, Cambridge: Cambridge University Press, 1995, pp. 290ff.

virtue-ethical claims in his account of morality, his virtue ethics seems to conflict with other aspects of his theory of morality, as we shall be seeing shortly.) Hume thinks of the natural virtues as requiring no grounding in social rules or conventions and no specifically moral thinking (no thinking about what is right or wrong or virtuous), and among the virtues he classifies as natural in this sense are benevolence, parental solicitude for children, gratitude, and meekness.[5]

However, Hume thinks some very important virtues are not natural in the above sense and are in fact and as a result more difficult to understand. Hume thinks that virtues like justice or honesty (by both of which Hume usually means respect for people's property), fidelity to promises, allegiance/obedience to government, and female modesty are artificial, rather than natural: unlike benevolence or meekness, they can exist only as the product of human conventions (though not necessarily of a social contract) and require a reference to their own obligatoriness. The virtue of fidelity, for example, requires there to be a rule or rules governing promises that individuals feel bound by and conscientiously obey. There is no natural instinct or impulse toward keeping promises the way there is a natural impulse of benevolence or compassion toward those one sees in distress. Rather, one keeps promises or respects another person's property in the complex ways required for civilized life, because one feels obligated to do so, because one feels bound by a rule or rules that forbid one to break a promise or make use in certain ways of another's possessions. (For the moment, let us ignore the question whether these rules are socially operative norms, or officially promulgated laws, or valid moral rules that may or may not be honored or have been promulgated.)

As an empiricist and sentimentalist, Hume thinks he can explain and understand how benevolence and self-interest naturally operate in the human mind and in human life, but he also attempts to explain how such motives, with the aid of human artifice or cleverness, can lead to the development of the/a system of strict rules that govern property, promise-keeping, female modesty, and allegiance to government. Without the institutions or practices of property, promising, etc., civilization cannot really get off the ground, and he thinks human beings benefit individually and collectively from these artificial, that is, cleverly contrived, institutions/practices/ virtues. Benevolence and the counterweight to selfishness that it represents are certainly useful to human beings and to human society, but Hume sees benevolence as a motive that adjusts flexibly to differences in circumstances and believes that civilization cannot get off the ground, much less flourish as it does in modern times, without rules that operate via more rigid attitudes of obedience that in given cases refuse to take heed of benevolent or self-interested considerations.

However, when Hume attempts to account for the artificial virtues, most especially justice and fidelity, his sentimentalist commitments are strained to the breaking point, and Hume himself in various ways acknowledges the challenge, the difficulty, of understanding these virtues in sentimentalist terms.

5. See, for example, *Treatise*, pp. 518–19, 574–76.

In fact, Hume at times seems to regard the whole idea of artificial virtues as problematic.[6] For example, he commits himself to a kind of virtue ethics by declaring that actions lack any moral quality in themselves and derive any moral quality they have from the motive that underlies them (that they express). So the obligatoriness or virtuousness of helping another depends entirely on (what we can say about) the motives of helping and not helping. If the motive or attitude of indifference to another person is morally vicious, then that is what makes it wrong not to help and obligatory or virtuous to help, and if benevolence toward another is admirable and good, that is what makes it virtuous for someone with that motive to actually help that other person.

However, Hume's commitment to virtue ethics seems to clash with (some of) his views about the artificial virtues. He says, for example, that honesty is basically motivated by a sense of the obligatoriness of not taking or tampering with other people's property, but he also claims that the virtuousness of such conscientious actions regarding property depends on there being some motive *other* than a sense of obligation or conscientiousness for doing them. Yet there appears to be no such thing as a natural motive (a motive operating independently of concern to do what is obligatory or virtuous) to respect the property or possessions of others. And he makes rather similar points about the keeping of promises.

Thus for Hume motive is what grounds the obligatory or virtuous character of an action, but our motive in cases involving justice or fidelity (to promises) is to do what is morally required of us or obligatory. And this makes it seem as if it is the character of the action that comes first in the order of ethical explanation. We then seem to be caught up in a vicious circle, because (given Hume's commitment to virtue ethics) the moral obligatoriness or goodness of any act needs to be grounded (noncircularly) in the moral goodness of its motive, but in the case of artificial virtues like property, promising, and obedience to the law, we can only specify good motives by reference to the moral obligatoriness or goodness of certain acts (since there is no natural desire or motive to keep promises, obey the law, etc.).[7]

---

6. On the problems or paradoxes of justice, see *Treatise*, pp. 480, 483, 528; and see also pp. 518–19, 534 on similar issues with promising. Promising in fact raises paradoxical issues additional to those that arise in connection with justice/property, but I don't think we need to enter into these (independently fascinating) issues here. However, see, for example, Rachel Cohon's "Hume on Promises and the Peculiar Act of the Mind," *The Journal of the History of Philosophy* 44, 2006. My own discussion of Hume is generally indebted to Cohon's work and to discussions with her.

7. Samuel Kerstein has reminded me that the fact that the notion of rightness or duty is essential to the motive of dutifulness or conscientiousness doesn't by itself show that it is circular to explain the rightness of actions as being due to the fact that they issue from a motive of duty. There is a circle of concepts here, but not necessarily of *explanations*. The virtue-ethical idea that the moral qualities of acts must be noncircularly explained in terms of the moral qualities of their underlying motives doesn't in itself entail that the specification of such motives can't make intensional reference to the moral qualities of actions. For example, the thesis that actions are right to the extent they are motivated by a desire to do what is right isn't explanatorily circular (though it could certainly be objected to on other grounds). Hume (*Treatise*, p. 478) seems to miss this point, but a circle of concepts would at the very least be damaging to his general empiricism. There is more to be said, but I am not going to try to say it here.

In the light of these considerations, Hume questions whether justice/honesty may not be based in sophistry and makes similar points about fidelity to promises. But the threatened circularity or sophistry here has been noted by countless commentators, and one way out of "Hume's circle" that has been suggested is to see whether obedience to the rules of justice, promising, etc. cannot be motivated and justified by natural motives that sentimentalism thinks it easier to understand, like self-interest and/or benevolence. There may be no natural motive of justice/honesty, for example, and when we adhere inflexibly to the rules of justice, we may well be confused or incoherent in our thinking about justice. But this inflexible behavior might nonetheless be justifiable or motivatable in less confusing terms and in particular in terms of self-interest or the virtue of benevolent concern for the public interest. It would be both philosophically interesting and humanly important, if one could show that that was the case.

Defenders of egoism and utilitarianism sometimes try to show that ordinary deontology or some other facet of commonsense morality can be justified in egoistic or utilitarian terms. Thus utilitarians frequently believe that ordinary deontological thinking is confused and irrational, and a utilitarian justification, say, for keeping promises is supposed to offer philosophy and ordinary people a justification for instances of a practice that the utilitarian thinks cannot be justified in terms of confused ordinary thinking about that practice.

Now Hume doesn't believe there is such a motive or therefore such a natural virtue as universal concern for humankind (*Treatise*, p. 481). But he does think it is possible to have concern for the public interest, and though such a motive is obviously more limited in scope than universal benevolence, it is closer to it than the egoism and partiality to family and friends that most people display most of the time. One way to view Hume's account of justice/property, fidelity to promises, and other artificial virtues might, then, be to see him as offering an egoistic or limited-utilitarian justification of or motive for ordinary deontological practices. The Humean circle described above (supposedly) indicates how confused our ordinary thinking about the artificial virtues is and how incapable, presumably, therefore, such thinking is of justifying our adherence to the deontological rules of honesty, etc. But, according to the present way of understanding or reconstructing what Hume is doing both in the *Treatise* and in the (second) *Enquiry*, we can present a moral justification or a motive for rigid adherence to the rules of justice by showing that self-interest or benevolent concern for the public interest dictates such adherence.[8]

Hume points out that just or honest people don't repay loans out of concern for the public interest; he thinks ordinary thinking about our reasons to repay a

8. David Hume, *An Enquiry Concerning the Principles of Morals*, in ed. L. A. Selby-Bigge, *Hume's Enquiries*, 2nd edition, Oxford: Clarendon Press, 1961. "Or a motive" is disjoined in this last sentence, because Hume is unclear whether to think of (the motive of) self-interest or self-concern as a virtue; but if we can show that doing something is required by self-interest, that can certainly, for Hume, provide a motive.

loan involves an aversion to "villainy" and injustice that makes no reference to (benevolent concern for) the public interest or egoistic concern for one's own self-interest.[9] And, given the circle, such ordinary thinking is confused. But (Hume may be thought to be saying) we can justify or motivate doing what just people do by reference to considerations that are far from the minds of those who behave justly, considerations (and in that sense reasons) having to do with the advancement of self-interest or the public good. Even if the reasons/motives of the just are confused or incoherent, there is or can be a quite unconfused and understandable (natural) reason or motive (or set of such) for doing exactly as just people do. In particular, we may be able to motivate rigidly just behavior by showing it to be in the interest of the agent and perhaps we can (alternatively or also) justify just behavior by showing that it serves the unproblematic virtuous motive of concern for public good or the public interest. (The motive is unproblematic, because even if it never actually exists in the absence of the artifices or conventions necessary to civilized life, it is concerned with human well-being, not with acting rightly or virtuously, and *its status as a virtue* in no way seems to depend on the existence of human conventions. So it seems fully natural in Hume's sense.)

On such a view, the artificial virtues are artificial because they depend on human artifice for their existence, but if they are virtues, they are not virtues on their own terms, in the terms in which they tend to see themselves. In other words, the establishment of social conventions and the emergence of strict rules governing property, promises, and the like is a work of human ingenuity, of human contrivance, but human contrivance, convention, and artifice do not produce a new way of justifying our attitudes and actions, do not offer a new foundation for something's counting as a virtue. If justice is an (artificial) virtue, it has that status because acting justly can be defended by reference to what is a very real virtue, concern for the public interest (or, if prudence or long-term self-interest is a virtue, by reference to it). But in order for people to possess and act on the artificial virtues, certain practices and certain (confused or problematic) motives or justifications have to be produced by human artifice or contrivance, and those practices and motives allow human self-interest or concern for the public interest to be *redirected* in new channels laid down by the artifice. Artifice and the artificial virtues thus represent a means by which benevolence or self-interest gains new opportunities, but aren't an independent source of moral reasons or justifications (or understandable, unconfused motives). In a word, artifice is the means to justice but not its justification.

Something like this interpretation or reconstruction of Hume's position can be found, for example, in David Gauthier's "Artificial Virtues and the Sensible

---

9. See *Treatise*, p. 481, for Hume's view that ordinary honesty/justice isn't motivated by concern for the public interest. In "Hume's Difficulty with the Virtue of Honesty" (*Hume Studies* XXIII: 104–05, 1997), Rachel Cohon points out that Hume also shows no signs of believing that ordinary honesty/justice is motivated by self-interest.

Knave."[10] Gauthier suggests that Hume may think that there are reasons or motives of prudence, of long-term self-interest, for individuals always to abide by the rules that govern justice and the other artificial virtues, even though people are sometimes tempted to break the rules because they underestimate the risk of being discovered or overestimate the advantage to be gained by running that risk (e.g., people sometimes don't see that violations of the rules are likely to weaken the whole system of social rules that they so greatly benefit from). According to Gauthier, the Hume who wrote the *Treatise* had hopes of showing that strict obedience to rules can be grounded in self-interest of a sufficiently enlightened or far-sighted kind, but, by the time he came to discuss the thinking of "sensible knaves" in the *Enquiry*, saw that the earlier approach wouldn't work.[11] And if this is so, then the Gauthier interpretation, however accurate to the *Treatise*, doesn't really represent a way in which Hume can justify adherence to the rules of justice. If, as the knave discussion suggests and reconsideration today makes plausible, there are occasions when breaking the rules of justice is in enlightened self-interest, then the attempt to justify or motivate deontology in terms of the natural motive of self-interest (redirected so as to embody and take into account the rule-guided practices that human beings have contrived to create) doesn't succeed. Self-interest cannot provide a motive for universal obedience to the rules that deontology or Hume seeks to justify, and we cannot, therefore, ground deontology on this sort of sentimentalist basis, though the thoroughness and intricacy of Hume's own discussion may help make it clear(er) to us why such an approach won't work.

But if self-interest won't work, perhaps (concern for) the public interest will. Hume's discussion of the sensible knave seems to argue or assume that there are cases where the knave could advance his long-term self-interest by breaking a rule of artificial virtue, and Hume also says that anyone with the horror of villainy that is typical of the honest or just individual will not think or act like a sensible knave. But perhaps the (confused or circular or at least problematic) thinking of those horrified by villainy is not necessary to make someone avoid rule-breaking in the circumstances of the sensible knave. Perhaps someone with concern for the public good will or would avoid rule-breaking, and perhaps a justification in terms of the virtue of public benevolence can put obedience to rules of justice on a firmer foundation than our ordinary circular thinking about justice will allow.

However, and as Stephen Darwall and others have argued, the point that adherence to rules of justice can occasionally be against self-interest can be extended to considerations of public interest as well, and Hume himself

10. David Gauthier, "Artificial Virtues and the Sensible Knave," *Hume Studies* 18: 401–28, 1992.

11. In "Hume's Difficulty with the Virtue of Honesty," p. 105, Cohon argues that the evidence even for the *Treatise* is more ambiguous than Gauthier seems to allow. *Treatise*, p. 497, for example, suggests that individual acts of justice may be contrary to the private interests of the agent *because* they are contrary to the vital interests of society.

provides examples where conformity to the rules of justice serves the public interest less well than violating them: as when we return money we owe to a miser or to a "seditious bigot."[12] So it looks as if we cannot justify our rigid (i.e., universal) adherence to the rules of justice, or to the rules associated with the other artificial virtues, by reference to the motive of public benevolence and so cannot show how (all) instances of artificial virtue can be justified by reference to a clear-cut, unproblematic, natural virtue. If this were possible, we would have a kind of sentimentalist justification for our deontological practices, rules, and motives, but it doesn't seem to work, and the reason, in the end, seems similar to and to anticipate what has later been found about utilitarian justifications for deontological restrictions/practices: such justifications don't seem to cover all cases where we intuitively think that violations of a certain deontological restriction/rule/practice are wrong.

This leaves us still without a plausible Humean justification for deontology, but we have not yet run out of possible interpretations, and there is another way in which Hume can be, and has been, understood that may well be more promising. As I mentioned earlier, Hume points out that someone who is just is fairly inflexible with regard to the rules of justice, but that benevolence involves much greater flexibility with regard to what to do in various circumstances. We are taught to regard the property of another person as sacred and inviolable, but these notions and the rigid attitude toward (the rules of) property that they express are not characteristic of natural motives, and according to Hume, it takes a lot of work—human conventions and rules need to be established and particular individuals need to be morally educated—to create such an attitude.

What I would now like to suggest as a way to construe and/or strengthen Hume's justification of the artificial virtues focuses not on the usefulness of particular acts that conform to the rules of justice or promising, but on the usefulness of the inflexible and possibly incoherent attitude that makes us unwilling to violate them (horrified at the thought of violating them) even in those instances when it might be more useful to us or others to do so. Hume says that society couldn't have evolved beyond its original primitive condition, if human beings hadn't contrived rules/conventions/institutions governing promising and contract, and, Enlightenment figure that he is, he thinks this shows the usefulness of the inflexible attitude toward rules that makes promising and its legally governed version, contract, possible (and effective).

Moreover, he may also think that that attitude cannot be sustained unless people are (generally) ignorant of the confusions or incoherence it involves and unless, and this is an additional point, they don't realize that social utility is what actually makes the attitude virtuous. To realize that the artificial virtues can only be justified by reference to their social utility (and not in their own terms) would leave one open to the "temptation" to violate their rules in those instances where such violation was, or appeared to be, socially useful, so (this

12. See, for example, *British Moralists*, p. 313n and, again, *Treatise*, p. 497.

interpretation of) Hume might be thought to be recommending a split between exoteric and esoteric moral thought, and a schizophrenia or split within the individual moral theorist as well, that are more than a little reminiscent (or anticipatory) of certain features or tendencies of utilitarianism. Schizophrenia or splitting and the related phenomenon of an esoteric morality are sometimes regarded as ethically problematic, sometimes not; but I in fact don't think they are as problematic as some philosophers have claimed, so I don't propose to press this aspect of our present interpretation of Hume *against* Hume. Hume runs into problems enough from a quite different direction.

I think we now need to say a little more about how, on the present interpretation, artificial virtues can be inculcated and justified. According to Hume, parents, educators, politicians, and others get children to disapprove of individual violations of the rules of promising or property either on their own part or on the part of others. Then, since Hume thinks disapproval can motivate people to avoid doing what they disapprove of (and there is a certain tendency for attitudes to generalize), we can understand how children come to be motivated to obey the rules of justice and of the other artificial virtues in a rigid fashion. And this motivation is precisely what is characteristic of someone who possesses the artificial virtues. Furthermore, Hume holds (roughly) that human beings tend (under conditions of relevant information) to feel a sentiment of approval about and only about traits that count as virtues, so if we can explain, in sentimentalist terms, how justice and the other artificial virtues come to be approved, we will then also have a sentimentalist *justification* for their status as virtues.

But a trait like justice *will* be approved if and when we recognize that the inflexible motivational attitude that lies at its core is more socially useful than more flexible attitudes/motives like (public) benevolence. Hume thinks that human sympathy with the effects a trait/motive has on human happiness can cause a trait to be approved, and this certainly accords with Hume's sentimentalism. But in that case, if we learn that the rigid attitude, say, of justice is more useful than relevant alternatives, sympathy with the traits' overall effects will make us approve of it, and that can lead the sentimentalist to the conclusion that justice is a virtue.

However, this entire train of reasoning depends on assuming that children can be made to disapprove of (all) instances of injustice, of infidelity, etc. via sentimental mechanisms, and it is not at all clear how this happens (or can happen). When parents and educators get children to disapprove, for example, of unjust actions, they typically don't do so by appealing to the disutility of the actions, so the mechanism of disapproval isn't sympathy with the unfortunate effects of an action on the happiness or well-being of others. (And also, as suggested earlier, it is difficult to see how disapproval grounded in such considerations could then be or become indifferent to utility in the way that Hume thinks is characteristic of just individuals.)

However, Hume thinks approval and disapproval can come about in other ways. He holds that we love and approve certain traits apart from their effects on people's happiness and independently of sympathy with such effects: certain traits are simply immediately agreeable or disagreeable to us. But this can hardly be the basis for our approval of justice and injustice, because there is nothing, or very little, that is amiable or agreeable in justice (as compared, say, with personal warmth or humor). It taxes credulity to suppose that children find justice to be immediately pleasant or agreeable, and indeed Hume's insistence on the need to train—and difficulty of training—children to approve justice and disapprove injustice seems to prove that such attitudes cannot be based on what is immediately agreeable. But Hume specifies no other mechanisms for the emergence of approval and disapproval, and so in his own sentimentalist terms, it is mysterious how children could ever become just or acquire any other of the artificial virtues.[13]

Thus Humean sentimentalism seeks to explain both why justice, fidelity, etc. are virtues and how people come to possess these virtues, and it seems in fact inadequate to the latter task. But Hume's attempt to show justice to be a virtue also faces a number of problems. Let us for the moment grant him the assumption that the inflexible attitudes characteristic of justice and the other artificial virtues are useful to society. Let us assume that we approve justice, fidelity, etc., because we are sympathetic with their good effects on or for society. And let us grant, finally, that all this vindicates the virtue status of justice, etc. But then consider someone who in a given instance doesn't do what is honest or just, because she knows (*knows*, not just *thinks*) that she can do more good by violating some generally useful (valid) rule concerning property. At least in the *Enquiry*, Hume seems to want to allow the possibility of such cases, but he also holds that it is wrong, contrary to obligation, for the woman to break the rule in a case where she can do more good by doing so, and this set of conclusions raises difficulties for Hume's theory.

To support his views, it is not enough for Hume to claim that a person who violated rules of property for the sake of producing more good would show herself to lack the inflexibility that is so essential to the usefulness of justice and the other artificial virtues. This only shows that the woman of our example has an attitude toward rules that is overall less useful and virtuous than an attitude of inflexibility, it doesn't show that she won't do more good in the particular circumstance because of the attitude she has. And how does the fact that she would do more good generally, if she had a different attitude toward rules, show that it is wrong of her to break the rules on an occasion when that is precisely what *will do the most good*? If justice as a general trait is virtuous

---

13. On p. 427 of the *Treatise*, Hume says that the opinion of another can have an influence on our own, but even if this allows us to explain, in appropriate sentimentalist terms, how disapproval can be transmitted from parent or educator to child, it doesn't explain how the disapproval came into being in the first place. And to suppose that someone originally saw the usefulness of justice, approved it, and then influenced others to have an approval not necessarily based on knowledge of the usefulness is to buy into a sentimentalist equivalent of the idea of an actual social contract.

and approved as such because of its usefulness, why shouldn't useful acts of *in*justice be approved and count as morally permissible?[14]

Now this question is more than a little reminiscent of act-utilitarianism and the charge of rule-worship that it makes against the rule-utilitarian view that we sometimes are obligated to perform less-than-optimific acts because they are required by optimific rules. And Hume's (implicit) response to this question is in fact determined by an assumption he makes that is somewhat analogous to the view just attributed to rule-utilitarianism. Rule-utilitarianism assumes that actions cannot be assessed directly (in terms of their consequences), but only indirectly and by reference to (the consequences of) rules; and Hume analogously assumes that we cannot morally evaluate actions in themselves, but can only do so by reference to their *motives*. We already noted above this commitment, on Hume's part, to a kind of virtue ethics. But I believe that the virtue ethics is in tension with Hume's other views, and I want to explain now why I think the problem just raised calls Hume's account of the artificial virtues into question. I think in particular that it is difficult if not impossible to combine virtue ethics with Hume's sentimentalist account of moral approval.

Hume not only makes the virtue-ethical assumption that the moral character of actions depends entirely on the character of the motive or trait that underlies it, but also ties that assumption to his sentimentalist account of moral approval and disapproval by claiming that we only approve actions in relation to (approving) their underlying motives/traits. But how does Hume know this, and how, indeed, can he justify it by reference to other (justified) parts of his views or to plausible philosophical assumptions more generally? After all, even apart from the truth of act-utilitarianism, there is the possibility of approving or disapproving along act-utilitarian lines. Bentham famously describes how reading Hume's account of the artificial virtues led him to act-utilitarianism and, in particular, to denying (Hume's belief in) the wrongness of optimific violations of useful social rules ("I felt as if the scales had fallen from my eyes");[15] and this means that Bentham at least learned (from Hume himself) to (dis)approve actions *without* (dis)approving of their underlying motives. So whether or not we accept Bentham's conclusions, the sheer empirical fact that he seems to have drawn them goes counter to Hume's theory of human approval and disapproval and the support that theory is supposed to give to his virtue ethics.

But we should also consider Hume's *philosophical* arguments for his view that our approval of actions depends on our approval of underlying traits or

---

14. The problem I am raising here doesn't particularly involve, or focus on, the circularity or incoherence of our *ordinary thought* about justice and the other artificial virtues. As we shall see more clearly in what follows, the difficulty stems rather from a certain incoherence or inadequacy within *Hume's account* of these virtues.

15. See Jeremy Bentham, *A Fragment on Government; with an Introduction to the Principles of Morals and Legislation*, ed. Wilfrid Harrison, Oxford: Blackwell, 1948, pp. 50n, 51n.

motives. Though at one point in the *Treatise* (p. 477) he tells us simply that it is "evident" that we praise (or disapprove) actions only in relation to the motives that produce them, he elsewhere claims that only underlying character and motivation "are *durable* enough to affect our sentiments concerning the person" (*Treatise*, p. 575, emphasis Hume's). And he immediately goes on to say that "[a]ctions are, indeed, better indications of a character than words, or even wishes and sentiments; but 'tis only so far as they are such indications, that they are attended with love or hatred, praise or blame." But this conclusion seems a *non sequitur*, given that the preceding argument only speaks of our sentiments about persons. How does the fact that only character and motivation are durable enough to affect our sentiments about persons show that we cannot have (moral) sentiments about actions that are independent of character and motivation? To be sure, earlier on the same page Hume says: "Actions themselves, not proceeding from any constant principle, have no influence on love or hatred, pride or humility; and consequently are never consider'd in morality." But this seems more to assume what is at issue here than to attempt to prove it;[16] and, as I indicated, Bentham and other act-utilitarians seem to be direct empirical counterinstances to what Hume is claiming.

However, the most powerful argument against Hume on this point may actually come from Hume himself. His explanation of how justice is acquired seems in fact to depend on the possibility of parents' and others' getting children to disapprove certain kinds of actions quite independently of their underlying motives; and several passages in the *Treatise* point explicitly to that possibility.[17] In that case, he cannot defend his commitment to virtue ethics without dropping other parts of his theory: in particular, his account of the acquisition of the artificial virtues. And so Hume appears to have no way to defend his view that it is wrong to break the rules of justice or fidelity even when doing so is socially useful or optimific and no way, therefore, to defend a deontology based in the idea of artificial virtues. And, of course, there is also, as I suggested above, the problematic character of Hume's rule-utilitarian-like assumption that (some) actions cannot be morally justified in terms of their own utility, but can be justified in terms of the utility of the general attitude/disposition they exemplify. It is difficult to understand why the test of utility

16. In *The Invention of Autonomy: A History of Modern Moral Philosophy* (Cambridge: Cambridge University Press, 1998, p. 362), J. B. Schneewind notes the weakness of Hume's arguments for tying the approval of actions to the approval of underlying character traits or motivation. But, as Elizabeth Radcliffe has pointed out to me, (the force of) those arguments may depend more on Hume's associationism (on principles of the operations of the mind that have their basis in book I of the *Treatise*) than Hume explicitly indicates. That would certainly limit their effectiveness in the context of present-day moral philosophy.

17. Cohon ("Hume's Difficulty with the Virtue of Honesty," p. 98) points up Hume's reliance on the possibility of disapproving actions apart from their motives, but doesn't (I believe) put sufficient stress on the problems this creates for his overall virtue ethics. For relevant passages in Hume, see *Treatise*, pp. 500, 533.

should be valid for general attitudes toward rules (or for the rules themselves), but not for the actions that may or may not accord with such rules.

It is worth noting at this point that the above objections to Hume in no way depend on the rigidity that he attributes to the motivational attitude toward rules that underlies or constitutes artificial virtue. Hume constantly stresses the inflexibility of our attitudes toward promise-keeping and respect for property (e.g.), but he somewhat surprisingly, in other places, stresses the need to make certain (generalizable) exceptions to ordinary rules governing property, promises, and obeying the law, so his own attitude toward these virtues is in fact a somewhat less rigid one than he in some places suggests.[18] But in any event it seems fair to say that Hume has and recommends a more rigorous attitude toward (what he calls) honesty/justice and the keeping of promises than what we find, for example, in W. D. Ross's *The Right and the Good* (aside from the fact that Ross doesn't seem to regard our deontological obligations here as having an artificial basis).[19] However, even if the rules of promise-keeping, etc. allow of the more extensive exceptions that Ross would or might defend, those rules require one to keep some promises that it would be optimific to violate. So even if Hume had such a relatively more flexible conception of what is required by the artificial virtues, he would still need to account for the wrongness of such optimific violations of the (valid) rules of promising and justice, and that account would be subject to the very same difficulties we have sketched above.

By the same token, we have also till now been assuming, with Hume, that an inflexible attitude toward deontological rules is socially useful, more useful than relevant alternatives. But even if the slightly less rigid attitude Ross favors would in fact be more useful to society, the basic problems with Hume's treatment of the artificial virtues remain. Nonetheless, Hume's account of the artificial virtues can be regarded, at the very least, as a "heroic failure". (A phrase once used in muted praise of David Gauthier's own *Morals by Agreement*.[20]) And I think we still have a great, great deal to learn today not only from Hume's insights, but also from his mistakes.

18. See, for example, the *Enquiry*, p. 206, and also *Treatise*, pp. 552–53.
19. Oxford: Clarendon Press, 1930.
20. Oxford: Clarendon Press, 1986.

7

KANT FOR ANTI-KANTIANS

In this essay, I want to talk about some contributions that Kant made to ethics that even an anti-Kantian like myself ought to accept and acknowledge. Even an anti-Kantian ethicist has an enormous amount to learn from Kant, and that is what I am going to try to show here to those of you who have doubts about this: care ethicists, virtue ethicists, perfectionists, consequentialists, and perhaps others. For those of you who are deeply committed to Kant or Kantian ideas, it might prove useful to know where Kantian ideas meet the least resistance from those generally opposed to Kant's conclusions or methodology. But you might wonder—everyone might wonder—why I have used the strong word "anti-Kantian" in the title of this essay. Why not speak instead of "Kant for non-Kantians"?

My reason has to do with the compliment or compliments I intend to pay to Kant. A non-Kantian, after all, might be on the fence and might easily acknowledge the validity or value of certain ideas of Kant's while doubting other ideas and/or finding other approaches also attractive. But it is more of a compliment to Kant if those who in major and fundamental ways disagree with Kant have to acknowledge the greatness of some, or many, of his ideas. I consider myself an anti-Kantian because I think the Kantian emphasis on autonomy misses out on the moral value of connection with others, because the emphasis on the conscientious application of principles also fails to see the moral value of more direct and emotional involvement with others, because Kant's derivation(s) of different versions of the Categorical Imperative seem fallacious or to make use of questionable assumptions, and I could go on. But I'm not going to, because I do really want to stick with my main purpose in writing this essay.

I am going to talk about a number of major contributions. There are Kantian ideas, ideas that historically originate with Kant, that I think every kind of approach to ethics or ethical theory ought to accept. And so we all have or should recognize a debt to Kant's innovations and, in many areas, his clarity of historical and conceptual moral vision. I am going to begin by talking of the distinction between categorical and hypothetical imperatives, which I think Kant was the first to draw in any explicit way. I am going to proceed to discuss Kant's distinction between das Gute and das Wohl, a distinction that I believe effectively makes Kant the *discoverer* of the idea of a good state of affairs, or at least the first to be really clear about the implications of that idea. And I am also going to talk about how Kant's distinctive emphasis on the inner character of morality contains important lessons for virtue ethicists and care ethicists, and may even have something, though less, to say to consequentialists, since a proper attention to what Kant is saying about the inner life can help consequentiialists to sharpen and differentiate their own contrary views.[1] But let me begin with the distinction between hypothetical and categorical imperatives.

7.1 Categorical versus Hypothetical Imperatives

I don't believe that anyone before Kant really had this distinction, and I think it is a distinction that needs to find its way into any moral philosophy, however (otherwise) distant from the Kantian. But I also have to be careful about *which* distinction I have in mind. In "Morality as a System of Hypothetical Imperatives," for example, Philippa Foot treats the distinction between categorical and hypothetical imperatives as tantamount to or at least involving the distinction between imperatives that derive from and are dictates of reason and imperatives that are not.[2] But this distinction probably isn't new to Kant and may well be discernible in Hume, if not earlier. I believe that moral claims or injunctions can and must be viewed as categorical imperatives in a way that certain claims or recommendations about the means we ought to take to our ends are not, and *this* distinction is, I believe for the first time, made in Kant's *Groundwork*. According to Kant, someone to whom a hypothetical imperative (e.g., if you want to fix that car, you ought to use a c-wrench) is addressed can plausibly beg off by arguing that she lacks the relevant desires or motives (e.g., I have no interest in spending time on that old junk heap). But, on the Kantian view, the absence of desires, motives, or intentions relevant to the fulfillment of a categorical imperative doesn't leave the person to whom it is addressed outside the scope of that imperative—doesn't make the imperative inapplicable to that person in the way that can be true for hypothetical imperatives.

This distinction is tantamount, I think, to (our sense of) the *inescapability* of moral injunctions, moral obligations (this last word comes from the Latin word for tying or being tied), but not of certain ordinary "ought"s or "should"s. But one can admit the forcefulness, the necessity, of the distinction while disputing about its boundaries. Kant, for example, held that only moral imperatives were categorical; but Sidgwick claimed that prudential imperatives can also be categorical (I tend to agree with him). And in the essay mentioned above, Philippa Foot argues powerfully for the conclusion that, in the sense just-mentioned, the "should"s of etiquette can be regarded as categorical. So the Kantian view

---

1. Kant's distinction between imperfect and perfect duties is not original to Kant and was quite familiar in his day—even though most of us hear of the distinction only through reading (about) Kant.

2. Foot's article is reprinted in S. Darwall, A. Gibbard, and P. Railton (eds.), *Moral Discourse and Practice*, New York: Oxford University Press, 1997, pp. 313–22.

that moral imperatives are categorical doesn't necessarily distinguish moral "ought"s from all others. But that doesn't preclude us from insisting on the categorical force of the moral ones, and in that case, non-Kantian moral philosophies had better have a way of allowing for the inescapability or categorical character of moral injunctions or claims.

In fact, I think other moral philosophies do allow for this. Hume, for example, never explicitly mentions the idea of a categorical imperative, and one might suspect that his sentimentalist approach would be too "soft," too lacking in the kind of strictness one finds in Kantian rationalism, to allow him to acknowledge the categorical status or force of moral claims or utterances. But remember how strict a view Hume takes of our obligations of justice (regarding property) and fidelity (to promises). Here, arguably, however, Hume's accurate sense of our ordinary moral feelings and thinking moves him toward rationalism—one might think a sentimentalist like Hume can't really insist on the strictness of our obligations to repay our debts and keep promises. And I think there is some truth to this.

But that doesn't mean that Hume can't allow for categorical imperatives (without ever mentioning the idea). Even in the area of benevolence, where our obligations seemingly lack the strictness one may feel attaches to deontological obligations of justice and fidelity, there is still a robust kind of inescapability and, therefore, of categoricalness. Someone who never wants to help anyone in need or danger doesn't escape strong moral criticism just because he or she has no interest in helping anyone else. And this is entirely consistent with the Humean sentimentalist view of the source and nature of virtue and vice concerning our helpfulness, or beneficence, toward others. Hume would certainly also allow that one doesn't get out of one's special obligations to help family members just because one has no interest in helping them.[3] By the same token, there is no reason why care ethicists, virtue ethicists, and consequentialists can't allow for the categorical force of moral "ought"s on basically similar grounds.

But unlike Kant, most consequentialists, virtue ethicists, and care ethicists don't call attention to this categorical force, and one might almost suspect that they didn't think moral imperatives have categorical force. They may, at least some of them, be under the impression that the less strict or absolute character of the moral duties they subscribe to—by comparison, say, with the absolute strictures against lying one finds in Kant—makes moral claims less than categorical. But if they think this way, they are just plain wrong. They are confusing strictness in the sense of absoluteness with inescapability. A moral imperative that allows for exceptions doesn't necessarily bind us less strongly than one that doesn't allow of exceptions. However, the confusion or mistake is

3. In "Categorical Requirements: Kant and Hume on the Idea of Duty" (*Monist* 74: 83–106, 1991), David Wiggins defends the idea that Hume can accept categorical moral imperatives and offers an interesting account of why some critics may have thought that Hume and other sentimentalists were incapable of allowing for such imperatives.

understandable here, because what doesn't allow of exceptions is for that reason and in a certain sense inescapable; so what does allow of exceptions is to that extent, and in that sense, *not* inescapable. And it might then be easy for a moral philosopher like a care ethicist, virtue ethicist, or consequentialist who thinks that ordinary moral injunctions (almost) always allow of exceptions to conclude that such injunctions are simply not, in any sense, inescapable or categorical.

But this is or would be a mistake because what we have in effect been seeing here is that there are two different kinds or notions of inescapability. Even though the consequentialist, virtue ethicist, or care ethicist allows for the moral acceptability of certain kinds of stealing or lying, some or most of them will still want to maintain the general wrongness of stealing and lying. But then the moral injunction against (say) lying that they accept (and as they accept it) will contain or allow certain exceptions and we can say that the exceptions are built into the *content* of the injunction or obligation they accept. There is, as a result, a certain escapability or non-inescapability in or vis-à-vis the content of what they say if and when they say lying is wrong. But there will be inescapability perhaps regarding the content of certain other obligations they accept, like the obligation not to kill people when there is no moral reason to do so.

In any event, the (in)escapability of the content of certain moral claims or injunctions is different from the (in)escapability of those claims or injunctions as such. Even if there may be exceptions to the injunction not to lie, that injunction can never be escaped (or made irrelevant) *as an injunction with exceptions built into (how we regard) its content*. Thus the content of an injunction may allow for exceptions or escapes, but what binds in this exception-allowing way is not itself escapable; it inescapably binds us or, as we can now say, it binds us categorically. So there are two notions of inescapability and only one of them corresponds to our notion of a categorical imperative.[4] The other kind of inescapability, inescapability of content, as I am calling it, isn't necessary to the first or categorical kind's being in place. More simply, a categorical imperative whose force is inescapable may allow of exceptions and thus be escapable with respect to its content.

Now the terms I have used to make this distinction are strongly suggestive of distinctions made outside of moral philosophy proper. Frege notably distinguishes between the content of assertions and the asserting of them, that is, between the content of propositions and the asserting of them. And in the area of intentionality generally, we distinguish act and object, and are aware of instances where language is ambiguous as between those two: what is called

---

4. Henry West has pointed out to me that the above discussion could (in a philosophically useful way) be further complicated by bringing in the notion of overridingness, that is, the idea—which many, but by no means all philosophers accept—that moral obligations (rationally) override all other sorts of considerations or reasons. The putative or supposed overridingness of moral judgments (concerning all-things-considered obligation) can itself be seen as a kind of justificational inescapability, so if we brought in overridingness, we would *really* have our hands full. But I don't propose to do that here.

"act-object ambiguity." The term "assertion" is just one example of this; we find the same thing with terms like "belief," "assumption," and "injunction." In such cases, attributes of the act may not hold for the object, or vice versa, and that leaves open the possibility that a certain adjectival term might apply in one way or sense to a certain act and in another to its object. This is what I believe we have uncovered with the notion of inescapability.

Our discussion could possibly be enriched or solidified, at this point, by folding it into a larger and systematic consideration of similar intentional ambiguities, if I can call them that. But I don't want to get into a general discussion of intentionality—that actually lies beyond what I would feel comfortably competent in attempting. It's enough, I think, to mention these larger possibilities and to indicate briefly how they might bear on the distinctions regarding categoricalness that I *have* been talking about. And those distinctions have been brought in for one main reason: to show that all moral philosophies ought to acknowledge and make room for the categorical character of their moral imperatives, their moral obligations. (This last "ought" is itself intended as a categorical imperative of ethical theory or theorizing.)

Hume and others have treated moral "ought"s as categorical imperatives without having that specific notion. But there is nothing anti-Kantian about that. After all, Kant seeks to uncover and describe ordinary people's (deepest) feelings and thoughts about morality, and he knows full well that ordinary people don't have an explicit idea of categoricalness. But nonetheless, he thinks, ordinary people implicitly treat moral imperatives as categorical, and Kant seeks, successfully, to bring out this fact in the *Groundwork*. It's no great wonder, then, that moral philosophers should treat moral "ought"s as categorical without knowingly doing so and even perhaps (though this is perhaps more surprising) while becoming confused enough by ambiguities to think, mistakenly, that they don't regard morality as categorical. We have tried to disentangle some of these issues here, but all of what we have said redounds to the advantage of Kant's original insight. The distinction between categorical and hypothetical imperatives is very important, and it is very important to try to be or stay clear and unconfused about it.

7.2 Good States of Affairs

To be at all clear about the notion of a(n impartially considered) good state of affairs, one has to be clear about the distinction between that notion and the notion of what is good for someone, what makes their life go better.[5] But as far as I can tell (and others more scholarly than I may just have to correct me here)

5. I use the words between parentheses because in recent years, philosophers have become aware that it is possible (also) to judge states of affairs in relation to some one person's point of view. But that is not the concept I shall be discussing in the text.

no one before Kant *was* aware of this distinction. In fact, when he explicitly introduces the distinction in the *Critique of Practical Reason*, Kant at the very least implies that he is the first to do so; but before I say more about why I think, and Kant may have thought, that previous philosophers hadn't been clear in this area, let me say just a bit about how Kant himself introduces the distinction.

Early in the *Groundwork*, Kant tells us that no impartial rational spectator could approve or be pleased by the prosperity of a vicious (or non-virtuous) person. Given the context and Kant's other views, Kant would presumably also say that no impartial spectator could be pleased by the *happiness* of a vicious person. And though Kant doesn't use the term "state of affairs," he clearly is talking of a certain state of affairs when he says no impartial observer could approve the prosperity of a vicious person. Since Kant is using this example as one among many illustrations of the conditional goodness of every good other than the good will, he clearly implies that the prosperity or happiness of a vicious person is not (a) good (thing). But Kant isn't disputing that the prosperity is good for the vicious individual, so he really seems to be distinguishing between the goodness of a state of affairs involving some individual and what is good, makes for a better life, for that individual.

At this point in his oeuvre, Kant isn't totally explicit about this distinction. He makes it without calling attention to the fact that he is making it. But before I bring in a later discussion in which Kant explicitly calls attention to the distinction, let me just say that as far as I can tell, even this less self-conscious distinction-making in the *Groundwork* is relatively rare in the history of ethics before Kant. We shall see shortly that Aristotle at one point comes fairly close to this idea, but I can't myself think of anyone else who explicitly says that it may not be a good thing for someone, a vicious person, to obtain what is good *for* him. (Perhaps others will be able to correct me on this.)

However, in the *Critique* (part I, book I, ch. I), Kant is quite explicit and self-conscious about the distinction we are talking about. He mentions that the Romans had a hard time making it because they had only one word "*bonus*" to cover both ideas; but German, he says, has two words here, and that helps one be clear that there really is a distinction to be made. The German "*das Gute*" and "*das Wohl*" both correspond to the Latin "*bonus*," and Kant makes it clear that moral considerations enter into our conception of *das Gute* but not into our ideas about *das Wohl*. Which is to say that the immorality of a man doesn't prevent him from being well-off (something the Stoics and Aristotle would have disputed),[6] but does, if he is well-off, prevent it from being a good thing that he is.

Now even in the second *Critique* Kant doesn't use any expression that can be translated as "state of affairs" in talking of *das Gute*. But in fact there

---

6. According to ancient eudaimonism, virtue is in the interest of the virtuous individual, so the idea of a vicious person's flourishing, or being well-off, is a far stretch from the point of view of ancient virtue ethics. Most modern philosophy is not, however, eudaimonistic in that sense, and certainly Kant isn't a eudaimonist of the this-worldly kind one finds in ancient ethics.

are a number of expressions in English (and corresponding expressions in German) that effectively pick out states of affairs and attribute goodness or badness to them. We can say that the prosperity of a vicious person isn't good, or a good thing; we can say that it isn't (a) good (thing) that a vicious person should prosper; we can say that prosperity of a vicious individual (is something that) shouldn't exist. All of these seem equivalent to talking *explicitly* about the non-goodness of a state of affairs (or situation), and I won't distinguish among these phrases in what follows. But once Kant has called our attention to the distinction between well-being or what is good for someone and goodness as characterizing states of affairs, he has certainly gone beyond anything to be found in previous philosophy. Even if Aristotle or others said some things that entail the distinction in question, even if they understood and/or sometimes made use of the distinction, it is quite another thing to be explicitly aware of it *as* a distinction and to call it to the attention of philosophers and others. And this Kant seems to have been the first to do.

But, as I said, the distinction seems to be implicit in some things said by previous philosophers. Most ancient ethicists were trying to figure out how to connect virtue and well-being, and the goodness of states of affairs didn't really come into the picture. But when Aristotle says that justice involves a proportionality between merit, or virtue, and benefits, or things that are good for one, I think one can't make full sense of what he is saying without bringing in the distinction between good states of affairs and what is good for individuals. The existence of a proportionality between virtue and well-being is a state of affairs, and in implicitly characterizing that state of affairs as just and the state of affairs consisting of an absence of such proportionality as unjust, Aristotle should be committed to saying, for example, that the former state of affairs is a good thing. If he did say this, he would be distinguishing between what is good for people and what constitutes a good state of affairs, but in fact Aristotle never says that proportionality between virtue and well-being is good or a good thing. He simply calls it just. And perhaps he avoided saying something like this in part because to have done so would be to have said something in some measure suggestive of Plato's Form of the Good, and Aristotle is strongly committed to denying the Forms. I am not sure about this last suggestion, though, because modern-day ethicists who talk about good states of affairs, or say that it is good that such and such happened, don't always consider themselves committed to universals of the Platonic variety. Still, the suggestion does push us in the direction of Plato, and I in fact think we should allow ourselves to be pushed a bit in that direction.

Another place in the history of ethics before Kant where I am aware of something implying a distinction between what is good for people and what is a good state of affairs or good "thing" is, in fact, in Plato's discussion of the Form of the Good and the other Forms. The Forms are said to be good, but Plato doesn't seem to mean that they are or have to be good *for* anyone. As Nicholas White has put it, the Form of the Good isn't the Form of Self-Interest or of Benefits for Individuals.[7] Rather, the Form of the Good is good in itself, as a metaphysical entity, rather than in relation to anything else, and Plato's description of the blinding goodness of the Form of the Good comes very close, I think, to anticipating Kant's admiring claim that the Good Will is the only unconditionally good thing in the universe. In both cases, what is said to be good is regarded as absolutely good and not as good in relation to anyone's interests, so I think Plato's emphasis on the Form of the Good represents an unusual point in Greek philosophy, a point where the usual Greek preoccupation with the good of the individual, with what is good for the individual, is attenuated in favor of focusing on a different kind of good altogether, and one that is held to be vastly superior to or more important than what is good for individuals. (Isn't this again reminiscent of Kant?[8])

I can think of only one other example, in the history of ethics prior to Kant, of philosophical commitment to a notion of good that isn't relative to the individual (and constitutive of his or her well-being), and this is the Stoic idea of the perfect goodness of the cosmos and its structure.[9] Perhaps there are other cases where philosophers prior to Kant have spoken of goodness in such absolute terms, but I am, nonetheless, willing to venture that the more self-conscious introduction of the distinction between well-being and absolute good that we find in the second *Critique* is altogether without precedent in the previous history of ethics. And the distinction is a mainstay of much present-day philosophical theorizing. Many of us make quite a lot of use of it, and this is especially true of utilitarians and consequentialists (though to some extent also of contemporary Kantian ethicists), which might make one wonder whether Bentham or some other early utilitarian had the distinction at about the same time Kant was developing it.

The answer, in a nutshell, is that I believe they, or at least Bentham, did. But the matter isn't entirely clear because Bentham was never as clear and self-conscious about the distinction as Kant was. In fact, one has to tease out the

---

7. Nicholas White, "The Rulers' Choice," *Archiv fuer Geschichte der Philosophie* 68: 24–46, 1986. Also see his *A Companion to Plato's Republic*, Indianapolis: Hackett Publishing Co., 1979, pp. 35–37. By the way, when *Genesis* says "And God saw that it [his creation] was good," that too doesn't seem a reference to goodness for anyone or anything, but to something (whose existence is) good in itself; and notice that to say something's existence is good in itself is basically to say that the state of affairs consisting in its existing is intrinsically (impartially) good.

8. Still, as Marcia Baron has reminded me, the Good Will is a state of some individual or individuals and the Form of the Good isn't tied in this way to individuals, so the two are different in that respect. But, as I said above, neither is supposed to derive its goodness from some connection to self-interest or human well-being, and that is an important resemblance. Moreover, Kant and Plato believe, respectively, that the Good Will and the Form of the Good are not only *unconditionally* good (things), but also *uniquely* good (things). This too is an important resemblance.

9. On Stoic views of the perfect goodness of the cosmos, see the discussion in Nicholas White, *Individual and Conflict in Greek Ethics*, Oxford: Clarendon Press, 2002, pp. 311–26. It is clear that the Stoic gods are supposed to recognize the goodness of the cosmos in something like the way the Jewish/Christian God is thought of as seeing the goodness of the created universe.

distinction from passages in which Bentham might easily be thought of as talking about something else, the welfare or happiness of individuals; and only careful attention to Bentham's precise words can assure us that he is committed to the notion of a good state of affairs—even if perhaps not aware that he is. In fact, utilitarians who require the distinction between good for people and good as a state of affairs have very rarely, even in recent years, made explicit reference to it, and I am not sure that the distinction was ever made by a consequentialist as strongly and clearly as Kant made it in the second *Critique*, until Amartya Sen did so in his 1979 article "Utilitarianism and Welfarism."[10] (Making and applying the distinction is one of the main purposes of the article.) But back to Bentham.

The reason I say that Bentham may not have been fully aware of the distinction between good for people and good as a state of affairs is that he never explicitly or self-consciously refers to it. But he did say things that entail or imply the distinction and let me now say what those are. In *An Introduction to the Principles of Morals and Legislation*, Bentham introduces a version of the "greatest happiness" principle, according to which acts are right when and only when they bring about the greatest happiness of those whom they affect.[11] This is rough, very rough, but it is less rough or approximate than what Bentham himself says in the *Introduction*; and in any case I don't want to enter into a detailed discussion here of how the principle of utility or greatest happiness should be stated.[12] What is important to note, however, is that this way of formulating the ultimate principle of utilitarian morality doesn't mention states of affairs or their goodness and *doesn't at all commit itself to these ideas*. And indeed there are later versions/developments of utilitarianism that focus on and advocate what most promotes well-being or happiness, without ever saying that what most promotes well-being has *better* consequences than its alternatives and can be justified, therefore, as being *for the best* or as resulting in an *overall better* state *of affairs* than its alternatives.

However, Bentham himself does talk about good consequences in a number of places in the *Introduction* (e.g., pp. 89, 114–15), and I believe that in the context of everything else he says, such talk implicitly commits Bentham both to the idea of a good state of affairs and to the conclusion that any action that produces the most overall human or sentient good, that is, well-being, that produces more such good than any alternative, produces better consequences or

---

10. "Utilitarianism and Welfarism," *Journal of Philosophy* 76: 463–89, 1979. By the way, G. E. Moore in *Principia Ethica* is very clear and explicit about the notion of a state of affairs—perhaps he is the first utilitarian to be that explicit about the notion—but *argues against, and in his own conclusions avoids, the whole notion of welfare or personal well-being*. So one really can't say that Moore was clear about the distinction between what is good for people and what counts as a good state of affairs.

11. Edited by J. H. Burns and H. L. A. Hart, London: Methuen, 1982.

12. In *Common-Sense Morality and Consequentialism* (London: Routledge, 1985, ch. 3), I argue that Bentham actually advocates incompatible versions of the principle of utility at the beginning of the *Introduction*. But that issue is orthogonal to my present purposes.

results than any of its alternatives and can be justified on that basis. This latter thought is certainly familiar to us nowadays; as Sen makes clear in the article cited above, almost any contemporary utilitarian will see the moral justification of acting to produce the most happiness, desire-satisfaction, well-being, or personal good as dependent on the assumption that any such action has better consequences (results in an overall better state of affairs) than its alternatives. The idea that acting to produce the most personal good or happiness is *acting for the best* seems to many contemporary utilitarians to be an essential element in the justification of their views (or would seem so, if they bothered to think about the matter). But the assumption that what produces the most personal good is what produces the best consequences is far from self-evident and non-utilitarians will reject it. Sen explicitly denies it in his article, and Kant implicitly denies it when he (in effect) says that what helps a vicious person to prosper can't be viewed as a good thing.

In emphasizing good consequences as he does and also advocating that one act in such a way as to maximize the happiness or personal good of those affected by one's actions, Bentham in effect says that one should perform the action that has the overall best results or consequences, and this is equivalent to saying that one should perform the action that results in the overall best state of affairs.[13] By the same token, if Bentham hadn't spoken of good consequences and had simply advocated producing the most happiness, etc., we would have no basis for saying that he implicitly relies on the notion of a good state of affairs. Let's be very clear about this. To say that a certain situation or state of affairs contains more personal good or happiness than some other is not (yet) to say that *it* is in any way better than that other; and to say that a certain act produces *more* personal good or happiness than some other is not (yet) to say that it produces *better* consequences than that other, and if Bentham had only made the former type of claims, there would be no reason to think that the idea of a (good or bad) state of affairs had ever surfaced in his discussion. Commitment to the greatest happiness principle in its original form doesn't involve one in talking about states of affairs, much less good or bad states of affairs, and it is only, therefore, because Bentham also invokes the notion of good consequences that we can say that he implicitly uses the notion of a state of affairs and implicitly distinguishes between what is good for someone and what makes for a good state of affairs.

Now I can see someone questioning what I have just said, on the grounds that no one could really advocate always producing the most good for people unless they thought, or were prepared to hold, that a situation in which people have more personal good than in some other is a better situation than that other. But I am not sure. The idea of producing the most good for people, or sentient beings, seems to me to have an intuitive appeal *independently* of any

---

13. There are complications about the effect an action may have on how we can characterize the past that I needn't enter into here.

thought or talk about what makes for a good situation or state of affairs. And if that is so, then, as I said above, it is only the talk about good consequences that shows or indicates that Bentham implicitly distinguished between what is good for individuals and what makes for a good state of affairs. But this is still only an *implicit* awareness. Bentham never self-consciously distinguishes these notions, the way Kant does in the second *Critique*, and in that case a certain element of surprise, even of paradox, emerges from the history of ethics in this area.[14] Present-day utilitarians speak of good states of affairs and of human welfare much more than present-day Kantians do, and from a contemporary standpoint it might seem surprising, and even, as I say, paradoxical that it should have been Kant rather than Bentham or some other early utilitarian who first explicitly made the distinction between personal good and goodness in states of affairs. But there are, after all—and as the poet e. e. cummings says—"things we cannot touch because they are too near." And I think that it is because utilitarians tied personal good and good states of affairs more closely together than Kantians do that they are and were less likely to clearly distinguish the two ideas. The utilitarian thinks the goodness of states of affairs is a(n additive) function of how much personal good they contain—this is the thesis that Sen in his article calls "outcome utilitarianism." And Kant, of course, rejects outcome utilitarianism because he thinks, for example, that it can be (a) better (state of affairs) if a vicious person isn't well-off than if he or she is. But if what makes for more personal good doesn't, according to one's views, automatically make for a better situation or state of affairs, then the distinction between personal good and good states of affairs is obtrusive and obvious in a way it might not be if one was (implicitly) assuming the nearest or closest sort of ties between personal good and goodness in states of affairs. That may be

14. Henry West has suggested to me that Bentham's claim (in *An Introduction to the Principles*, pp. 158ff.) that "all punishment is mischief: all punishment in itself is evil" involves the distinction between what is bad for people and (objectively) bad states of affairs. But I think this is far from obvious. Bentham constantly contrasts mischiefs and evils with benefits, and the notion of (a) benefit is clearly a notion of what is *good for* someone. To be sure, Bentham talks of what is evil "in itself," but the distinction between what is good in itself and what is extrinsically or instrumentally good can as easily apply to personal goods or benefits as to objectively/impartially judged states of affairs. My own belief is that in his discussion of punishment, Bentham is simply talking about what is good or bad for people. The idea that punishment, the pain of imprisonment, is an objectively bad thing to have happen that can nonetheless sometimes lead to an objectively good overall state of affairs doesn't make any clear appearance in Bentham's discussion, even though we are inclined to think that Bentham held—*must have held*—such a view of punishment. Given the arguments made in the text above, it seems to me that the notion of a good state of affairs makes a *clearer* appearance in what Bentham says about good consequences; but even if we were to hold, with West, that Bentham is implicitly using it in his discussion of punishment, Bentham never draws our attention to the distinction between what is objectively or impartially good and what is good for individuals, in the way that Kant does. Since it is one of the virtues of philosophy that it makes us explicitly aware of what we previously only understood or used in an implicit fashion, my idea that Kant has made a special contribution to our understanding of the above distinction seems borne out by our discussion taken as a whole.

why Kant, rather than Bentham, was the first to explicitly distinguish between good states of affairs and personal good or welfare.

Once we are aware of this distinction, furthermore, we can see why it is so important. In the present state of ethical theory, for example, utilitarians and Kantians sharply disagree about the truth of outcome utilitarianism, about whether the goodness of a state of affairs depends solely on how much personal good it contains. (I am here disregarding the issue of total versus average utilitarianism and am for simplicity's sake assuming that we are talking about a fixed population.) Indeed, this is one of the sharpest, most important, disagreements between utilitarianism and Kantian ethics. (Remember that both Kant and classical utilitarianism assumed something close to hedonism in regard to personal good.) And in this dispute, it is clearly Kant who is on the side of common sense. That is why the example of the vicious person who is prospering has such force with us even nowadays, after we have heard so many utilitarians defend the opposite viewpoint, that is, defend the idea that it is good for a vicious person to flourish and not be punished unless better results for all could be produced by means of punishment.

However, I don't want to discuss the merits of the philosophical case any further here, because my main purpose has been to argue for making the kind of distinction between good states of affairs and personal good that allows the important issue of the truth of outcome utilitarianism to come to the fore. The validity of utilitarianism as a whole does seem to me, and others, to depend on the viability of assuming outcome utilitarianism (though hardly just on that assumption), and so the distinction that Kant was the first to make explicitly is of enormous importance for contemporary and ongoing ethical theory. And both Kantians and those who oppose Kant in various ways have reason to acknowledge that fact.

But before we conclude this section of the present essay, I do want to mention a further distinction that might confuse some of the issues we have been speaking of. Most or all philosophers are familiar with the distinction between intrinsic and extrinsic, or instrumental, goods.[15] And one might wonder whether the distinction between good states of affairs and personal goods can't be subsumed under, or isn't made otiose by, the distinction between intrinsic and instrumental goods, between what has value or is good in itself and apart from its effects and what is valuable (only) in virtue of (potentially) leading to or resulting in valuable consequences. But I would like to show you now that the two distinctions are in fact quite independent of one another and that we need both to understand ethical phenomena; and we shall also see how and why a failure to recognize these facts might lead one to downplay or ignore the importance of the distinction between personal goods and good states of affairs.

---

15. To keep matters relatively simple, I will not discuss, though I am implicitly adjusting my account to, the distinction between conditional and instrumental goods that both Christine Korsgaard and I have discussed and emphasized. See her "Two Distinctions in Goodness," *Philosophical Review* 92: 169–95, 1983; and my *Goods and Virtues*, Oxford: Oxford University Press, 1983, ch. 3.

Although in some, even many, cases the distinction between intrinsic and instrumental personal goods may be vague or difficult to apply, some personal goods are typically regarded as merely instrumental to a good life or personal well-being, while others are seen as part of, constitutive elements in, personal well-being or a good life. For example, the distinction between money and what it makes possible is clearly considered relevant to differentiating intrinsic from instrumental/extrinsic personal good(s). According to many, the mere possession of wealth/money is not even partly constitutive of a good life or personal well-being, and is merely a means to living well, merely an instrumental personal good; and though this last assumption is probably more difficult to defend than is usually conceded,[16] its point is clear enough and should help to make us clear or clearer on the difference between intrinsic and instrumental personal goods.

But all this gets us nowhere in any attempt we may wish to make to reduce the distinction between good states of affairs and personal goods to the distinction between intrinsic and instrumental/extrinsic good(s). For the very same distinction between intrinsic and instrumental can also be applied to the evaluation of states of affairs. The existence of a proportionality between moral merit and well-being (in individuals) is not valued by Kant on instrumental grounds, but rather, quite clearly, for its own sake. And that is, I think, how we commonsensically regard this issue. However, once one acknowledges that certain states of affairs are good in themselves, or intrinsically, it is clearly possible to regard other states of affairs (or events) as valuable means to the latter; and if, for example, it is considered intrinsically good for morally bad people not to prosper and actually to endure punishment for their wrongdoings, then one can easily regard the fact that a certain evil person is being tried for his crimes—regard that state of affairs—as an instrumentally good means to the intrinsically valuable or good state of affairs of such a vicious person's not prospering.[17] So the evaluation of states of affairs allows of an intrinsic/instrumental distinction that seems no less valid than that between intrinsic and instrumental personal goods, and, as a result, it seems clear that the distinction between good states of affairs and personal goods cannot be equated with or reduced to the familiar distinction between the instrumental and the intrinsic. And in fact, given the interests most of us have as ethical theorists, the distinction between good states of affairs and personal goods is effectively and most importantly a distinction between two kinds of intrinsic goodness. Indeed, the fact that the intrinsic/instrumental distinction cuts across the distinction between personal goods and good states of affairs may help to explain how and why the latter is (and was) so frequently (or long) ignored or confusing to philosophers. The idea that there are two kinds, or even two concepts, of intrinsically good things doesn't naturally or easily occur to one after

16. On this point, see *Goods and Virtues*, ch. 6.

17. I am here ignoring the problems that would be introduced and the complications that would be necessitated by a consideration of the Good Samaritan Paradox.

one has already taken the trouble to differentiate intrinsic from instrumental goods, and the further fact, as it appears, that a philosophically clarified and distinct concept of intrinsically good states of affairs took so long to appear in the writings of philosophers may therefore indicate how difficult it is to go beyond the distinction between instrumental and intrinsic goods to the further and independent distinction between good states of affairs and personal goods. All the more reason then to admire Kant for having made this latter distinction clear for the first time. However, a look through the recent literature of ethical theory, and, most particularly, through the introductory textbooks that have been written, say, over the past thirty years, might convince one (I am not going to try to document this here) that the distinction is still often not noticed, or treated in a confused manner, by philosophers. And that means that we have to keep making or insisting on Kant's distinction (even) to professional, academic philosophers. But I'm sure I haven't been doing anything as obnoxious as that here.

7.3 The Inward Character of Morality

It is time to turn to a third area or issue where Kant's innovative thinking is of great importance even to anti-Kantians, the question of the extent to which moral rightness and/or goodness depend on internal/psychological factors. I believe Kant thinks morality and valid moral judgment entirely depend on such factors, and although most contemporary ethicists don't hold this sort of extreme view, I think its merits have been greatly underrated. Or so, at least, I hope to persuade you in what follows.

Now even (act- or direct-)utilitarianism involves agential factors in its evaluations of actions. Expectabilist versions of utilitarianism that conceive rightness as dependent on the expectable utility of a given action often treat that expectability as (to some extent) relative to the state of mind of the agent whose action is being evaluated. An action is wrong if, given the evidence available to or known by the agent, its expectable utility is less than that of other actions the agent could perform instead. However, even an actualist form of utilitarianism typically involves internal factors in its evaluations. After all, utilitarians apply the term "rightness" itself only to intentional or voluntary actions. Accidental slips on banana peels that somehow have wonderful consequences still don't count as morally right because they aren't in the appropriate sense actions; so to that extent even actualist utilitarians consider factors in the agent in deciding what moral evaluations to make.

But clearly the typical utilitarian (or consequentialist) allows factors outside the agent to enter into assessments of her or his actions, and this is what Kant is unwilling to do. He considers the actual usefulness or fruitfulness of an action to be irrelevant to its evaluation. As long as we make every effort to do our duty, our will shines "like a jewel" and has the greatest kind of value. And this view has seemed and still seems to many ethicists to be much too extreme, to be as extreme and dubious in its own way as the opposing actualist-utilitarian viewpoint may also appear to be. However, I think Kant's view—that is, his emphasis strictly on internal factors, rather than the particular aspect(s) of our inner life that he claims are the basis for valid morality—actually fits our intuitions about hypothetical and actual cases pretty well. This might be surprising to many of you, and that is why I want to say more about this issue here. If I can persuade you, then Kant's "internalism" is more important and more philosophically useful than most of us have thought.

I am not, however, assuming that Kant was the first or only philosopher to have stressed internal factors exclusively. A case could, I think, be made that the Stoics also conceived virtue/morality in strictly internal or inward terms, and Kant was very probably influenced by Stoic thought.[18] But even if this is so, we can still say that in reviving the Stoic emphasis on internal factors, Kant was making available to modern philosophy a point of view that might otherwise have been forgotten or ignored, and if that point of view can be cogently defended, then Kant's revival of Stoic inwardness will count as a very important contribution. In addition, there is also the fact that Kant puts his defense of inwardness in much more modern terms than what we find in Stoicism: his talk of acting from duty and of making one's greatest efforts to fulfill one's obligations/duties sounds much more like how we nowadays think of morality than anything one finds in Stoic discussions of virtue. So Kant not only revives Stoic ideas, but expresses and develops them in terms that are more modern and to that extent, perhaps, more compelling than what we find among the Stoics.

But are they compelling enough? Will these ideas look plausible if we apply them to cases? Many among us will argue they won't, or don't, and perhaps the first and most obvious line of attack stems from the plausible thought that "the road to hell is paved with good intentions." Any morality that emphasizes only intentions will fail to criticize people or actions in cases where the best of intentions lead to or are followed by disastrous consequences, and the fact that this is so has led many ethicists to conclude that consequences need to be taken into account when we morally assess acts or actions.

However, in the *Groundwork*, Kant shows that he is aware of just this sort of problem. He says that mere wishing (to do the right thing) doesn't constitute a will as a Good Will, and he stresses that the Good Will is one that "summons all means in [one's] power" and makes the "greatest efforts" to accomplish one's (moral) ends. And what applies to wishing also applies to good intentions. Having good intentions doesn't mean that one makes one's greatest efforts to do what is right, so someone who has a good intention and lets it lapse will not count as having a good will, according to Kant, and Kant can then certainly allow that such a person ends up not (even) fulfilling their

---

18. On the Stoic influence on Kant, see, for example, Klaus Reich, "Kant and Greek Ethics II," *Mind* 48: 446–63, 1939.

duty. Someone who promises to return a book and who sincerely intends to do so, but who allows herself to be distracted from that goal and never *acts* on that intention will be considered by Kant to have acted wrongly, and so it seems to me that Kant himself could agree with the adage that the road to hell is paved with good intentions.

Now in speaking just now of what Kant would or would not say about the morality of certain actions, I was thinking of his actual moral views. But in what follows I don't want to stress those views. Kant was trying to capture and account for our ordinary moral thinking, but he said some things—for example, about masturbation—that most of us would never agree with. So instead of following Kant's specific moral views, I shall try to speak in present-day commonsense terms and, using actual and hypothetical examples, show why I hold that we should emphasize inner factors in moral evaluation more than most of us think we should. The example just mentioned—of someone not making every (reasonable) effort to return a book—shows you that in that kind of case, at least, an inner criterion or focus of evaluation corresponds quite well with what we commonsensically, or intuitively, think.

But we now need to consider some harder cases. Aren't there situations, for example, where someone meets that Kantian criterion of putting forth his or her greatest efforts to do right or good, but does harm instead? And isn't it clear or obvious that in at least some of those cases, the person in question ends up having acted in a way that most of us would consider to be morally wrong? I don't think so, and I think we can come to understand why if we pay attention to particular examples and certain classes of cases.

To begin with, there are many cases where someone's actions yield bad or unsatisfactory results as a result of the person's ignorance of important factors in the situation. In some of these, the person couldn't help—and there is nothing wrong about—his or her ignorance, and we are (therefore) not inclined to blame or criticize their actions in moral terms. Imagine someone, for example, who promises to bring important medicine from New York to Washington, DC, and knows that if she doesn't get the medicine to Washington within six hours, a patient will suffer a horrible deterioration in his condition. Assume further that she learns of this need and makes her promise only at the last minute, when it is already too late to arrange a leisurely trip down to DC that would still allow her to give the patient everything he needs in good time. Imagine, in other words, that the woman of the example is *presented* with an emergency that requires immediate action.

So what does she do? She rushes down to Penn Station and takes the first train to Washington, but the train gets into an accident and never arrives, so the patient never gets the needed medicine. Has she acted wrongly? Most of us would say that she hasn't—at least it doesn't go counter to common sense to hold that she hasn't; and at least part of the reason lies in the fact that serious train accidents are not the sort of thing one can be expected to anticipate.

If, on the other hand, we transpose this woman to another country where train wrecks occur frequently and/or trains almost always run very late, then it may be wrong for the woman to take a train. For she can be expected to know better and to go by car (if necessary borrowing one), rather than take a chance on the train in such an emergency situation. Knowing what she knows, she will evince a rather cavalier or careless attitude toward (helping) the patient who needs her help, if she decides to take the train. It is that attitude that, intuitively, makes her count as having acted wrongly in such a case, but such a woman also hasn't exerted her greatest efforts, or tried her hardest, to help the person who needs the medicine. So we still don't have a case where someone really does do their best and yet ends up acting immorally. And the case just discussed is also an example of how inner or internal factors can determine the moral evaluation we intuitively want to make.

But what about cases involving culpable ignorance where we clearly want to morally criticize what someone does? Can't such cases at least be used to challenge the Kantian reliance on inner factors in making moral judgments? Again, I don't think so, and my reason is that (I believe) culpable ignorance can itself arise only through morally criticizable inner factors. Take someone who backs out of his driveway in his car and runs over and kills a small child. He wasn't aware that there was a child there and wasn't even thinking about that possibility, so he certainly didn't have malicious or cavalier *intentions*. But we would accuse such a person (nonetheless) of gross negligence and careless-ness with regard to human life, and this is clearly a moral criticism. In harming the child, we think the person acted wrongly, even though he had no intention of doing any harm and wasn't thinking in advance that he might kill a child while backing out of his driveway.[19] Now the fact that there is no evil or mali-cious intention (no *mens rea*) might make the accusation of negligence seem to depend partly or wholly on external factors. After all, in many cases, ignorance of a potentially harmful or disastrous factor in a given situation doesn't bring with it any accusation of wrongdoing—we saw that in the case of the woman here in the United States who gets into a train accident going from New York to Washington. So ignorance by itself doesn't support an accusation of wrong-doing, and the culpability of the ignorance in the case of the negligent driver doesn't result from any immoral or malicious intention or desire on the part of that driver. Therefore, it would seem that there must be external factors that (at least in part) account for the moral criticizability that attaches to the driver or his actions.

But I don't believe this has to be so. The culpability of the driver's igno-rance and the moral criticizability of what he does can be unpacked in terms

---

19. If the man backs out carelessly but doesn't hurt anyone, then we will think of what he has done as less *seriously* wrong than if he *has* killed or injured a child. This is one aspect of the so-called problem of moral luck, and if common sense is right to make this sort of moral distinction, then external factors do enter into our moral thinking, even if they don't, say, affect what we call right or wrong *tout court*. All theories have difficulties accounting for intuitions about moral luck, and I don't have anything useful to offer on that topic here. Certainly, this whole issue offers a chal-lenge to what I am saying in the main text, but I am just not clear how strong a challenge this is.

of internal, mental factors that existed in the past and that may have persisted into the present. The driver who runs over the child presumably knows that cars are dangerous and knows that, because children are more heedless than adults, someone who drives has to be especially concerned about the safety of children. He has been told things like this and presumably has some direct experience of relevant facts—has, just to take two possible examples, seen children run heedlessly out into traffic or ignore dangers that are coming right at them. So what does it mean if, knowing these things, he backs up in his driveway without checking to see if there is anyone small behind him or moving swiftly in that direction? What I think it means is that when he was told or observed that children act heedlessly, he didn't really take that knowledge to heart. Someone who really cares about the welfare of (the) children (around him) will impress upon himself the dangers of driving a car in an area where children live and will not drive as negligently, carelessly, or incautiously as the driver who kills the child has driven. If someone cares enough, the possibility of children will be on her mind (or in the back of her mind) when she backs her car out of her driveway. Or, alternatively, she will have instituted a habit-checklist of things to do when she drives that includes automatically checking around the back of her car when she backs out of her driveway. Such a practice or habit might allow her not to be thinking about children at the precise moment she backs out of the driveway. But then her habituating herself to using such a checklist will itself be a sign of the concern she has for children and free her from any charge of (culpable) negligence.

This point can perhaps be reinforced by considering another kind of example. Someone driving a car in summertime with groceries in the back might suddenly realize that they have a quick errand to do and then drive to where the errand is to be done. They might park their car and then, after doing the errand, get caught up in a way they hadn't anticipated in some activity that leads them to forget the groceries. As a result, when they several hours later return to their car, they could easily find that much of the food had spoiled. All or most of us have had such things happen. But contrast such a case with one in which a person who is driving during summertime with his child in the back seat has to do a quick errand. Imagine that he leaves the child in the back seat while he does the errand and then gets distracted by some further activity or interest, forgets the child, and returns several hours later to find that the child has died of suffocation due to heat and/or lack of air. Such cases are very, very rare (thank heavens!), much, much rarer than cases where one neglectfully allows groceries to spoil. And there is a reason for this difference in frequency.

We care much, much more about the life of our children than about any bundle or bundles of groceries, and although we know both that groceries can spoil and that children can suffocate or die from heat, the latter knowledge is much more vivid to any decent parent than the former. A parent who would allow a child to die of heat in a car while they were distracted by activities in the vicinity treats the child as if they were a sack of groceries, simply doesn't love their child the way a parent should. If we are good parents, or even half-way decent parents, we don't *let* ourselves entirely forget (for some hours) a child we have left in our car. And we don't leave a child in a car at all unless the errand we have to run is very, very quick and the neighborhood where we park is entirely safe, etc. Any parent who acts otherwise lacks the kind of motivation we think of as necessary to being a morally decent person, because every parent knows that there are dangers in leaving a child alone in a car on a hot summer's day.

The terrible culpability and wrongdoing of the (very unusual) parent who allows a child to die in a car in the kind of circumstances just mentioned can be understood in internal psychological terms, and in fact the moral character of such a case is similar to what we have uncovered in the case of someone who runs over a child while heedlessly backing his car out of his driveway. Both the person who allows his child to die in his car and the person who runs over the child ignore, and are ignorant of, the dangers they are imposing on others, but this absence of knowledge differs from the ignorance that exists in cases where we aren't inclined to make moral criticisms. Their ignorance is attribut-able to a morally criticizable lack of concern for certain other people, whereas the woman who gets into a train wreck going from New York to Washington with badly needed medicine doesn't show a lack of moral concern when she decides to take the train. But, of course, and by the same token, the woman who knows that the trains in her country are unreliable but nonetheless takes a train rather than a car in order to deliver badly needed medicine also exhibits a lack of sufficient concern for the person whose life is in danger. Even though such a case doesn't involve any particular ignorance, culpable or otherwise, the woman acts wrongly because she has a slapdash or careless attitude toward the welfare of the person she has agreed to help. So the upshot of our discussion is that we still haven't seen any examples where internal/psychological factors aren't sufficient to yield the kinds of moral judgments and moral distinctions most of us want to make.

But there is yet another kind of case that we should probably also consider, cases involving the learning of moral lessons. Imagine that a food-aid agency has been successfully providing famine relief in a given country for about a year, when all of a sudden there is a coup d'état there and a new regime takes power. This new regime terrorizes and tyrannizes over the people of the coun-try, and it confiscates the food the foreign agency has provided and sells it to people outside the country, thereby consolidating its hold on power and caus-ing the situation of most people inside the country to further deteriorate. Such cases have actually occurred (e.g., in Africa), but I want to prescind from the question whether this has ever actually happened. My point, rather, is that the first time something like this happens, one may not want to fault the food-aid organization whose act of sending food to a given country ended up doing more harm than good. If no government has ever before confiscated food aid, then it is perhaps not culpable not to think of that possibility when one ships food to another country, and there will presumably be nothing inhumane, negligent, or thoughtless about doing so. Thus the first time something like this happens there may be no moral criticism to make, but *if it happens a second time*, then criticism may well be appropriate.

Once again, the difference here can be understood in terms of internal factors. When there is no way to have anticipated a certain problem, then the fact that a given agency or organization didn't anticipate it can show nothing untoward or morally criticizable about its (employees' or officials') motives. But once a certain problem has occurred and has led to dire results, the agency whose executives (say) ignore, or allow themselves to forget, that problem shows a morally criticizable lack of concern for the people it has committed itself to helping. The moral difference, once again, can be accounted for in terms of internal factors.

Now there are still some kinds of relevant cases I haven't yet spoken of. For example, very young children often do things that it would be wrong for an adult to do, like poke a(nother) child with a stick in the eye, and we don't blame the child or think it has acted wrongly, if we think it is ignorant, say, of the damage its actions may cause. This is something all mentally competent adults know, but since some ignorance is culpable, one can ask what makes the child's ignorance blameless; and the first or most natural response may be that the child is simply be *too young* to be held accountable, say, for damaging another child's eye. But this is a rather superficial answer, because it leaves us with the very important question *why* extreme youth and the ignorance that normally accompanies it are automatically free of moral culpability. (After all, some forms of ignorance *are* culpable.)

One possible answer to this question is that a child who is young enough will lack moral concepts, and we presumably don't morally criticize wild animals for that reason as well. But I think more can usefully be said, and once again it involves tying ignorance to motivation. We saw above that where ignorance is due to bad motivation, it can be culpable and the basis for moral criticism. But there are also cases where what we can say about the moral goodness or badness of motives depends on how ignorant we think someone is, and this occurs in situations involving young children and animals. (I won't speak further about animals, but what I say about children also applies, *mutatis mutandis*, to them.) Young children don't usually have a very clear idea about the reality of other people and their inner states, so even when a child in some sense knowingly harms another child, its understanding of what it is doing and causing may be much less clear than what adults in a similar situation would have. It may not fully understand what harm or well-being are, and it will certainly lack the idea of long-term harm or well-being and be rather unclear about what it means for a human being, including itself, to endure and have changing experiences over long periods of time.

So let's say a young child sees another child cry out for help: for example, ask for food because they are hungry. The child may not offer the food, but that failure to act (assuming the child actually does have food it can offer) will be different from an adult's failure to provide food in similar circumstances. The adult will have a very good idea, let us assume, of the reality of others and of what it is for them to feel hungry and need food. So in refusing to help, the adult would show real indifference to the well-being of another human being. But it makes less sense to accuse a young child of this kind of indifference if he or she fails to help another child, because the child doesn't completely understand the nature and consequences of what he or she does.

Indeed, it may not be possible, in the fullest sense, *either* to care about *or* to be indifferent to other people, if one lacks a clear conception of what another person is and feels. So one reason why we may not make full-blown moral criticisms of young children may be due to the fact that they are too ignorant of relevant facts to have morally criticizable definite or unambiguous motivation toward others. We can't accuse them of indifference or, for that matter, of malice in the full way this accusation can be made to stick for adults, and that fact can be due, as I have just suggested, to the fact that they are (inevitably) ignorant of certain facts in a way that makes it impossible for them to have "completely formed" morally good or bad motives. Similar points also apply to someone with very low intelligence; they too may not be able to understand other people or their feelings well enough for us to be able to attribute fully formed good or bad motives to them.[20] Finally, let me mention a somewhat different kind of case that I have often written about in the past. It is sometimes objected to sentimentalist ethical views that they allow someone with good motives to get away with things, with actions, most of us regard as morally criticizable. If one places, for example, a great emphasis on benevolence or caring as a moral motive, doesn't that let a benevolent or caring person off the hook if, through ignorance, they end up harming someone they wished to help? And didn't I earlier, for example, let the presumably benevolent food-aid agency off the hook because they couldn't have been expected to know (and because it doesn't derogate from the goodness of their motives that, the first time around, they didn't know) that some corrupt and brutal governments would be capable of playing lethal politics with food aid? But since common sense treats such cases as showing no moral fault, one needs to find some different sort of case where sentimentalist approaches lead to unpalatable conclusions through a failure to take issues of ignorance about consequences seriously enough.

Perhaps the kind of case such an objector has in mind is one where someone intent on doing, desiring to do, good for another person provides them with precisely what they don't need, precisely what will in fact most harm them, and where this is something that wouldn't have happened if they had bothered to find

---

20. Marcia Baron tells me she is inclined to think the very young child who pokes another in the eye has acted wrongly, just not culpably. But I think (even) the accusation of wrongness has to be attenuated for cases like these. It is difficult, however, to know how to express that sense of attenuation. Perhaps one should say that the child doesn't act *as wrongly* as a similarly circumstanced adult presumably would do if they poked someone in the eye. Or one could say that the child's act is wrong to some degree, but not completely. But I do think most of us would want to say something like this.

out relevant facts. But what is the word "bothered" doing in this last sentence? If the person described as desiring to help *can't be bothered* to find out relevant facts, that substantially undercuts the claim that they really did want to help. A person who genuinely cares about the welfare of another person and who is trying to help that other person will ipso facto *not* think it a bother to learn some relevant facts. Rather, they will *seek to learn* such facts, and that is because if one is really concerned to help in a certain way, one will be concerned to learn facts that one thinks may be relevant to one's actually helping. The cases that are supposed to show the untoward moral consequences of sentimentalism in this area—cases where a caring individual doesn't bother to find out relevant facts and ends up doing harm or no good—are just not possible.[21] And, once again, it is motivational/internal considerations that allow us to understand such cases the right way. But I think I have now said enough about the ways in which our moral judgments can be accounted for in terms of internal/psychological factors. And what we have said, as far as it goes, is certainly some sort of vindication of Kant's ideas about the inwardness or internality of the moral.[22]

Interestingly, too, at least one Kantian ethicist has anticipated some of what I said above about negligence and some other aspects of the present discussion as well. In her lovely essay "What Happens to the Consequences?," Barbara Herman discusses some of the ways in which a Kantian needn't find fault with the present maxims or actions of a person who acts negligently or incautiously, but can nonetheless criticize what the agent has willed and done previously.[23] And Herman makes a further point that isn't at all discussed in what I have said above and that could and probably should be added to that discussion. In cases where one fails to do what one has intended, but is not subject to any moral criticism for that failure, one can become subject to criticism if one doesn't appropriately follow up on one's failed actions. If, through no fault of one's own, for example, a book one promised to return is destroyed before one can return it, one may well not be criticizable for not returning the book (on time), but one

21. Sometimes when a person fails to find out relevant facts, that failure in no way shows a lack of strong concern for someone's welfare, but rather indicates some intellectual deficiency that the person can't be held morally responsible for. The Aristotelian can still criticize such a person, or her actions, as showing a lack of (overall) virtue. But if we think in commonsense *moral* terms, we might see intellectual/cognitive defectiveness rather than moral fault in such a case. This is very much in keeping with the Kantian idea of the inwardness of the moral. (I am indebted here to discussion with Eric Silverman.)

22. Henry West has suggested to me that Kant's ideas about inwardness are simply taken from common sense and therefore not as original as I am saying and supposing. But if Kant, in modern times, brings out the inwardness of our ordinary moral thought more explicitly and fully than anyone else, that is a considerable achievement. Just as we have said it is a great achievement on Kant's part to have brought out the distinction between categorical and hypothetical imperatives, a distinction that is arguably implicit in ordinary moral thought, more explicitly (and more fully and clearly) than anyone else had done.

23. See Barbara Herman, *The Practice of Moral Judgment*, Cambridge, MA: Harvard University Press, 1993, ch. 5.

will be criticizable if one fails to "make amends"—either by buying another copy of the book or by doing something else to show (as best one can) that one takes seriously what has happened and how someone else's interests have been compromised. And, of course, at the very least one has to apologize.

Herman places considerable emphasis on the ways that there can be moral responsibility and criticizability for willings both *before* (and leading to) and *after* (and leading from) a given failed act that is itself not to be faulted morally; and this seems to me to be a very insightful way of presenting the issues. But, not surprisingly, Herman's whole discussion is put in Kantian terms—with considerations about the universalizability of maxims and other parts of the Kantian moral-theoretic armamentarium playing a central role. Her emphasis is as much on the inner as my own (though I believe the above discussion covers a different, and perhaps a broader, range of examples than she considers). But the interesting point, from the perspective of the present essay, is the manner in which Kantian ideas about inwardness and morality can be replicated within and be helpful to thoroughly non-Kantian (and commonsensical) approaches. In a way, that has been my whole point in this present section, and it also represents, expresses, and illustrates the more general theme of the present essay. Kantian ideas can be extremely valuable to anti-Kantians.

8

RECONFIGURING UTILITARIANISM

I am not a utilitarian, but I have been fascinated and even moved by utilitarianism over many years. I say "moved" because I think the spirit of Bentham, the spirit that says no to aristocracy and monarchy and to entrenched institutions like the Church of England and that says human happiness should be the test of everything—everything!—is a humane spirit that philosophy and philosophers should be proud of. (I think philosophy has somewhat similar reason to be proud of the way it has historically faced down the arguments that have been given for God's existence and engaged itself in conceiving or building a secular vision of how things are and ought to be.) However, many philosophers find utilitarianism intellectually and morally repugnant, and I don't blame *them* either. Bentham's uniform and unifying vision narrows the possibilities and the interesting ideas available in the universe of morality; the insistence on quantity and quantifying seems very one-sided; and the refusal to acknowledge anything *higher* in the moral life seems a betrayal of some very deep human ideals and aspirations.

As I said, I am not a utilitarian. But I have spent a lot of philosophical time considering different versions of utilitarianism and comparing utilitarianism with commonsense or intuitive morality. However, this essay will address some aspects of the history of utilitarianism I have never before spoken of—and that I don't think anyone else has, either. The critical comparisons I have made between utilitarianism (or consequentialism more generally) and common morality have all presupposed a widely accepted (and to my mind plausible) contemporary view about how to state or present utilitarianism and how to state or present commonsense morality. But that view is itself of fairly recent origin, and the fact that the relation between utilitarianism and common sense was presented in at least two different ways in the past is usually now ignored in philosophical discussions. And in purely philosophical terms, it is probably all right that it is. However, a better understanding of the *history* of utilitarianism requires us, I think, to recognize and say something about the different ways its relation to common sense has been conceived and presented, and I believe we can in fact tease out from this history of differences some interesting implications or morals for our understanding of moral phenomena.

I am indebted to Roger Crisp for helpful suggestions.

I hope what I am about to say to you will seem familiar and uncontroversial. For some decades now, our understanding of the nature and implications of commonsense morality has been based on *contrasting it with (act-) utilitarianism*. Or, to put it slightly differently, those wishing to state commonsense views have first stated utilitarianism in all its clarity and distinctness and then pointed out the respects in which common sense disagrees with it. For example, utilitarianism or consequentialism holds that actions are morally assessable solely in terms of the overall impartially judged goodness of their consequences, and common sense is said, for example, to believe that certain deontological considerations require us to evaluate some actions as wrong even when their consequences are the best possible; as well as to believe that, independently of deontology, there are times when one is permitted to choose what favors one's own self-interest or certain personal projects even though this will mean not producing overall best consequences.[1] Now this way of understanding commonsense morality is so widespread that I hope I may be forgiven for not giving appropriate references. And, following many others, I have myself configured utilitarianism in the way just indicated whenever I have in any detail compared its merits with those of commonsense moral thinking.

But in fact there have been at least two other major ways in which utilitarianism has been represented, and in each the relation to common sense has been framed differently from the way I presented it just a moment ago. These differences are the main subject of this essay, and I propose to consider them in chronological order, starting with Sidgwick. I could begin, of course, with Bentham or even earlier, but the shifts or reconfigurations that occur between Sidgwick and intuitionists like W. D. Ross and between Ross and the present day are interesting and complex enough to occupy us fully. And, in a way, the points to be made here seem or will seem all the more forceful, given that the two reconfigurations I am going to describe have occurred within roughly one century. It wouldn't be surprising if utilitarianism in Sidgwick's version had been seen differently, in relation to common sense; but the fact that, as I say, within one century this relation(ship) has been overhauled twice in major ways is interesting and indeed striking. So there is some reason for me to confine myself to the later changes in the way I am proposing to do here.

So let's begin with Henry Sidgwick and concentrate on his masterwork, *The Methods of Ethics*.[2] I don't plan to make an exhaustive or thorough examination

---

1. I am and will be focusing on the consequentialist dimension of utilitarianism; but some utilitarianism also disagrees with common sense in holding a hedonist view of human well-being and in holding that the goodness of consequences (at least relative to a fixed population) is solely a matter, a function, of the amount of well-being they contain. I won't discuss these differences from common sense any further in this essay, but they are discussed somewhat in another essay in this book, "Kant for Anti-Kantians."

2. Seventh edition, London: Macmillan, 1907.

of that book or even of the way it relates utilitarianism and common sense; but I do want to highlight certain themes in and aspects of the book, and much of what I shall be saying will almost certainly be familiar.

In relation to what we nowadays think, Sidgwick downplays or underplays the conflict between common sense and utilitarianism. He sometimes points out what he seems to think of as divergences and perhaps even as tensions between the two. But, of course, a tension is not an outright contradiction or incompatibility (the tensions between husbands and wives don't always amount to incompatibility), and the notion of divergence is broad enough to include many differences other than sheer inconsistencies. So, unlike so many contemporary moral philosophers, Sidgwick never says, and I don't believe he thinks, that common sense and utilitarianism are ever, that is, in any cases, *simply inconsistent* with one another. To illustrate this point, let's consider a specific issue regarding which most of us nowadays believe act-utilititarianism and common-sense morality to be inconsistent: the question of the nature and extent of our obligations of beneficence to people we may or may not personally know.

At one point, for example, Sidgwick speaks of the utilitarian doctrine (roughly) that we should consider the happiness of any other person as equally important with our own, and says: "it seems to me difficult to say decidedly that this is *not* the principle of general Benevolence, as recognized by the common sense of mankind. But it must be admitted that there is also current a lower and narrower estimate of the services that we are held to be strictly bound to render to our fellowmen generally" (pp. 252–53). Here Sidgwick seems to be saying that common sense is of two minds about the validity of utilitarian "doctrine" and the main tension seems actually to exist *within* common sense rather than between it, taken as a whole, and utilitarianism. However, later on (p. 499), he says that "Utilitarianism is more rigid than Common Sense in exacting the sacrifice of the agent's private interests where they are incompatible with the greatest happiness of the greatest number" and this is certainly to assert a difference or divergence (in tendency or flexibility) between common sense and utilitarianism. But, once again, what Sidgwick says appears to amount to far less than an imputation of genuine incompatibility or inconsistency between the two "methods."[3]

Moreover, in other places in *Methods*, Sidgwick seems to want to treat common sense as simply coincident with utilitarian views. On p. 436, for example, he says that if an unforeseeable calamity occurs to someone—anyone!—we are bound to make as much effort to relieve them of pain and suffering (or danger) as will not entail a greater loss of happiness to ourselves or others.[4] And

---

3. Roger Crisp has pointed out to me that on p. 497 of *Methods*, Sidgwick says that there is some sort of "discrepancy in details between our particular moral sentiments and unreasoned judgments on the one hand, and the apparent results of special utilitarian calculations on the other." Crisp thinks Sidgwick might have wanted to cash out "discrepancy" in terms of inconsistency, and that may be so. But I don't think the matter is at all clear.

4. This is almost precisely what Peter Singer argued for in "Famine, Affluence, and Morality," *Philosophy and Public Affairs* 1: 229–43, 1972.

Sidgwick makes it pretty clear, in the context, that he is speaking of common-sense thought and its latent utilitarian tendencies or underpinnings. The idea that common sense latently or unconsciously tends toward act-utilitarianism is a major theme in *Methods*,[5] and that idea seems at the very least *itself* in tension with any assumption of an incompatibility between common sense and utilitarianism. Of course, the issue of beneficence is just one area, albeit a major one, of potential incompatibility or conflict between utilitarianism and common sense, but the fact is that Sidgwick never explicitly asserts any such incompatibility and, as I think we know, Sidgwick was pretty good, very good, at asserting and maintaining his beliefs. So when he speaks of the latent utilitarianism of common sense, I think we have to assume that he doesn't (definitely) think of the two as incompatible even with respect to the deontological issues or cases that are highlighted in present-day discussions.

Now it may seem odd that Sidgwick didn't see the incompatibility, with regard to such cases, that nowadays seems to stare us in the face. But the fact is that the cases, say, that we nowadays reach for in order to show students the incompatibility between commonsense deontology and utilitarianism are cases Sidgwick never talks about and probably had never thought of. The well-known, even (in contemporary terms) hackneyed example of the omnicompetent surgeon who can kill someone lying asleep late at night in a hospital corridor and use his organs to save five automobile accident victims and who knows she can do all this without anyone's ever finding out, certainly seems to establish an incompatibility between the dictates of common sense and those of utilitarianism. Utilitarianism says the surgeon should kill the sleeping person in the circumstances we just described, but common sense sharply disagrees. So we might well wonder why Sidgwick doesn't think of such examples and see the resultant, obvious incompatibility between common sense and utilitarianism.

But the case of the surgeon is a science-fiction one, and Sidgwick, as far as I can remember, never makes use of such "far-fetched" or "unreal" examples. We nowadays tend to think of such examples as relevant to and indeed as sometimes offering the best way to defend or attack moral claims, but it isn't clear to me what Sidgwick would have said about this. If, as I suspect, he would have had to grant the relevance of science-fiction cases to moral theories or claims, then moral philosophers subsequent to Sidgwick discovered a method or set of methods for investigating moral phenomena that Sidgwick himself, great as he was, missed out on. This indeed suggests a kind of progress within the field of ethics—even if it is progress that hasn't at all enabled us to settle the issue between common sense and utilitarianism in a definitive manner. But the point is that Sidgwick's ignorance or ignoring of the relevance of science-fiction methodology led him to believe in a compatibility or reconcilability between these two approaches or methods that we nowadays would deny. I am

5. See, for example, pp. 435, 438; but Sidgwick says this in a number of ways in many places in *Methods*.

not sure when science-fiction cases entered the picture for moral philosophers (historians of ethics might find this an interesting subject to investigate); but one doesn't have to go all the way to science fiction in order to see how limited a diet of examples Sidgwick fed upon.

By the time I entered the field of philosophy in the early 1960s, there were (at least) two sorts of examples that were frequently used to discuss the merits of common sense versus utilitarianism, but that Sidgwick never mentioned. There were desert island cases where someone living on a desert island with a dying friend promises, say, to water the friend's petunias after he dies and then has to decide whether to incur the inconvenience of doing so once the friend does die. And there were cases of race rioting where a sheriff has to decide whether to frame a black man for a serious crime he didn't commit in order to prevent race riots in which both whites and blacks will almost certainly be killed. By the time I entered philosophy, everyone agreed that utilitarianism dictates that the friend not water the petunias and that the sheriff should frame the innocent man, but that common sense disagrees with both these verdicts. Now these examples aren't science-fictional, but they *are* out of the realm of everyday life (or so one hopes). Somehow Sidgwick never mentions anything like either one of them, and since both do, I think, show the conflict, the incompatibility, between act-utilitarianism and common sense, there is a sense in which, meticulous and systematic as Sidgwick was about commonsense moral thinking, there were nonetheless aspects of that thinking that his limited methodology prevented him from seeing. Once again, this is a sign of progress on the part of moral philosophy since the time of Sidgwick, something that should make many of us (more) hopeful about its future prospects and results. At any rate, by the time we get to W. D. Ross and his form of commonsense intuitionism, the idea that common sense and utilitarianism are incompatible with respect to certain kinds of cases was a philosophical commonplace.[6]

Ross was confident that commonsense morality disagreed with the dictates of act-utilitarianism on the basis, among other things, of examples involving the keeping of a promise when someone could do slightly more good by breaking it. But this confidence also depended, I think, on his confidence in commonsense morality itself. He was an intuitionist and he believed, in particular, that our basic prima facie duties are self-evident to mature reflection—even if not obvious, for example, to young children. His list of such duties includes duties of fidelity to promises and promise-like undertakings or commitments, duties of gratitude, duties of beneficence toward others generally, duties of non-maleficence, and other duties as well. But his confidence in his list of

---

6. As it presumably had been, long before Sidgwick, in utilitarianism's early days. Godwin's famous case of the fire notoriously illustrated the divergence and inconsistency between utilitarianism and common sense, but I am focusing on the history from Sidgwick to the present, and Sidgwick (to say the least) downplayed that divergence and inconsistency. Perhaps all this is a reason *not* to be so sanguine about the progress that has been and can be made with respect to our understanding of these issues.

basic duties made him also confident about the clash between utilitarianism and common sense, because the principle of utility is equivalent to *just one* of the duties on the list, the duty of beneficence. Since Ross thinks that moral judgments about particular cases and ordinary moral decision making depend on appealing to various different prima facie duties on the list, rather than just to a single one of them—and holds, in particular, that no single duty on the list constantly outweighs any other such duty—he confidently assumes that common sense delivers some judgments that differ from those that can be derived from the utilitarian principle, from the duty of beneficence taken on its own.

But the most important point, for our present discussion, is the fact that Ross lays out common sense in terms of a list of principles and treats utilitarianism as if it were an extremely truncated version of that list, namely, the prima facie duty of beneficence taken on its own and therefore raised to the level of a universal actual duty. This makes our understanding of utilitarianism dependent on our understanding of commonsense morality. That is, according to Ross's scheme of things, utilitarianism is to be understood *by contrast with* an independently understood (and validated) commonsense conception of morality, and this treats utilitarianism as at the very least conceptually secondary to common sense.

That is the very opposite of the way we tend to view common sense and utilitarianism/consequentialism nowadays. And it is my main purpose here to make this point, and then try to explain it, because as far as I can tell no one else has called attention to the striking reversal of perspective that has, historically and in particular since Ross's day, occurred in regard to these two major components of moral thought and theory. In discussions of utilitarianism (or consequentialism) versus common sense over the past three or four decades, common sense is understood by contrast with utilitarianism and the latter is treated in some sense as basic to (our understanding of) morality. And this is the very opposite of the way Ross and others of his time saw things.

Now many of those who would recognize this shift once it was pointed out to them might claim that it is or involves a matter of sheer convenience. (This is how I used to view the matter.) They will or can say that utilitarianism is much simpler than common sense, in fact as simple as it is possible for a full-fledged moral theory to be, so it is simply *easier* for a discussion or morality or moral theory to first introduce utilitarianism and then explicate common sense in terms of the several ways in which it diverges from and conflicts with utilitarian thinking. According to this view, the method of introducing common sense—the fact that it is introduced *after* utilitarianism is described—suggests and implies nothing about the relative merits of the two views/approaches.[7]

Permit me to disbelieve this! I think there is and has been more going on than this "convenience" explanation encompasses or allows for, and in what follows

---

7. This is what opponents of Hempel's covering law model of explanation might say about the way their own positive views often take off against a background of criticism(s) of that model.

I want to say why I think so. I believe that at least part of what is happening involves a major shift, over the past several decades, in the balance of power as between intuitionistic moral commonsensism and utilitarianism (or consequentialism, but I shall henceforth drop this qualification). By balance of power, here, I am referring to the perceived relative strength of the two theories within the field and profession of philosophy, and I believe the shift I am referring to is itself in turn largely due to the increasing(ly perceived) strength of Kantian ethics within ethical theory as a whole.

Ross, as I have said, treated his prima facie duties as self-evident; and he felt no need to derive them from or justify them in terms of some single more basic, and thus more general, moral ideal or criterion. Now, of course, Kantianism is at least as critical of utilitarianism as Ross was, but Kantianism also is or has been critical of the idea of an intuitionistic list of commonsense duties that isn't backed by anything deeper and more unifying. This is certainly Kant's attitude in the *Groundwork* but one also finds something like the same attitude in Rawls's *A Theory of Justice* (Cambridge: Harvard University Press, 1971); and I believe that it is Rawls's influence that has made the most important difference to the balance of power, as I like to put it, between intuitionism or common sense and utilitarianism. Rawls says he is a Kantian, but in fact some of his students—Onora O'Neill, Barbara Herman, Christine Korsgaard, and others, but not, I believe, T. M. Scanlon, Thomas Nagel, or Joshua Cohen— thought that Rawls hadn't gone far enough in a Kantian direction. In any event, Rawls's influence on moral philosophy in the last half of the twentieth century was greater than that of any other person, and I believe that that rather Kantian influence made it harder to "get away" with simply asserting the self-evidence of some list of prima facie duties. It was and has been thought, rather, that one should try to *explain why* commonsense duties are as valid or correct as we think they are, and this implies that we should be somewhat unsatisfied with and dubious about common sense if it turns out that such an explanation *and justification* are not forthcoming.

And the rest is, really, history. It has proved to be difficult, if not impossible, to come up with any sort of explanation of why commonsense thinking is valid, and that, in turn, has led to some sort of reversal between common sense and utilitarianism. If common sense needs a justification but can't in any obvious or compelling way be given one, then the ways in which common sense diverges from utilitarianism don't *necessarily* or *obviously* redound to the advantage of common sense, and that has been a major factor (though not, as we shall see shortly, the only factor) in making it seem less than obvious that utilitarianism should be understood in intuitionistic Rossian terms as contrasted with and as a truncated version of independently conceived common sense.

But let me back up for a moment. I think more should at least briefly be said about the reasons why it seems to have proved so difficult to say anything by way of justifying and unifying common sense in terms of more fundamental moral ideas. As I indicated above, common sense diverges from utilitarianism in at least two ways: it involves deontological *restrictions* or *side-constraints* on what one can do in the name of overall good consequences and it involves giving moral agents the *prerogative* of weighing their own interests, projects, and commitments more heavily than those of others (and contrary to overall impersonal optimality) in deciding what to do. (The reader will notice that I am doing the same thing I have said almost everyone does nowadays, namely, conceptualizing the commitments of common sense by contrast with those of utilitarianism.) But of these two modes of divergence, I think ethicists, but especially Kantian ethicists, tend to pay more attention to and place more weight on the difference deontology makes to our ethical thinking. My strong impression, and it is an impression born of reading much of the recent and not-so-recent literature on commonsense morality, is that those who are intent on understanding/explaining/defending common sense put more weight on doing this with respect to deontology than on doing so with respect to our prerogatives to favor ourselves. Part of the reason, I think, is that we, as moral philosophers, tend to be a bit (do I dare to say it?) moralistic, or at least morally rigorous both with ourselves and others; and to deny deontology, to say we can kill, etc., if that leads to better consequences, seems to be letting us all to a certain extent off the moral hook. By contrast, to say that we lack prerogatives to favor ourselves and our projects is precisely *not* to let us off the hook of morality, but rather to place us even more securely on that hook. For if we lack prerogatives, what may intuitively seem to be morally optional turns out to be morally required of us, and what is required in particular is that we always do the best and most we can to promote human or sentient happiness. So I think it does just seem to us more morally (or moral-theoretically) important to justify deontology than to justify commonsense prerogatives, yet the former, as I indicated, has proven to be an extremely elusive goal.

Thus recently reviving noncontractualist Kantian ethics has attempted to rethink and/or reformulate different versions of Kant's Categorical Imperative in order to use it to justify ordinary morality (in the way Kant himself sought to do). But notable problems have arisen regarding all these efforts— though I hope I don't have to go into the details of this here. And as Samuel Scheffler pointed out in *The Rejection of Consequentialism*, many Kantian and quasi-Kantian efforts to support deontology over consequentialism fall afoul of a new sort of example that has surfaced in the literature of ethics in recent decades.[8] I am speaking of cases where someone has to choose not merely between honoring some part of deontology and producing overall better consequences in some way that would have been familiar to Ross, but also, and this is the new part, where one also has to choose between violating commonsense deontology and permitting a greater number of violations of deontology on the part of others. Bernard Williams's famous "Pedro" example of the man who a local dictator gives a choice between killing one person in a village where he

8. Oxford: Oxford University Press, 1982.

is visiting or else allowing that dictator to kill twenty of the villagers is of this new type if, as many assume, the choice of refusing to kill is what common sense requires.[9] For the choice is basically between violating deontology by killing one person and allowing a *greater number* of deontology-violating killings (with overall less good consequences) on the part of someone else.

Scheffler examines a number of familiar defenses or justifications of deontology and shows that they all have some difficulty in dealing with the new kind of example. Thus it is sometimes said that if we kill one person in order to produce overall better consequences, we violate that individual's personhood or show a lack of respect for her as a rational being, but if we use this kind of consideration to justify ordinary deontology's presumed take on Pedro-type examples, our justification seems less than compelling and what deontology says about such cases can, as a result, be put in doubt. For if, for example, it is so morally objectionable for someone to violate another's personhood or show them moral disrespect, isn't there in fact some reason to do such things if that will help minimize the number of objectionable violations of personhood or manifestations of moral disrespect that will occur as a result? If killing the one villager will prevent nineteen others from being killed, then one's violation of personhood or manifestation of disrespect will prevent a greater number of such violations and manifestations from occurring, and given the moral badness of the violations and manifestations, isn't that a reason to prevent a greater overall number of these morally bad things by doing the more limited violating of personhood and manifesting of disrespect oneself? But that precisely calls (what we have been considering to be) commonsense deontology into question—and might even convince us that in the case just mentioned, killing an innocent person isn't really violating their personhood, etc. So the new sort of example puts pressure on commonsense deontology, and if we were to decide to reject the specific part of deontology that this sort of example directly engages, one might start questioning more of deontology as well, and a landslide toward utilitarianism might not be all that far away.

So I think the Kantian emphasis on justifying our moral intuitions in deeper and unifying terms—and its at least premature confidence about being able to do so—have, ironically, led to a weakening of commonsensism both in itself and in relation to utilitarianism that (at least as I see it) Kantians aren't likely to find desirable. And the insistence on justifying deontology has, therefore, made it more natural and/or acceptable to understand common sense by reference to utilitarianism than it would have seemed sensible to do in Ross's day and given Ross's assumptions. But there is another factor in the shift that has occurred that I haven't yet mentioned, but that some philosophers have recently discussed, namely, the fact that Ross has no room for the notion of a moral prerogative.

As Stephen Darwall and David McNaughton (and no doubt others) have pointed out, Ross thinks only another duty can override or outweigh a given duty

9. See his essay in J. Smart and B. Williams, *Utilitarianism: for and against*, Cambridge: Cambridge University Press, 1973.

in justifying and determining our actions.[10] But our moral permission or prerogative to spend a certain amount of money on ourselves when we could do more good beneficently spending it on (sick or starving) others *isn't a duty*. And the proof of that is that common sense considers it morally meritorious (supererogatory)— rather than contrary to duty—if one spends the money on the sick and starving rather than, permissibly, spending it on oneself. This sort of example shows us a major defect in the way Ross presents commonsense, intuitive moral thinking, shows us an aspect of ordinary morality that finds no expression or acknowledgement in Ross's scheme of prima facie duties and what he says about it. So in fact the main difference(s) between common sense and utilitarianism can't be viewed as a matter of taking Ross's list of duties and simplifying it to a single duty of beneficence. And that is another reason, I think, why it seems so much more natural and plausible today to state/conceive common sense by reference to utilitarianism rather than take the exactly opposite path favored by Ross.

I say another reason, rather than the main reason, because I still think that the Kant-inspired felt need to justify deontology has been the main reason, in historical terms, why it no longer seems plausible to conceive utilitarianism simply by contrast with a self-evident pluralistic conception of common sense. But even those, like Darwall and McNaughton, who point to the inadequacy of Ross's scheme for capturing the highly important prerogatives aspect of commonsense morality haven't noted the way that (partly in the light of greater awareness of prerogatives, partly as a result of increased emphasis on justifying deontology) statements of the relationship between common sense and utilitarianism have reversed themselves since Ross's time. The way we now state and conceive utilitarianism, common sense, and their relation to one another is in a very important sense the very opposite of the way Ross and others of his time conceived these things, and it has been one of my main purposes here to call attention to that fact. But in doing so, I have also called attention to the ways in which emphasizing and knowing about certain sorts of examples, or counterexamples, has influenced our acceptance of or confidence in one or another approach to morality; and the overall historical process both from Sidgwick to Ross and from Ross to the present can, I think, therefore, be usefully seen as to some extent powered by increasing awareness of the sort of hypothetical and science-fiction cases that most of us nowadays assume are relevant to the justification of one or another approach to morality.

10. See Stephen Darwall, "Under Moore's Spell," *Utilitas* 10: 286–91, 1998; and David McNaughton, "Intuitionism," in ed. Hugh LaFollette, *The Blackwell Guide to Ethical Theory*, Malden, MA: Blackwell, 2000, especially pp. 278–79. Darwall also argues that Ross ends up treating the prima facie duties other than beneficence as mere qualifications of or exceptions to the duty of beneficence; but I don't think his discussion shows this, and in the same *Utilitas* symposium, Jonathan Dancy's "Wiggins and Ross" seems to me to make a good case for *denying* such an understanding of Ross's (ultimate) views. Dancy focuses on the final paragraphs of ch. II of Ross's *The Right and the Good* (Oxford: Clarendon Press, 1930) as indicating Ross's actual attitude toward utilitarianism, and the reader can check for herself or himself whether Dancy or Darwall has the better take on that attitude. But my own view is, as I have said in the main text above, that the idea that non-utilitarian considerations are to be seen as qualifications of or exceptions to the principle of utility or some basic duty of beneficence had to wait for a good while after Ross to be fully expressed and/or accepted by moral philosophers.

9

UNDER THE INFLUENCE: A VERY
PERSONAL BRIEF HISTORY OF
LATE-TWENTIETH-CENTURY ETHICS

I don't know of any scholarly history of ethics in the late twentieth century, and I am certainly no historical scholar. Still, I have lived through a lot of changes and developments in our profession, and I believe it might be interesting to fellow philosophers (or academics) and useful to students to hear what someone who has been through those changes and developments thinks about and has taken from them. (I don't know of any other ethicist who has published the kind of personal historical study—if I may dignify it to that extent—that the present essay represents.)

I began studying philosophy in the later 1950s, first as a high-school student with the (for that time, and perhaps even now, rare) opportunity to take a course in philosophy and then, in college, as a major in philosophy and psychology (what at Harvard was called Social Relations). I am not going to do much gossiping here, but I can't forbear mentioning—as an illustration of the somewhat awkward transition I had to make between precollege and college philosophy—what happened when I went to see Burton Dreben, the director of philosophy undergraduate studies at Harvard in the fall of 1958, to sign on as a (joint) major. When he asked me why I wanted to study philosophy, I told him that I had been inspired by Whitehead's philosophy in high school and thought it was wonderful to be able to study his thinking at Harvard, where he had, after all, taught. Dreben's laconic response was: "We don't do that sort of thing here." That was a remark it took me a long time to digest.

As an undergraduate, I was very interested in ethics, and, given my joint major, I decided to write an undergraduate honors thesis on "The Concept and Definition of Health in Psychology." A young transitioning assistant/associate professor, Rogers Albritton, agreed to be my advisor, and my introduction to late-twentieth-century ethics really began with him.

9.1 Foot and Rawls

Albritton immediately came right out and said to me that the two best people in ethics were Philippa Foot and John Rawls, and he advised that I make use, especially, of Foot's work in writing my thesis. This was some years before Rawls came to Harvard and was the first I had heard of him. But Hare's and

Stevenson's differing forms of noncognitivism were at that time dominant in academic ethical thinking (or so it seemed and still seems to me), and it would have been very useful to me to read Foot's trenchant critique of such views in "Moral Beliefs" and "Moral Arguments." These papers had just appeared, but when I tried to locate them in one or another library, I found that they were missing. And that made a big difference to my thesis, which remained stuck in stereotypical noncognitivist thinking, though it had benefited enormously from the onslaught (it felt that way) of Albritton's criticisms of every draft, one after the other. Albritton isn't well known now because he didn't publish very much, but he had a considerable influence on Thomas Nagel and Saul Kripke (I think he's the only person Kripke really acknowledges as a teacher), and I learned a great deal myself about how to think analytically from seeing him take apart my ideas.

At any rate, I didn't learn the lessons Foot had to teach us about Stevenson and, especially, Hare till some years later, when, as a Harvard graduate student, I took a course with her at MIT. I had a chance to see her in action and saw how powerful her critique of Hare really was. Some of this came out in her article "Goodness and Choice," which appeared after I wrote my undergraduate thesis, and although I don't want to enter into the details of anybody's work here, let me just mention very roughly or programmatically what I took to be her main message. Foot argued (against Hare) that we can't just will or choose whatever we want to be our ultimate moral value, that there are constraints having to do with human welfare and human practices, so that no one's ultimate or fundamental moral value could be, for example, never to turn southeast after turning northwest. We take such conclusions for granted nowadays—at least many of us do. But at the time she wrote, Foot's arguments were a revelation (at least to me); and I saw how (her) philosophical incisiveness could undercut what seemed initially plausible as a model, say, of moral utterances and attitudes.

I got to know Philippa Foot pretty well, and I don't think I have ever met another moral philosopher who is as incisive as she. I remember her making that sort of comment in response to a paper given by Martha Nussbaum at the Joint Meeting of the Mind Association and Aristotelian Society in Oxford in the summer of 1984—but, though I was very impressed at the time (I thought to myself: this is not something that would have occurred to me), I can't remember exactly what she said. So to illustrate this incisiveness to the reader, let me refer to an incident that I have merely heard about, and, unfortunately, I don't remember when and where it occurred. But I hope and believe it will tell you something about the power of Foot's mind.

Apparently, Hilary Putnam was giving a talk on the subject of possibility and certainty and had said that for all he knew for certain, it could turn out that his head was stuffed with straw rather than brains. Foot replied that that was in fact impossible, because if something is sustaining thoughts and language, it simply can't be *straw*. This is more than a little reminiscent of Kripke's views about the metaphysical necessity of certain facts about material substances, except that it was said many years before Kripke had lectured (or thought?

who knows? Kripke was so precocious) about this issue. Foot was no metaphysician, but out of the blue was able to come up with her reply to Putnam, and I think the example nicely illustrates the power of her mind. (Of course, what I am saying about Foot will not convince anyone who doesn't think well of Kripke's views or who doesn't agree that Foot's reply represents a forceful response to Putnam's point.)

But now I think it is time to bring in John Rawls. For me, one of the most interesting things, from an historical standpoint, about present thinking in ethics is how invisible Foot's main contributions are in comparison with Rawls's. Rawls's accomplishments in *A Theory of Justice* (*TJ*) and later work are a constant focus of present-day philosophical discussions in a way that Foot's trenchant criticisms of noncognitivism are not, and I would like to speculate a bit about the reasons why this may be so.

First, one might say that Foot's early efforts were only some among the many that were made to undercut/overcome views like Hare's and Stevenson's (and Ayer's). Elizabeth Anscombe and Peter Geach in England and Paul Ziff in the United States were part of the same naturalist/descriptivist "movement." So Foot has to share some of the credit for her accomplishments, and one might argue that that is why her work of those early days doesn't get mentioned so much nowadays. Except that the "movement" as a whole doesn't get that much mention either, and, if I may say, Foot's critique has always seemed to go to the heart of the issues surrounding prescriptivism and emotivism more directly and relevantly than what any of the others said about these matters.

Perhaps, then, the explanation has to do with the fact that Rawls published a book based on his earlier articles much much more quickly than Foot did—or perhaps with the fact that Rawls has attracted far more followers and students than anyone else in the field of ethics during the past fifty years. But another possibility—and the one I myself favor—is that Foot did her job too well. The lessons Foot taught (some of) us are now just presuppositions of the way we work and think, things we take for granted and that lie for us in the background. Whereas Rawls's ideas, for all his influence, are controversial. In fact, the history of political philosophy since Rawls's first book was published can plausibly be seen as (mainly) a history of ways in which political philosophers and theorists have disagreed with Rawls on fundamental issues. Nozick's libertarianism, Sandel's communitarianism, and various forms of feminism and virtue ethics *present themselves* as reactions to and disagreements with Rawls's Kantian liberal individualism. So, far from giving us lessons we can accept and put into the background, Rawls's importance to a large extent consists in the ways he has stimulated others into disagreement and/or insights that contrast with and are not reckoned within his own approach to political philosophy (whether in *TJ* or in later work).

Of course, from the point of view of those who more or less agree with Rawls's fundamental orientation (I don't mean his particular conclusions or arguments), it is important to resist some or all of the resistance to Rawls that has emerged during recent decades. But that is, in a way, just my point. Those who like Rawls's Kantian liberal approach have had and still have to defend it against a host of critiques coming from all sorts of different directions. Rawls's work in itself seems to me a great contribution. But in addition it has a central place in present-day political thought because of all the rich and (to my mind) important work that takes issue with Rawls.

But there is another point worth making about the contrast between Foot and Rawls. I sat in on Rawls's courses as a graduate student, rather than taking them for credit, and that was partly because I was mainly studying epistemology in those days (my dissertation was on the topic of empirical certainty). I was also in those days interested in German philosophy (I had taken a semester at the University of Munich between my undergraduate and graduate work), and Rawls knew that. So he and I had a number of lunches and dinners together, but the subject (alas!) was almost never political philosophy and was usually Kant or Hegel. But for all that I saw and heard of Rawls as a graduate student, I never saw him make the kind of criticisms I had seen Foot make: criticisms that involve difficult conceptual distinction-making and that at a single blow undercut some familiar and seemingly plausible position. His mind didn't seem to me to work like that. If Foot was the paradigm of ethical incisiveness (the kind of moral-psychological incisiveness last found, perhaps, in Bishop Butler), then Rawls was something different, something, actually, more positive and sustained. Darwin has been described as having an alluvial mind, one that was always accumulating and organizing more and more material in the pursuit of a chosen intellectual goal, and that term, "alluvial," seems to me to be very apt for Rawls as well. In fact, I know of no one else in value theory who represents such a good example of an alluvial mind; and we have seen how fertilely it has contributed to and shaped political philosophy over the past few decades.

But let me now say just a bit about how Rawls's way of doing things influenced me. As I said, I didn't work in ethics as a graduate student—and I sometimes nowadays wish that I had. After all, I am an ethicist and also work in political philosophy, and think what benefits I would have reaped if I had worked officially with Rawls! But what may be most interesting—not just to me, but perhaps to you—in this connection is the fact that Rawls exerted an enormous influence on my thinking nonetheless: that he did so, if I may put it this way, at a distance. Rawls got philosophers to do normative ethics once again—after a gap of some fifty years during which metaethics dominated and ethicists thought doing metaethics was the only way to be philosophically respectable, to make a genuine contribution. Students nowadays may not realize what an enormous difference Rawls made with respect to this issue, but those of us who were influenced by Rawls (and we are getting older now) recognize the difference he made here, and this particular difference may in fact be like the difference Foot made. As I have said, Foot did such a good job of convincing people that values weren't totally arbitrary that we nowadays don't (have to) focus on her ideas. But by the same token, Rawls so thoroughly convinced ethicists and political philosophers that they could do respectable work in normative ethics that those today who want to do such work don't ever have to consider whether it is all right for them to do so. And so Rawls's contribution to this issue, this effect, is somewhat buried. Buried at least by comparison with the specific views and arguments he advocated as a (normative) political philosopher. Again, I think this is something graduate students nowadays might find an interesting fact—and perhaps they can expect and will look for similar developments over the course of their own careers during the next few decades.

But how all this relates to myself is fairly straightforward. I had worked on ethics as an undergraduate and took up the subject again about ten years after I received my PhD. At that point, I was convinced by Rawls's arguments and example that I could and should do normative ethics; and since I had entered philosophy during the heyday of metaethics (actually things were in the process of changing, but much of that change was only beginning to manifest itself), it felt liberating, when I got back to ethics, to feel or think that I could work on normative issues—which always somehow had interested me more than metaethics.

But Rawls made a difference to me in another, related way. When *TJ* came out, it presented itself as offering a theory, rather than a mere definition, of justice, and Rawls in *TJ* puts a great deal of emphasis on theoretical virtues like simplicity and explanatory power (most importantly, perhaps, in his arguments against ethical intuitionism). The idea that one could do normative ethics in a systematically theoretical way, that is, in the "grand manner" of earlier historical work in ethics and political philosophy, seemed to me very liberating—though I recognize that ethical anti-theorists will consider this to be the sign of a corrupt mind, or of a mind corrupted by Rawls. In any event, Rawls's theory exhibited a boldness and ambition that I found exhilarating and sought to some degree to emulate, and I consider that particular influence to have been the greatest any philosophical ethicist has exerted over my intellectual development/thinking. But, of course, lots and lots of philosophers have felt Rawls's influence in one way or another—and for late-twentieth-century ethics and indeed for twentieth-century ethics generally, no other philosopher (with the possible exception, I think, of G. E. Moore) has exerted as great an influence. I would like now to say a bit about some other recent ethical thinkers whose work was influenced by or bears important relation to Rawls's and who have also made an important difference to my own thinking.

9.2 Nagel and Parfit

What I am going to say now about Nagel and Parfit is here kept separate from what I shall be saying in the next section about Williams and Stocker. But it would in fact be difficult for me to separate out how they respectively affected my work in any kind of strict *chronological* order. (Parfit, Nagel, Stocker, and I are roughly of the same philosophical generation; Williams was somewhat older.)

I came to be influenced by Thomas Nagel's work almost despite myself and at a point not absolutely at the beginning of the period (around 1977) when I entered the field of ethics on a permanent and fairly exclusive basis. I had accepted a professorship at Trinity College, Dublin, and was living in Ireland when I started being interested in rationality and rational choice. And my ideas developed in a very specific direction. I came to believe and was able to develop arguments in favor of the idea that self-interested rational choice (that occurs outside of moral contexts) is not necessarily optimizing or maximizing of the choosing individual's self-perceived welfare or good. I became convinced, for example, that when it comes to promoting our own well-being, we are often satisfied with what we consider to be good enough and sufficient, even though we know we could do somewhat better for ourselves by choosing more or differently.

Now this is a controversial idea even nowadays and after the work that I and others have done to support or defend it. But at the time it occurred to me, no philosopher had ever advanced such theses; and the one economist, Herbert Simon, who had famously gone in this direction and who had borrowed (from old Scottish Gaelic) the term "satisficing" to describe the willingness to do something other than optimize or maximize one's good, hadn't gone as far as I was prepared to go in defending the rationality of an entire range of satisficing choices. So I was actually somewhat frightened of what I was thinking and preparing to write about. I was about to go against what everyone else at least in philosophy thought about the character or basis of rational choice, and that gave me pause. But I was also at the time reading Nagel's *The Possibility of Altruism*, and, as I shall now explain, my reading of Nagel helped me become resolute about what I wanted to say about satisficing.[1]

When Nagel's book had first come out, more than ten years earlier, I read it somewhat cursorily and was put off by its "extreme" views about the influence of reason on choice. Nagel argued that we can derive a motivating reason for certain actions from a certain kind of rational understanding of our situation and its possibilities and without basing our reason on some sort of antecedent desire, and this thesis, while it is in line with much that Kant says, certainly goes against what almost every Anglo-American thought at the time Nagel's book appeared. I remember, for example, speaking to Joel Feinberg about the book and hearing him say that he had been talking about it with (his then colleague) Donald Davidson and that both wondered why Nagel would try to defend something so clearly indefensible. And I remember at the time chiming in agreement.

But when I reread the book years later—read it for the first time really carefully—I had a different reaction. The idea that motivation for action needn't be grounded in desire still seemed to me outré and counterintuitive; but Nagel's arguments began to seem more and more powerful, the more I thought about what he was saying. Nagel's example of having a reason to study Italian now because one knows one will have reason to (want to) speak Italian at some

1. Oxford: Oxford University Press, 1970.

near future date (one will be in Italy) came to seem fascinating and forceful, when I realized, as Nagel asserted, that the force of that reason doesn't seem to depend on one's having the antecedent general desire to do (other things being equal) anything that will help one prepare for actions that one knows one will later have reason to perform. And Nagel's comparison of such practical thinking about the future with ordinary means-end reasoning also came as something of a revelation (though I actually think Nagel doesn't make as much as he could or should of this comparison). When, having an end that I have reason to pursue, I learn that some action will serve as a means to that end, I automatically take myself to have reason to perform that action and that assumption or disposition doesn't appear to depend on my having some kind of general antecedent desire to do whatever is a means to my ends. And an argument by analogy from means-end cases to cases having to do with one's own future reasons is intellectually very forceful.

I say "intellectually" because, although it is very difficult to fault Nagel's argument in philosophical terms, I am actually still not entirely convinced that he was correct; my inclination to believe that desire is necessary to the motivation of action is somehow just too strong. Still, and as I just indicated, Nagel had provided an argument for moral-psychological rationalism that it is very difficult to fault in philosophical terms, and, as I realized when I read his book for the second time, that is a considerable accomplishment. That realization then seemed to me also to have bearing on what I was thinking and planning to write about satisficing. Here we had Nagel boldly arguing against what everyone thought, and perhaps he was wrong in what he was arguing. But the fact that his views could be defended in strong philosophical terms made them in some sense worth defending, or at least important to consider; and I came to think that if I could mount strong enough arguments in favor of satisficing, then even if these ideas went completely against current philosophical opinion and even if there was a strong risk that most people wouldn't change their minds, the philosophical force of the arguments could and would justify presenting and publishing them. And such thinking, helped along by my view of what Nagel had and also what he perhaps hadn't accomplished, made me feel less anxious about committing my ideas to print.

Parfit's influence came a bit later, but was somewhat similar. It occurred at a time when I was becoming more and more committed to virtue ethics and made itself felt through or in his book *Reasons and Persons*.[2] Most defenders of virtue ethics up to that point had been anti-theorists. They regarded Aristotle and virtue ethics as a kind of antidote to (what they considered) the inappropriately theoretical and quasi-scientific model of moral philosophy that one finds exemplified in Kantian ethics and utilitarianism. But I had been impressed by Rawls's frankly theoretical approach, and then along came Parfit who seemed to me to push the idea of theory even harder than Rawls had. Rawls's idea of

2. Oxford: Clarendon Press, 1984.

"reflective equilibrium" gives considerable importance to antecedent intuitions/ values in the construction of an ethical or political theory, but *Reasons and Persons* uses enormously inventive theoretical arguments to undercut many of our strongest intuitions, and this clearly tips the balance against ordinary thinking and in favor of theory/theorizing. (While Parfit isn't a utilitarian, his willingness to sacrifice intuitions is highly reminiscent of utilitarianism.) The lesson I (thought I) learned from Parfit—on top of what I had taken from Rawls— was that a good enough theory can give one reason to take back things, many things, one has long accepted and found plausible.

And this somehow made me think that the virtue ethics that was then reviving in the philosophical world needn't remain committed to anti-theory, but could, if one found the right framework, present itself as a theoretical alternative to Kantian and utilitarian ethics. Thomas Kuhn in *The Structure of Scientific Revolutions*[3] had told us that it takes a theory to beat a theory, that a scientific theory will not be given up simply because more and more evidence against it is accumulating. And so it occurred to me that not only were there positive reasons to try to push the idea of theorizing within the virtue ethics movement, but also that one could effectively counter utilitarianism and Kantian ethics— and what one found implausible in their implications or limited or distorting in their approaches to morality—only by developing virtue ethics in theoretical terms. And this is something I sought to do in the book *From Morality to Virtue*.[4] But that book went beyond Rawls's ideas about reflective equilibrium and in the more heavily theoretical direction mapped out by the utilitarians and, more recently, by Parfit. In it I heavily criticized and then rejected ordinary moral concepts and categories, using structural arguments/considerations that were more than a little reminiscent of the way Parfit had approached things (though I wasn't at all moving in the direction of his *conclusions*).

This was the furthest I ever moved away from relying on and allowing for ordinary thought and intuition, and in fact in subsequent work on or in virtue ethics, I pulled back from my theoretically driven rejection of some aspects of the commonsensical and (once again) relied heavily on both theoretical considerations and ordinary intuition. That work and some of what I had done earlier were greatly influenced by my reading of Bernard Williams and Michael Stocker, two philosophers who have generally opposed or been suspicious of theory in ethics. It is time I spoke about them.

9.3 Williams and Stocker

In the case of both Williams and Stocker, I was influenced more by articles than by the books they (eventually) wrote. And what I think I saw them both as

---

3. Chicago: University of Chicago Press, 1962.
4. New York: Oxford University Press, 1992.

doing—though I wasn't self-consciously aware of this at the time—was bringing moral philosophy down to earth: in particular, offering a more humanly realistic and less intellectualistic understanding of the kind of thinking and motivation that are relevant to ethics.

In writing about friendship, for example, Stocker argued that the rather Aristotelian emphasis on friends' acting for the sake of friendship does less than full justice to the importance, in friendships, of acting *out of friendship*. And in his seminal article "The Schizophrenia of Modern Ethical Theories," Stocker made the related, and perhaps even more significant, point that a normal person who visits a friend in the hospital will do so out of fellow feeling, sympathy, or friendship rather than in conscientious obedience to some rule or principle that speaks of the duties of friendship.

Stocker's examples and arguments hit me like a ton of bricks. I spent hours and hours thinking about their implications and rethinking some of my own ideas about moral psychology; and in the end, I believe I was able to see some problems with what Stocker was saying that go along with his insights. Stocker had concluded that modern ethical theories entailed an ethically undesirable split between the moral agent's motivations and the justifications we or he can give for having such motivations, but I eventually came to believe that Stocker's ideas led toward the very different conclusion that the schizophrenia or split Stocker was the first to describe was an inevitable and not necessarily undesirable feature of the moral landscape. I won't give the arguments or try to convince you of this, but what I concluded was that there were important aspects of morality and the good life that were not appropriately subject(ed) to the supervision of self-consciously followed explicit principles or rules. And this certainly runs counter to what Kant and other rationalists (Rawls in *TJ* is a fairly good example) tell us about the importance of following rules or principles and not relying on or being subject to (mere) natural motivations like sympathy and benevolence or, for that matter, ambition.

In the end, it seemed to me that Stocker had led us away from Kantian ethical rationalism and toward a less austere or more humane form of moral thinking and acting. (This is something, by the way, that the playwright Schiller had attempted to do in the early nineteenth century.) But of course in questioning the high importance of acting for the sake of friendship (and in many other points made in other articles and books), Stocker was also questioning certain aspects of rationalistic *Aristotelian* moral psychology. And I believe the same tendency to question rationalism in general, to question highly intellectualistic accounts of moral psychology or ethics, is to be found in Bernard Williams's work. (I believe these philosophers worked out their views fairly independently of one another.)

Williams's famous article "Persons, Character and Morality" makes virtually the same point Stocker did about the influence of principles upon action. If a husband sees his wife and a stranger both drowning and can rescue only one of them, then, if he is any sort of husband, he will not (have to) think about moral principles that tell him it is morally all right or obligatory for him to save his wife, before he goes in and saves his wife. Moved by love for her and realizing that it is his wife (or, say, that it is Jane) who is in danger, he will be impelled to go in and save her; and if he clears his way toward saving her by thinking that it is morally permissible/obligatory to save one's wife (or Jane) in such circumstances, then, as Williams so felicitously puts it, he will have had "one thought too many." Such an argument goes against Kantian rationalism, which has no way of explaining why conscientiousness should ever be morally questionable or uncalled for. (I have questioned Kantians about this.)

Williams also challenges Rawls's highly rationalistic assumptions about the desirability and appropriateness of life plans, of having a plan for the whole of one's future life, and here too I found what he had to say compelling. But by way of a caveat, I should also mention that I found myself less than convinced by Williams's more general onslaught against the Kantian view of duty as such and what he took to be its centrality to moral thinking generally (what Williams called "the morality system"). It struck me that the connections Williams drew between blameworthiness and reasons for action were less than obvious, and that his argument against the whole idea of external reasons (reasons we might have for action than don't spring from anything we actually want) just didn't work. If there are no external reasons, then Kantian ethics is totally undermined, but one can defend external reasons, for example, of prudence on a non-Kantian basis, and this is something Sidgwick did in *The Methods of Ethics*.[5] I have, in fact, my own arguments for believing in external reasons, and I have spelled them out in a book entitled *The Ethics of Care and Empathy*.[6] But I don't want to go into these issues any further here, and my point has mainly been to indicate to readers that there are limits to what I have taken from Bernard Williams. (Remember too that I believe in ethical theorizing in a way Williams didn't.)

So I don't think either Williams or Stocker got everything right (what else is new?); but their work made me question the rationalist tradition much more than I would have done otherwise—and it led me gently and through the further influence of others that I am about to describe in the next section, toward the sentimentalism that I advocated in the book just mentioned. But before I move on to describe these other influences, I do want to say something by way of conclusion about the differing mentalities of the philosophers who have influenced me and made, as a group and individually, such a difference to the history of ethics during the late twentieth century.

I have already characterized Rawls as having an alluvial mind, one whose strong sense of intellectual purpose was well served by an ability and willingness to accumulate and organize ideas of others that might be useful to his own philosophical enterprise. And I contrasted all this with what I said about Foot, whose incisiveness, more than any other quality, was what most impressed me about her and her work. But having said what I have in these past two sections

5. Seventh edition, London: Macmillan, 1907.
6. London: Routledge, 2007.

about Nagel and Parfit, and Stocker and Williams, I think I and we are in a position to characterize at least some of what is so outstanding about the way *their* minds work and about the way *they* were led to make the important contributions to ethics they have made.

If I had to pick out one description of Nagel and Parfit that pinpoints what I so much appreciated about their minds and their work (perhaps I don't *have* to do this, but I am going to try nonetheless), then I would say that their work exhibits a remarkable degree of boldness and ingenuity. Now I am not saying that there was little boldness or ingenuity in what Rawls or Foot did—quite the contrary. But nonetheless those qualities aren't what comes to the fore when I consider their contributions and/or the mentalities (if that is the right word) that led to those contributions. And certainly this is highly personal; others might see things very differently. But it is my hope at least that students and some more mature philosophers who read what I am saying here will think about the philosophers I have discussed in the light of what I have been saying about them and see whether the shoe fits. (This might require reading or rereading their work.) But let me continue with Stocker and Williams.

If I had to choose one phrase to describe Michael Stocker's work, I would say that it is marked by great sensitivity to moral-psychological subtlety and nuance. But Williams is also subtle, very subtle, so if I choose mainly to characterize him in other terms, that is because to me at least those other terms seem better to display or express what is distinctive about him and/or his contribution, seem closer to the immediate sense one gets or I have got from reading his work. And that immediate sense is a sense of his scintillating brilliance and the wit or humor it demonstrates. The "one thought too many" discussion is just one example of this. That phrase itself seems to me the most scintillating and witty aspect of the discussion, and it is no accident, I think, that that phrase has been cited and quoted by almost everyone who ever refers to or argues about Williams's example of the husband who has to decide about saving his wife. The example/discussion is called (roughly) Williams's "one thought too many" example/discussion, and I believe that is a tribute to how memorable and also humorous that phrase is. But as I said, there are many, many examples of coruscating, or scintillating, wit or brilliance throughout Williams's work. Some of it is in fact *wickedly* humorous, as, for example, when he described the rationalistic idea that we should romantically love someone only if, on the basis of their character or actions, they *deserve* our love, a conclusion that one of Rawls's followers had advocated in print, as "this righteous absurdity." And he was correct, I think, but also cruel to express it in that way.

If all or most of these characterizations are on the mark, then they may be interesting for the way they illustrate (some of) the different forms of excellence in the ways philosophers do ethics. This is something students and professors might find worth knowing, and though in advancing and to some extent defending these characterizations I have been writing/doing history, the history of ethics, in anything but a standard way, I still believe that such an approach has its uses and its historical interest. But I would like now to turn to two other intellectual figures whose ideas influenced me as the twentieth century was coming to a close (though I am, as with those already mentioned, also personally acquainted with them).

9.4 Gilligan and Noddings

Though neither Carol Gilligan nor Nel Noddings has ever taught (as far as I know) in a philosophy department, they have strong philosophical interests and their work has had an enormous impact on philosophers and others working in the field of ethics. Gilligan's ideas developed in reaction to what her teacher and colleague Lawrence Kohlberg had said about moral development. Following in the footsteps of Jean Piaget, Kohlberg's studies had led him to conclude that moral development occurred in various stages and that the stages involved increasing cognitive sophistication culminating in a (rarely achieved) final stage in which universal or universalizable principles featured as the focus or basis of morality. This was rather Kantian, as Piaget had been something of a Kantian. But Gilligan "blew the whistle" on Kohlberg's ideas when, in her 1982 book *In a Different Voice: Psychological Theory and Women's Development*, she pointed out that Kohlberg's studies had been done exclusively on males.[7] When further studies then indicated that women typically reach a less advanced stage of moral development than men, that might (Gilligan said) simply show that women's moral development is *different* from, rather than inferior to, that of men (hence the title of her book). Gilligan went on to argue that men almost always conceive morality in terms of autonomy from others and the just and rational application of universal rules or principles to problem situations, whereas women more frequently think of moral issues in terms of emotionally involved caring for and connection to others.

Two years after the publication of Gilligan's book, Nel Noddings, in *Caring: A Feminine Approach to Ethics and Moral Education*, sought to articulate and defend in its own right a "feminine" morality centered around the ideal of caring, and since that time there have been numerous further efforts to develop the kind of ethics of care Gilligan had said (and this was not entirely uncontroversial) was more typical of women than of men.[8] But I didn't hear or hear much about either Gilligan's or Noddings's work until about ten years after it had appeared, and when I did hear about it, I was in the middle of trying to work out some sort of theoretically grounded virtue-ethical alternative to Kantian and utilitarian/consequentialist ethics. My initial reaction was perhaps predictable. I decided not to let what Gilligan and Noddings were saying influence my own thinking, and my principal reason was that if they were on the

7. Cambridge: Harvard University Press, 1982.
8. Berkeley: University of California Press, 1984.

right track, it looked as if there were two moralities, one for women and one men, rather than the universal human morality that I was seeking and wasn't ready to give up on.

Interestingly, and as Gilligan herself pointed out in a personal memoir of Lawrence Kohlberg, Kohlberg himself had rejected Gilligan's ideas for roughly the same reason as mine. Largely because the facts of the Holocaust cry out for a universal human standard of moral judgment and condemnation, he was unwillingly to give up on the idea of a single standard of human or rational morality, and since he thought Gilligan's ideas led in that unfortunate direction, he sought to partially accommodate them through modest adjustments to and within his own univocal theoretical framework, rather than give up on the framework.

By contrast, I wasn't committed to Kantianism and wasn't prepared to accept Kohlberg's framework, so I continued my pursuit of a universally applicable human morality along virtue-ethical lines and also continued to hear and read more and more about care ethics as others were articulating and pursuing that approach. But a funny thing happened. My work in virtue ethics eventually led me to believe that virtue ethics would do better to follow the example of Hume than that of Aristotle, and care ethicists like Noddings had already claimed Hume as their own (forerunner). I began to see, in other words, that the kind of virtue ethics I found most attractive—the kind that emphasized benevolence and sympathy rather than focusing on *phronesis* and medial rational choice—had a great deal in common with what the care ethicists were doing. And I also began to see or think I saw that an ideal of caring could be the basis of a morality that governed or was applicable to both men and women. Gilligan's ideas and Noddings's didn't have to lead to a moral division between men and women; they could help us develop a morality of caring that was in the end more humanly plausible or valid than the more "masculine" theories that had centered around ideals like autonomy, rights, and justice and had made the conscientious application of universal principles the focus or goal of moral psychology. Since it would be implausible, to say the least, to give up on the notion of social justice or that of autonomy, this would mean *rethinking these notions from the general standpoint of caring for others*; but this was something I and others were prepared to do.

My first efforts were directed at articulating an ethics based on caring within a virtue-ethical framework. In doing so, I focused on Noddings's work and sought to generalize its findings: for example, in her early work, Noddings had said that the only important kind of caring was caring for people one personally knows, but I argued that caring was also significantly applicable to our relations with distant others. In fact, Virginia Held said very similar things at about the same time, but she was unwilling to join me in taking the further step of claiming that *social justice* is (entirely) grounded in caring. (Noddings herself eventually came to believe that caring is an important basis for justice.)

However, more recently—and now we are finally in the twenty-first century—my focus has shifted back toward what Gilligan said in *Voice*. As I tried to articulate a general ethics of care, I realized I would need to say something about ideals like respect and autonomy that are central to Kantian ethics and political liberalism and that are too appealing and powerful to be simply rejected or discarded. What I wanted to say turned out to involve a sustained appeal to the concept and phenomenon of empathy and to the recent psychological literature on the relevance of empathy to moral development. But when one treats respect for others' autonomy as crucially and centrally involving empathy with their point of view and the desires, fears, aspirations, and beliefs that arise within that point of view, the relevance to the feminist critique of patriarchy fairly leaps out at one. Gilligan had said that women tended to become debilitatingly selfless or self-abnegating because, under patriarchy, no one listens to their voice(s); and I realized that one could unpack this metaphor in terms of empathy and empathy-based respect. When, under conditions of patriarchy, women are told they don't really want to become doctors and that they really would prefer being nurses, when, under patriarchy, women's self-assertion is treated automatically as a form of immoral selfishness, this demonstrates a lack of empathic concern for women's own point of view, for their desires, aspirations, and thinking. And I was inclined to say that this also and therefore shows a lack of respect for women's or girls' autonomy and constitutes a kind of (social) injustice.

As I moved in this direction, I also thought I saw that the issue of whether virtue ethics was the right way to "do" an ethics of care was perhaps less important than I had thought. Care ethicists like Virginia Held think virtue ethics has to be more individualistic and less grounded in ideals of relationship than a care ethics ought to be; but I think that when one emphasizes empathy within care ethics, one ends up placing an enormous emphasis on relationship(s); and I now think it is more important to put empathy at the center of care ethics than to insist on doing or ask whether one is doing virtue ethics. The notion of empathy not only allows care ethics to articulate feminist ideals and criticisms, but (as I say in *The Ethics of Care and Empathy*) makes it possible to treat issues like autonomy, respect, social justice, and (even) deontology in distinctly non-Kantian, non-liberal terms. Such an empathically oriented care ethics might therefore help to further revive the (Humean) moral sentimentalist tradition that care ethics so frequently appeals to but that has long been eclipsed by Kantian liberalism and utilitarianism/consequentialism.

What I think I have taken from Gilligan and Noddings is both an increased willingness to see morality in sentimentalist rather than rationalist terms and a sense of the importance of centrally including feminist ideas and aspirations within any fully articulated humanly plausible (theory of) morality. I have no doubt that the philosophers whose ideas and whose influence on me I have discussed in previously sections would in varying degrees disagree with the conclusions I have recently reached and the direction(s) I have gone in. But I also think that Williams and, especially, Stocker would probably disagree less with these developments than the others; and that is the main reason why I discussed them in the section immediately before this one.

9.5 Some Thoughts about the Writing of History

When I look at the (slightly?) pretentious title I have just given this final section, I am inclined to chuckle. I am not an historian, not a scholar of the history of philosophy; and although I said that at the beginning of this essay, the point should be all the clearer or more obvious now that I have said what I have said within the previous pages. But the fact that I am writing at all reflects, I think, an important historical fact, the fact that, given that we are in the twenty-first century, the twentieth is now fair game for the history of ethics. This is perhaps obvious, and similar points can be and probably have been made in others fields about the previous century or others. But I think some other points can usefully be made, and whether or not they have been anticipated *mutatis mutandis* by others, I would like to make them.

Having lived a long time in the twentieth century and having made the transition to the next, it has occurred to me that in now writing the history of (the whole of) twentieth-century ethics, we will be somewhat prejudiced in favor of what occurred later rather than earlier in that century. Right now, as it seems to me, we ethicists are full of the influence of Rawls, Williams, Gilligan, and other late-twentieth-century figures; and these ethicists loom much larger for us than Stevenson, Ayer, Hare, Moore, Ross, Prichard, and other philosophers who did their work during the earlier years of the century. Now all this may be justified. It may just be that various more recent figures are simply more important, more significant for the history of ethics, than the earlier philosophers I just mentioned. It may be that good normative ethics outranks good metaethics—though Ross and Prichard were primarily normative ethicists. It may be that, following Rawls and Foot, ethics was *freed up* to flourish in ways that were impossible under the strict, self-denying regime or regimen of metaethics.

However, it is also possible that genuinely important work done earlier in the twentieth century is simply foreshortened for us from our particular temporal/historical position of being closer to the late twentieth century. We are likely ourselves to be more philosophically influenced by what is more recent, and we are not perhaps in a position to make allowance for the limitations of our own thinking in ethics. Our ethical views and allegiances may very well shape our sense of what is historically important, and if this is so, then perhaps a better understanding of (what is important to or in) twentieth-century ethics will have to wait for fifty or a hundred (or more?) years.

Think of how the history of eighteenth-century ethics would have been written right after the end of that century. Would Hume have been seen as the absolutely central figure he now appears to us to be? I doubt it. To be sure, Kant thought Hume important and Kant was regarded as important during his own time and subsequently. (But in England and France? I actually don't know.) Still, it was Hume's metaphysical/epistemological views that Kant regarded as so important, and Kant was rather dismissive of moral sentimentalist views like Hutcheson's. I believe Hume's importance as a moral philosopher and more generally came to be more and more recognized with the passing of time, and I think it is possible that this could happen with one or more of Moore, Ross, Hare, et al. Also, with the passing of time, Rawls's influence and achievement might loom less large. I think this might well happen if virtue ethics or care ethics became (even) more prominent or central to ethical thought and theorizing, though I am far from predicting that such a thing will occur. I was recently at a conference in which one very prominent virtue ethicist declared that Rawls's influence had not been a beneficial one; and certainly from the point of view of care ethics, Rawls's views—like those of Kohlberg, who was greatly influenced by Rawls—can seem to do less than justice (sic) to feminist ideals and to the emotional, caring side of morality that care ethics emphasizes.

So I think we may not be in a position to write a fair, good history of twentieth-century ethics, and the point may carry over to what I have been saying here about ethics in the late twentieth century. Perhaps I have placed too much importance on the more recent work of care ethicists rather than on what those who have followed Rawls, Nagel, Parfit, and others have been doing well into the twenty-first century. But I at least have the excuse that this essay is supposed to be a very personal history and to focus on how one ethicist was and has been influenced over the years. That is also my excuse, or justification, for not (more) considering the contributions of other ethicists during the late twentieth century. The figures I focused on may not, all of them, be more significant than some others I could have discussed: philosophers, for example, like Christine Korsgaard, T. M. Scanlon, Shelly Kagan, Rosalind Hursthouse, Virginia Held, and others, certainly, as well. But none of these figures had an influence on me at least that is comparable to what Rawls, Foot, et al., had. And in fact Korsgaard, Scanlon, Kagan, and the others just mentioned all were greatly influenced by one or more of the figures I have concentrated on in this essay. Perhaps, then, they could help to fill out what I have said (and move it in a more objective direction) by writing *their own* personal histories of late-twentieth-century ethics. This, I believe, would serve further to underscore the importance of the philosophers I *have* focused on, and that might be a very fitting ending to or continuation of what I have been doing here.

CAROL GILLIGAN
AND HISTORY OF ETHICS

When Carol Gilligan wrote *In a Different Voice: Psychological Theory and Women's Development*, it was in large measure in reaction to the work of Lawrence Kohlberg. Kohlberg, following Piaget, had offered a six-stage account of moral development, but when women were studied, it turned out that they on average advance less far through Kohlberg's stages of moral development than men do. This seemed to imply that women are morally inferior, less advanced, than men, but Gilligan blew the whistle on Kohlberg by pointing out that since the six-stage sequence had originally been developed in response to *studies done solely on males*, the fact that women advanced less far through those stages could at most show that women think *differently* from men about moral issues, not that they are morally inferior to men.[1]

Gilligan's book adduced evidence for such a difference, and at least partly on the basis of that evidence she argued in particular that men tend to think of moral issues in terms of justice, autonomy, and rules, whereas women are more likely to approach such issues in terms of caring for and direct connection with others. A great many people have subsequently questioned the *empirical validity* of Gilligan's findings, that is, have questioned whether women really differ from men as much as Gilligan originally suggested. But at least in part as a result of Gilligan's book, the so-called ethics of care began to emerge, and today, more than twenty-five years after the appearance of *Voice*, many, many people both inside and outside philosophy are working on and/or committed to doing care ethics. And much of this new care ethics rests not on Gilligan's original claims about the differences between men and women, but on the philosophical/moral appeal of care ethics itself as a way of thinking (and feeling) very different from that which Gilligan had attributed (mainly) to males. (Gilligan has subsequently modified her claims about the differences between men and women, and she

---

I am indebted to Virginia Held for her extremely helpful suggestions about this essay.

1. Carol Gilligan, *In a Different Voice: Psychological Theory and Women's Development*, Cambridge: Harvard University Press, 1982.

too thinks that the plausibility and appeal of care ethics are independent of actual gender differences.)[2]

Now the emergence of care ethics is not entirely due to Gilligan's work. Far from it. Around the time her book appeared, others were exploring care-ethical ideas or ideas very closely related to what eventually became known as care ethics, and I am thinking here of Sara Ruddick's "Maternal Thinking" and Lawrance Blum's *Friendship, Altruism, and Morality*, both of which appeared in 1980, and also and most particularly of Nel Noddings's *Caring: A Feminine Approach to Ethics and Moral Education*, which appeared in 1984, two years after *Voice* was published, and which was the first attempt explicitly to develop an ethics of care.[3] All of this work, together with Gilligan's book, served to advance and promote the idea and actuality of care ethics. And it did so very effectively. Many others began to work on care ethics and continue in (what I believe are) increasing numbers to do so. In fact, nowadays encyclopedias and handbooks of ethical theory typically contain separate articles or entries on care ethics, and the importance of care ethics as a fairly new—though as I shall indicate further, below, a historically rooted—approach to ethics is often stated or assumed in those articles/entries and by the editors who commission them.

The development of care ethics was partly encouraged by what Gilligan had said about the difference or divide between two (basic) moral voices, but this latter idea exists or can be seen somewhat independently of that historic development. What Gilligan says about the difference(s) between the voices is original with her, and I believe that it constitutes in itself a contribution to ethical thought, to the field of ethics. But in this essay I will try to show that Gilligan's work has an additional or further significance that has gone largely or entirely unnoticed. What Gilligan said about the difference between two "voices," two fundamentally different ways of approaching moral issues that turn out to correlate only very imperfectly with gender differences, may have major implications for how we should understand and write the *history of ethics*. So in my view, Gilligan made a highly significant difference to or within the history of ethics, but is additionally important for the way she can and does help us understand or write that history.

But I need to begin by saying a bit more about what Gilligan claimed in *Voice*. Gilligan distinguished between the voice of justice (what has sometimes, subsequently, been called justice ethics) and the voice of caring that

2. See Carol Gilligan's "Moral Orientation and Moral Development", in eds. E. Kittay and D. Meyers, *Women and Moral Theory*, Totowa, NJ: Rowman and Littlefield, 1987, pp. 19–33; and her "Letter to Readers, 1993" in later printings of *Voice*. In the Introduction of *Voice*, Gilligan also makes it clear that she doesn't think the significance of her idea of two moral voices depends on assuming a correlation with sex or gender.

3. See Sara Ruddick, "Maternal Thinking," *Feminist Studies* 6: 342–67, 1980 (and her 1989 book with the same main title); Lawrence Blum, *Friendship, Altruism, and Morality*, London: Routledge and Kegan Paul, 1980; and Nel Noddings, *Caring: A Feminine Approach to Ethics and Moral Education*, Berkeley: University of California Press, 1982.

care ethics has sought to articulate and develop. The former emphasizes the autonomy of the individual and issues of justice and of rights *against* others; and it also crucially appeals to moral rules and principles for decisions about what it is right (or just) to do; and I would say—and I think others by and large agree—that the contemporary paradigm of such an approach is Kantian/rationalist liberalism as found in the work of Rawls, Dworkin, Nagel, and Scanlon (and many others). By contrast, the voice or ethics of care downplays rules and principles because it implicitly sees the conscientious and self-conscious use of these as getting in the way of a morally desirable direct interest *in* and connection *with* or *to* other people. When we genuinely care about someone, our concern for their welfare and our actions on their behalf don't have to be mediated by rules or principles, and such points are central to the ethics of care that has been developing and gathering influence over the past quarter century.

Now this emphasis on two and only two voices implies that the divide between liberalism and care ethics is the principal divide for and within ethics or ethical theory. Gilligan never says this, but certainly if one reads her book as someone acquainted with the history and contemporary situation of ethical theory, one can well wonder what place (utilitarian) consequentialism or (neo-Aristotelian) virtue ethics can have in her scheme. Those of us who have done ethical theory over the past two or three decades have tended to see the clash between three of four major theoretical approaches to normative ethics as defining the field of normative ethics in contemporary terms. (This was certainly true of me before Gilligan and care ethicists like Nel Noddings and Virginia Held began to influence my thinking.) But Gilligan offers a bimodal or bipartite scheme, and this makes consequentialism, virtue ethics, and some other views seem much less important than Kantian liberalism and care ethics.

It also influences how we understand the import and implications of these other views. If one buys into the idea that the clash or difference between justice ethics in the paradigm form of Kantian liberalism and care ethics as developed by Noddings and others is the major issue for normative ethical thought or theory, one will also start seeing other views in relation to the two major ones. Thus care ethicists have noted the resemblance between their approach and Hume's and Hutcheson's moral sentimentalism, with its related emphasis on the feeling/motive of benevolence; but since utilitarianism also brings in (universal) benevolence, utilitarianism will be seen as to that extent bearing an important resemblance to care ethics, rather than to a rationalistic Kantian liberalism that is thought (by some philosophers) to play down the importance of feeling. Similarly, Aristotelianism stresses friendship much more than Kantian ethics and even contemporary liberalism tend to do, so contemporary Aristotelian virtue ethics to that extent seems more like care ethics, which also places great importance on relationships. But, of course, Aristotelian ethics attempts to ground moral thinking and choice in reason or rationality, and to that extent it resembles Kantian liberalism more than it does care ethics, which plays down or denies that caring has a rational(istic) basis.

In addition (and this is my main point), what Gilligan says about the divide between the two moral voices makes a difference to how we see or ought to see the previous history of ethics. If there is only one major or basic choice in ethics, between justice ethics and care ethics, then, for example, Christian agapism will loom large as the historical source (as most scholars acknowledge) of much of moral sentimentalism and therefore, in some sense, of a care ethics that acknowledges its debt to eighteenth-century British moral sentimentalism. (Of course, the Christian idealization of agapic love has *its* historical roots at least partly in Judaism's emphasis on compassion and kindness—something which Greek ethics never emphasized.)[4] Furthermore, if we accept the way Gilligan sees things, British sentimentalism will seem of greater historical (and contemporary) interest than it recently has to many (especially to Kantian) ethicists, because of the way it anticipates one side of the most central issue ethical thought and theory face. And Aristotelianism will appear commensurately to be of somewhat less importance because it really doesn't anticipate the primary or central clash of justice ethics versus care ethics.

Now it is important to note that none of this requires one to prefer care ethics over justice ethics or liberalism. Gilligan, others, and I myself definitely prefer the former, but certainly in the main text of Gilligan's book the emphasis is on difference rather than superiority or inferiority of one voice vis-à-vis another. (In the preface to later printings of *Voice*, she strongly hints that she hopes something like care ethics will replace justice ethics.) Gilligan's main point is that the difference or clash between the two voices is of central importance to ethical thought (and theory), but that means that all the changes I have just mentioned in how one views various (other) ethical theories and how one sees the history of ethics don't depend on taking sides between justice ethics and care ethics. It's as if, if I may say, liberalism and care ethics were ganging up on all other views and treating them as important mainly as illustrating issues liberalism and care ethics were interested in, or as being located at different places in the middle of a spectrum whose endpoints liberalism and care ethics defined. But, of course, this is just how Gilligan implicitly encourages us to see things (I hope she won't mind what I am saying about what is implicit in her views). However, the Kantian liberal would probably reject this view of the history of ethics and of the contemporary scene in ethics and might, for example, grant virtue ethics and/or consequentialism a much more important place in both than the different voices approach does.

Nonetheless, it is worth noting that what I have said about how Gilligan's view impacts or would impact our understanding of both the history and

4. Seeing things Gilligan's way also makes certain Eastern philosophies that focus on and idealize compassion and sympathy seem more important. I am thinking here both of Confucianism and Mohism in China and of Buddhism in general. Although I want to leave that vast topic alone for the purposes of the present essay, the reader can find further discussion, earlier in this book, in the essay "Comments on Bryan Van Norden's *Virtue Ethics and Consequentialism in Early Chinese Philosophy.*"

contemporary situation of ethical thought is *much less tendentious or partisan* than what one finds in some work on the history of ethics. For example, and as I read it, J. B. Schneewind's *The Invention of Autonomy* accepts or assumes that Kantianism had triumphed in the field of ethical theory during the late twentieth century.[5] And his reading of the previous history of ethics sees that history in the light of the eventual advance toward Kantian views. If one disagrees with Kantian ethics, one may well not buy this way of either writing or seeing the history of ethics, but what I have just been saying about the implications of Gilligan's views doesn't force us to accept, or presuppose the acceptance of, any one normative ethical position. It just requires us to see liberalism versus care ethics as the most important *issue* in the field of ethics, *and this is something that even a Kantian liberal might accept.* (Though, of course, and as I indicated just above, they don't *have* to view things this way.)[6]

But there is actually more to what Gilligan's ideas suggest about the history of ethics than I have yet had time to indicate. Her views allow one, I think, to understand the history of ethics, and indeed the current scene as well, *more deeply* than other approaches. Gilligan originally based her discussion on the work of psychoanalyst Nancy Chodorow, whose *The Reproduction of Mothering* had argued that the fact that men and women have both been primarily raised by *mothers* makes a difference to how they regard issues of separation versus connection.[7] Chodorow had said that men value separateness and autonomy more than women do because they need to separate from their mothers in order to model themselves on their fathers and become the kind of men they are expected to be. But the book also argued that women don't have to push off from their mothers and so don't have to place (so) much value on separateness, in order to learn from and become like their mothers in the way *they* are expected to do. Ideally, we all start off deeply connected with or to our mothers, but women don't have to forswear, and fear, such connection in order to meet social/familial expectations.

Now there certainly is anecdotal evidence available that indicates that men are, on average, more fearful and less valuing of connection than women— after all, it is generally men, not women, who get accused, by women, of being commitment-phobic. But the issue of the relative importance, for our lives, of autonomy/separateness and connection/commitment can be addressed independently of gender differences, and I have especially emphasized that point in my own work on and in care ethics. In a recent book, *The Ethics of Care and*

5. See J. B. Schneewind, *The Invention of Autonomy: A History of Modern Moral Philosophy*, Cambridge: Cambridge University Press, 1998.

6. To see the clash between Kantian liberalism and care ethics as the most important divide or issue in ethics is not necessarily to predict that others will (eventually) see things that way or that care ethics will (eventually and as a matter of sociological fact) displace consequentialism or virtue ethics as the alternative to Kantianism that most philosophers favor.

7. See Nancy Chodorow, *The Reproduction of Mothering*, Berkeley, CA: University of California Press, 1978. The empirical bases of Chodorow's ideas can be and have been questioned, and my discussion in the main text reflects that fact.

Empathy (henceforth, *ECE*), I argued that because of the great value they place on separateness/autonomy, Kantian liberals defend freedom of speech even when it amounts to offensive and quite possibly harmful *hate speech.*[8]

With regard, for example, to the famous question whether neo-Nazis should have been allowed to march and demonstrate in Skokie, Illinois, where a large population of Holocaust survivors lived, Kantian liberals like Thomas Nagel, Ronald Dworkin, and Thomas Scanlon all say that the march should have been allowed; and they all rely on considerations of (our rights of) autonomy in arguing for that conclusion. But for a care ethicist who insists on the value of our connection with and concern about others more than on our autonomy rights against others, it makes sense to intervene and not allow such a march and demonstration. The fact that the march and demonstration were likely not only to offend, but very possibly also to retraumatize (many of) the Holocaust survivors and thus to harm them in a very serious way is likely to be decisive from this point of view. And it is interesting, in this connection, to note that the liberals who defend (the right to give vent to) hate speech all actually ignore the just-mentioned danger to Holocaust survivors—they focus, in fact, on much less significant or less harmful potential consequences of allowing or not allowing the march/demonstration. (I am indebted on these points to Susan Brison.) However, *and this is more than ironic*, the neo-Nazis themselves seem to have been much more aware of this danger than the liberals. They chose Skokie for the march and demonstration *because* it was a place where many Holocaust survivors lived, and this likely means, I think, that the neo-Nazis were well aware of and happy about the traumatizing or at least damaging effects their planned march would have on (many of) the Jews of Skokie.

On the other hand, the fact that an ethics of care that doesn't emphasize (rights of) autonomy to the extent liberals do would want to question what the liberals say about the right to give vent to hate speech in Skokie-type cases (as Joel Feinberg usefully calls them) doesn't mean that care ethicists think lightly of (the right to) free speech. As I point out at some length in *ECE*, there are care-based reasons to want and insist on freedom of speech over a vast range of social and individual situations. However, when such reasons clash with something as humanly important as what was at stake in Skokie, the care ethicist is likely to take a less absolutist line about free (hate) speech than liberals do.

It would appear, then, that views about Skokie-type cases correlate with and even are anchored in views about the importance or value of connection or separateness, an issue that arises, presumably, in every childhood. Men may emphasize autonomy and become liberals more often than women, and

---

8. *The Ethics of Care and Empathy*, London: Routledge, 2007. For specific references to work by Nagel, Scanlon, and many others, see that book. My discussion there and here was/has been greatly influenced by Susan Brison's "The Autonomy Defense of Free Speech" (for data, see *ECE*), which incisively criticizes the many arguments Kantian liberals (including some women) have given for the importance of (traditional) autonomy and for allowing even Skokie-type hate speech.

women who become liberals may (for reasons we at this point don't know very much about and would do well to empirically investigate further) value autonomy and separateness as much as many men do.[9] But the point is that, independently of any strong correlation with gender, the issue of what to say about Skokie-type cases and, more generally, of whether to prefer a liberal or a care-ethical approach is one that has a background in psychosocial issues and normative preferences that arise for or in children. This has great bearing on the significance of Gilligan's work for understanding the history of ethics.

If the choice between Kantian liberalism and care ethics can be viewed as emerging from an ethical/evaluative issue about the (relative) importance of connection versus autonomy/separation that children—*both girls and boys*— have to face at least implicitly in the course of growing up and if, further, con- sequentialism and Aristotelian virtue ethics don't correspond in anything like this way to the evaluative issues and preferences/decisions that enter into every normal life, then these latter views should seem less important as theories and the choice between liberalism and care ethics all the more important to ethical theory and theorizing. This, then, in turn, gives us a reason, or more reason, to hold that Gilligan's discussion of the different "voices" can give us a unique and valid insight into the *history* of ethics. It moves us toward thinking of the historical development of consequentialism and virtue ethics *in terms of* or *in relation to* a long-standing dispute or disagreement about the relative impor- tance of connection versus autonomy, a disagreement that has more explicitly or fully come to the surface in recent ethical theorizing because of Gilligan's insights in *Voice*.[10]

But not *just* because of Gilligan's book. The autonomy/connection divide wouldn't, I think, have come to loom so large if people hadn't also been working

9. In e-mail correspondence, Carol Gilligan has said to me: "[W]ithin a culture that values autonomy and separateness (bill of rights, declaration of independence), it is not surprising that women as well as men hold these values." But if this is the explanation of why so many American women tend to emphasize autonomy in their moral thinking, then presumably European (and Afri- can, etc.) women will place less emphasis on autonomy. There is anecdotal evidence that this is the case (remember Robert Kagan's "Americans Are from Mars, Europeans Are from Venus"). But it would be helpful to have empirical studies of this issue.

10. The ethics-theoretical issue of individual autonomy versus connection with others arises more clearly in modern times than in the ancient world, where, as with Plato and Aristotle, the (moral) separation of the individual from and as against the community was to a large extent unthinkable. The question which factors made this idea and issue (more) thinkable in the modern world is an important one, but one I don't feel should be addressed here. But I am saying that the issue of autonomy versus connection, and therefore that between liberalism and care ethics, has more importance for understanding the modern history of ethical thought than for understanding the ancient. That problem was just more buried or hidden in ancient philosophy and thought. However, I should mention, finally, that in speaking here and elsewhere in this essay of autonomy, I mean autonomy as traditionally conceived by philosophers. In recent decades, feminists, care ethicists, and others have been working out a notion of relational autonomy that isn't subject to the criticisms care ethics would make of the original notion. In *ECE*, I discuss some of this new history and I myself advocate a relational view of autonomy that folds into the ethics of care.

on care-like ethical ideas around the time Gilligan wrote. As I mentioned earlier, Sara Ruddick, Lawrence Blum, and Nel Noddings were all developing care ethics or care-related ideas around the time *Voice* appeared, and what they wrote—and what others inspired by them and by Gilligan have written (and edited) subsequently—has helped to solidify the sense, among those addressing these issues, that the contrast Gilligan had drawn between an emphasis on autonomy and an emphasis on connection was central to ethical thought. But I also think that none of this would have been so convincing if there hadn't been—and if people hadn't recognized that there was—an underlying psychological reality to the issues that emerged in this fashion.[11]

Now at this point a Kantian, or others who oppose care ethics, might ask why psychological or social/psychological issues should be regarded as so important to questions of ethical theory and of the history of such theory. I am assuming, of course, that they are, but making this last question explicit can help us, I believe, to understand what this essay, and Gilligan's take on ethics, can contribute to our historical understanding. Perhaps the best way to do this would be to contrast what I have just been saying with a psychological approach to philosophical theories that I believe *doesn't* have the theoretical implications of what Gilligan, following Chodorow, saw.

William James famously distinguished between tough-minded and tender-minded philosophical views, but, although this distinction is indeed helpful in understanding or thinking about the history of philosophy and about philosophical/theoretical choices that arise from or within that history, it doesn't, I think, cut as deeply as Gilligan's distinction between two different voices.[12] James doesn't try to anchor his distinction within childhood, doesn't at all explain in social/psychological terms how or why some philosophers come to be tough-minded and others tender-minded. However, as we have seen, Gilligan *does* makes this sort of explanation possible at least in a very rough way that needs to be improved upon or developed further. But why, the Kantian liberal might still ask, should any of this be considered relevant to questions of ethical validity and to the historical perspectives that, as I have admitted, depend upon such theoretical/philosophical issues (Schneewind's book being an illustration of this last point)?

The/an answer to this question, or at least one that I think a care ethicist ought to give, lies in a certain way of understanding the epistemology of ethical

---

11. I am indebted to Virginia Held for pointing out to me how important the work surrounding Gilligan's book has been to vindicating or supporting its views about the opposition between autonomy and connection. Held herself has played an important role in communicating and defending these ideas to and for a younger generation of care ethicists.

12. See William James, *Pragmatism: A New Name for Some Old Ways of Thinking*, New York: Longmans, Green, 1907. Incidentally, one can question some of the specific ways James applies his distinction to the history of philosophy. For example, he says that empiricism is tough-minded and rationalism tender-minded, but surely the moral "side" of empiricism, its sentimentalism, is more tender-hearted or tender-minded than the ethical rationalism that is associated with rationalism in the larger philosophical sense. (The latter involves less of what we stereotypically associate with women.)

theorizing. Both Margaret Walker and Alison Jaggar have claimed that in developing and defending an ethical view, we ought to be interested in or concerned about the social and (I would add) psychological origins, in us or in others, of that view.[13] A view ought to be able to stand up to that sort of investigation, not seem narrow, prejudiced, hysterical, motivated by self-interest, etc., if we look into its origins. Now Jaggar, in particular, addresses this point specifically to contemporary, or traditional, ethical rationalism, which typically claims that such empirical issues really *aren't* relevant to questions *within* ethical theory. And this criticism of rationalist liberalism is important to our purposes in the present discussion. But let me first point out that others have said rather similar things in much more general terms. The idea that ethical thought should be able to withstand, not be undermined by, an investigation and understanding of its psychological or social origins is a theme familiar from the work of Bernard Williams, and I argued for roughly the same view in a 1977 *Journal of Philosophy* paper entitled "Morality and Ignorance," which, among other things, sought to show that Marx, Nietzsche, and Freud all accepted similar views about the relevance of origins to ethical believability. (This article is reprinted in my *Selected Essays*, Oxford University Press, 2009.)

If this sort of empirical factor or consideration is relevant to ethical believability, then any Kantian or other rationalist is wrong to insist on the purity and totally nonempirical character of our understanding and justification of ethical ideas. The question we put in his or her mouth above has an answer, the answer just offered, and if, *if*, one thinks that answer is on the right track, then that further supports what I have been saying about the historical understanding or insight that flows from Gilligan's distinction between voices. I believe, in other words, that it can help to justify a normative ethical view if one has a view of how someone might come or actually came to have that view that doesn't jar with it or call it into question and that makes it understandable in human terms why or how someone might come to hold such a normative view of things. Gilligan offers us the possibility of just this sort of account of Kantian liberalism and of a caring approach to morality, but nothing similar is apparently available for consequentialism or even Aristotelian ethics, and this serves to support the former pair over the latter and make the issue between Kantian liberalism and care ethics seem the central issue in normative ethics. And, as I have said, once one recognizes or grants all of this, the whole history of ethics is naturally seen in a new light.

This still leaves us, or at least me, with some interesting unanswered questions. Gilligan is not a philosopher, but consider how great her influence has been on what philosophers have had to say, and are saying, about ethics. Has any other nonphilosopher had as great an impact on the field? Well, I can't

13. See Alison Jaggar, "Ethics Naturalized: Feminism's Contribution to Moral Epistemology," *Metaphilosophy* 31: 452–68, 2000; and Margaret Walker, *Moral Understandings: A Feminist Study in Ethics*, New York: Routledge, 1998.

myself think of anyone outside of philosophy who has had as great an impact as Gilligan has had on ethics as a philosophical discipline. For example, her influence is arguably greater than what psychologists like Freud, Kohlberg, and Erik Erikson have exerted on the field, and I think it would be helpful to try to understand why this is so.

The answer to this question, and it is fairly obvious once one hits upon it, is that these other thinkers didn't bring to light a new way of thinking about ethical issues. Gilligan was the first to suggest the idea of different moral "voices," and she was the first person I am aware of to explicitly mention—though she did this somewhat tentatively—the idea of an ethics of care; and though, or perhaps because, she embedded those ideas within an overall picture of the underlying *psychology* of ethical thought and theory, her influence, her book, helped to launch a whole new way for philosophers to think about and do ethics or ethical theory. This can't be said about Freud, even though one has occasionally heard of such a thing as "Freudian ethics." It always turns out that the talk of "Freudian ethics" is false advertising and doesn't mean or refer to an/the ethics that Freud advocated or that follows out of his ideas and approach to psychology or to individual psychological problems. Freud didn't much like philosophy and he sometimes expressed the opinion that the well-analyzed patient would automatically be ethical, but this doesn't correspond to or express a particular ethical theory. Phrases like "Freudian ethics" or "psychoanalytic ethics" can refer to Freudian or psychoanalytic views about how it is proper or right to treat patients; or it can refer to psychoanalytic views about how the superego overdoes things and should be modified toward a more humane and less punitive set of moral demands within individuals. But even though this idea, these ideas, move us toward certain moral conclusions and away from others (working against the idea, e.g., that we should always love our enemies or the idea that homosexuality or too much sexual activity is immoral), they don't represent an overall take on the normative issues that any approach to ethics needs to address. Gilligan's idea of two voices is/was specific enough to encourage or allow the development of such a total ethical picture, or of many different such, based (to a substantial extent, but certainly not exclusively) in or on her ideas, but this is precisely what doesn't seem possible with Freudian ideas.

By contrast, Kohlberg does seem to have a total (if sketchy) view of or about normative ethics, but he doesn't offer us a new ethical/moral approach, but simply, or not so simply, stands by the Kantian ideas that flowed to him, at least, through the work of Jean Piaget. Gilligan did encourage us to move toward something normatively new and potentially systematic, and the new field of care ethics to some extent supports that view of things.

However, Erikson is the hardest case to understand in these terms. After all, Erikson does offer us a (to my mind) brilliantly insightful ethical picture of the goods and virtues of human development and aging, but philosophers haven't paid as much attention to him as they have to Gilligan, and one may well wonder why. Well, for one thing, Gilligan had the wind of the women's movement at her back. Her work came at a time of increasing interest (and not just among women) in women's issues and/or feminist issues, and her ideas did serve to advance and support feminist thought and social progress. To be sure, Nel Noddings's work on and defending care ethics has been attacked for idealizing a kind of selflessness that seems to legitimize, and leave undisturbed or uncriticized, patriarchal attitudes and behavior toward women. But whatever may be the validity of this depiction of Noddings's views, Gilligan's discussion of caring explicitly rejects selflessness or selfless caring as an ideal, and her work is fully within and helpful to feminist thinking and women's progress. So the effectiveness or influence of her views may in part reflect the social and philosophical force of recent feminism, a force that doesn't and didn't similarly serve to advance (the influence of) Erikson's explicitly ethical ideas.

But there are other reasons why Erikson may not have had as great an influence on the doing of ethics by philosophers. For one thing, even though Erikson advances a conception of the good life and its (developmental) virtues, he doesn't contrast his view with or defend it against other ideas about the good life, for example, Aristotle's. Gilligan does juxtapose the ethics of care to another, familiar and entrenched, approach to ethical issues, one mainly associated with Kant and contemporary Kantian liberalism. She therefore *jumps into* the field of ethics more than Erikson ever does, and that fact may be part of what is reflected in her greater influence *within* that field.

However, another factor may be more important. Within the discipline of ethics, philosophers are more interested in questions of moral right and wrong than in questions about what makes for a good or bad life, and Gilligan's ideas bear on the former, central topic of ethical theory, whereas Erikson's are (explicitly) relevant only to the latter. This may be a major part, then, of the reason why Gilligan's influence has been so much greater within ethical theory than that of any other nonphilosopher we have mentioned.

But I should also, finally, mention Nancy Chodorow, whose work Gilligan made so much use of, for, given her influence upon Gilligan, one may wonder why we shouldn't say that she has had at least as great an influence on philosophy as Gilligan has had. But things we have already said help us to an answer here. Chodorow's discussion of separateness versus connection doesn't explicitly focus on ethical issues in the way Gilligan did, and that, from my point of view as an ethicist, seems to me to be the chief advance that Gilligan makes on or with Chodorow's ideas: she shows us their relevance to ethical/ moral thought in a way Chodorow never thought to do. So, although Gilligan's work may be unthinkable in the absence of Chodorow's, it is more specifically ethical or ethics-oriented than what Chodorow did; and until one turns what Chodorow did in that specifically ethical direction, the possibility and actual development of an ethics of care seems highly unlikely. So Gilligan's influence on or in ethics just is, or seems (to me), greater than anything that can be attributed to Chodorow.

We have said that Gilligan's work gives us a better or at least a different perspective on the history of ethics (or of philosophy?). But it would be helpful at this point to move toward a clearer or more focused historical perspective on (the work of) Gilligan herself. We have already begun to do this by stress-ing the difference, and the reasons for the difference, between her influence on ethics and that of others, mostly psychologists. But in trying to understand Gilligan's historical place, her historical importance, I think we need to say a bit more about the character of her accomplishment in *Voice* (and also later on, but I shall focus on *Voice*).

To have seen the issues in ethics as boiling down to a choice between two rather richly described voices (think of the variety of things she said about each voice) represents a very large break (or leap) from previous ways of seeing the issues of or in ethics. Most of us before Gilligan tended to see the normative field of ethics as including a number, though not a huge variety, of conflicting and incompatible isms or approaches, and if you think about it, that is how the field is presented nowadays in typical philosophical text-books or anthologies (and in the ethics courses or seminars typically offered by philosophy departments). We are presented with the clash, say, between utilitarianism, common sense (or intuitionism), and Kantianism—or we are told that another approach, virtue ethics, has to be added into this mix. In such thinking, texts, or courses, Gilligan's bimodal approach isn't evident, and yet it strikes me, as an ethicist of care (who also likes virtue ethics), that if we take Gilligan's ideas, Gilligan's insights, seriously, they can lead us to reconfigure our understanding of the field of ethics in a very deep way: our understand-ing not merely of normative ethical theory, but, as I have argued here, of the history of ethics as well. That is why I think there is a touch of genius to what Carol Gilligan has accomplished.

INDEX